THE

DOMINICAN REPUBLIC

GUIDEBOOK

CW00550107

The Most Complete Guide
to the
Paradise Nation of the Caribbean

From The Minister of Tourism, Dominican Republic

At last, a truly comprehensive guide to the Dominican Republic! We have been waiting for a definitive work like this for a long time, and here it is, with everything that the visitor could possibly want to know about our beautiful country.

It is a delight to find a book that is well-organized, well-researched, and well-written; that allows a visit to be planned so that the sand and the city, the destinations, the nightlife and the history, the music and the stars are all drawn together to weave an unforgettable vacation or business trip.

H.E. Fernando Rainieri

I congratulate Marta Lugo and her co-writers for their broad coverage of the many facets of our country, the thoughtful organization of the factual detail, and the wonderful descriptions of our friendly and romantic people.

This book will be very helpful in making your visit to our country a happy memory. I sincerely recommend this book to you. I shall be keeping my copy close at hand.

FERNANDO RAINIERI
Minister of Tourism
Dominican Republic

THE

DOMINICAN REPUBLIC

GUIDEBOOK

Marta Lugo
Marc Paulsen, Carlos Ginebra C.

A Eurasia Press Book

MARC PAULSEN PRESS
Portland, Oregon
CARGIN, S.A.
Santo Domingo

COLUMBUS GUIDE SERIES

Commemorating
500 Years of History
in
The Americas
1492–1992

COPYRIGHT © 1989 by Marc Paulsen Press

*

Distributed to the book trade in the Dominican Republic by
Cargin, S.A., Gustavo M. Ricart esq. Ave. Tiradentes,
Apartado 210 ens. Naco, Santo Domingo,
Dominican Republic

*

FIRST EDITION, 1989
First Printing

*

Typography by M.E. Sharpe, Inc. and Genesis Typography, Inc.
Text set in Times Roman.
Cover designed by Lis Dimarco; cover photograph courtesy
Ministry of Tourism, Santo Domingo, Dominican Republic.
Text photographs by Marc Paulsen.

LIBRARY OF CONGRESS CATALOGING-IN-PUBLICATION DATA

Lugo, Marta, 1949—
   The Dominican Republic Guidebook
      Includes index
      1. Dominican Republic — Description and travel — Guidebooks.
I. Paulsen, Marc E.   II. Ginebra C., Carlos
F1934.5.L84   1989   917.293 '0454   88-26806
ISBN 0-932030-29-7

MARTA LUGO wrote the major sections on the history of the country, descriptions of geographical areas, and was an important contributor and consultant on other areas. A graduate of Marymount College and Fordham University's Master of English Literature program, she returned to the Dominican Republic in 1978 to pursue a career as a writer in advertising and to publish her own travel magazine for the Caribbean area. A compulsive traveler, she knows and loves all parts of the island country, and currently resides in Santo Domingo with her Welsh husband, John Harris.

CARLOS GINEBRA C., a native Dominican, studied engineering in the United States and Puerto Rico, learning to speak English in the process. His family background goes back over one hundred years of Dominican history. He currently operates an architectural design firm and has real estate businesses in Santo Domingo and Puerto Plata. An armchair journalist, he occasionallly writes feature articles related to tourism for the local newspapers. Mr. Ginebra provided much of the inspiration that lead to the birth of this book. He contributed his insights into the history, people, and lore of this romantic land, and suggested usual, out-of-the-way places to explore.

MARC E. PAULSEN is founder and publisher of Marc Paulsen Press. A longtime dealer and collector of rare books, his background also includes heavy construction, fine art, interior design, and real estate. Mr. Paulsen has served as project manager on assignments ranging from trade show exhibitions of national scope to high rise office construction and large sawmill machinery installations. While serving with the U.S. armed forces in Europe, he wrote many feature articles on tourism. He has traveled broadly, visiting many countries, and has toured the Dominican Republic extensively.

6

CONTENTS

I ■ THE DOMINICAN REPUBLIC AT A GLANCE

II ■ GENERAL INFORMATION: TIPS FOR THE TRAVELER

III ■ EARLY HISTORY

VI ◼ HOTELS AND LODGINGS

VII ◼ DINING OUT IN THE DOMINICAN REPUBLIC

VIII ▣ SHOPPING IN THE DOMINICAN REPUBLIC

IX ■ DAY AND NIGHT IN THE DOMINICAN REPUBLIC: RECREATION AND ENTERTAINMENT

X ■ EDUCATIONAL OPPORTUNITIES

XI ☐ INVESTMENT, THE ECONOMY, AND BUSINESS IN THE DOMINICAN REPUBLIC

XII ▪ APPENDIX

Chapter 1

THE DOMINICAN REPUBLIC AT A GLANCE

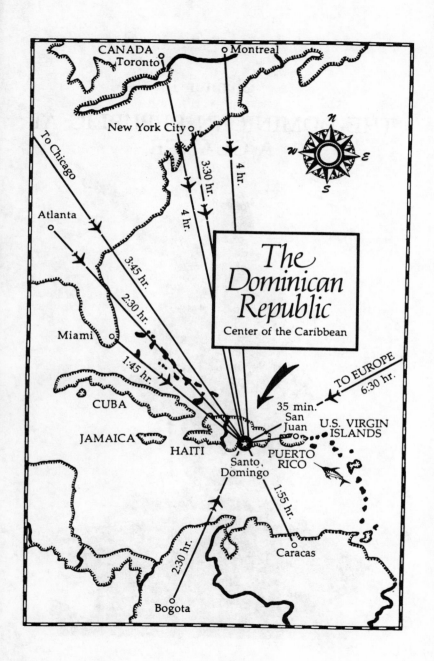

THE DOMINICAN REPUBLIC AT A GLANCE

Location and Size. The Dominican Republic is the heart of the Caribbean. Over 18,700 square miles in size, it occupies the eastern two-thirds of the island of Hispaniola.

Entry Requirements and Tourist Cards. Citizens of the United States and Canada must show a valid passport or proof of citizenship such as an original birth certificate with the raised seal. Visas are not required for citizens of the United States and Canada. Canadian and U.S. citizens must purchase a tourist card when departing from the U.S. or upon arrival in the Dominican Republic. It is available at the airline ticket counter for US$5.

Tourist Destinations. The principal destinations are the capital, Santo Domingo, on the Caribbean coast to the south, and Puerto Plata, located on the Dominican Republic's Atlantic coast to the north.

The famous beach resorts of the northern coast extend eastwards from Puerto Plata: Playa Dorada, Sosúa, Cabarete, Rio San Juan, Las Terrenas, Portillo, and Samana. The eastern coast offers the Punta Cana Club Med and the Bavaro Beach Resort. The southeastern coast stretches from the resorts of Boca Chica and Juan Dolio to La Romana, where you will find the jet set resort of Casa de Campo. The mountain regions of Jarabacoa and Constanza are also ideal vacation spots.

Population. 6.5 million (1987 estimate), with a labor force of 2 million.

Telephone Communication. Direct dial is available to the United States, Canada, Europe, and parts of Latin America. (dial 1 + country, state, or code + number). The area code for the Dominican Republic is 809.

Language. Spanish is the official language of the country. English is widely spoken in the tourism and business sectors.

Political Status. A thriving democracy. Since 1966, the Dominican Republic has enjoyed free elections every four years in a system similar in structure to those in the U.S.

Airports. There are two principal airports that are international facilities: one at Las Americas Airport in Santo Domingo that serves the southern coast, and one in Puerto Plata, Puerto Plata International, that serves the northern coast. Punta Cana and La Romana both have international airports for smaller jets.

Capital City. Santo Domingo dates back to 1496 and is the oldest city in all the Americas, the very first city in the New World. It is a thriving cosmopolitan center with many fine shops, restaurants, and intense nightlife. The colonial sector of Santo Domingo alone is worth the trip. It was here that Spain anchored all its activity in the New World. See the Alcazar Palace (the Columbus house), old fortresses, museums filled with antiques, priceless artwork, and galleon treasure! Excellent pubs and restaurants in this part of the city as well. Climate is warm, sunny, and very tropical. Temperatures range 70 to 80 degrees Farenheit.

Currency. The rate of exchange was relatively stable for many years until just recently. The country financed some of its growth in recent years with foreign borrowings as did most of the Latin countries. One major result has been a dramatic increase in inflation causing the exchange rate to move from a 1987 RD$3.30 per US$1, to as much as RD$6.40 per US$1. Do not exchange more currency than you think you need, as the banks are not allowed to exchange *pesos* back to dollars (July 1987). The airport bank, for example, will only exchange US$10.00 worth for departing passengers! All major credit cards can be used and the exchange rate applies to transactions.

Electrical Current. 110–120 volts A.C.

Ports. There are 5 major cargo ports and 2 principal tourism ports (Puerto Plata and Santo Domingo's San Souci).

Natural Resources. Rich in gold, silver, ferronickel, bauxite, coal, tin, marble, salt, and gypsum.

Investment Panorama. Stable and Promising. GNP for 1987: US$5.7 billion. The GNP is enjoying a substantial growth rate as a result of an investment boom. The United States and the Dominican Republic enjoy strong ties of friendship and commerce. U.S. investors have invested US$80 million in new direct investments in the country in the past year.

In the last four years, the U.S. has granted $490 million in economic aid to this island country, an indication of U.S. commitment to the future of the Dominican Republic. The other side of the coin is that the Dominican Republic is an excellent market for U.S. goods. The 1987 figures are US$560 million in imports from the U.S. to the Dominican Republic. In addition to agribusiness and tourism, there are substantial investments in offshore manufacturing. The Dominican Republic has seven Industrial Free Zones in operation, five under construction and over a dozen in the planning stage. The country offers a large work force with a minimum wage, excellent tax incentives, and adequate banking and communication systems.

Tipping. A customary 10% over the service charge included in the bill may be left at your discretion.

What to Buy. Terrific buys in handicrafts, island art, jewelry, Dominican gold and silver jewelry, handmade linen clothing, children's clothing, and shoes for the entire family.

What to Wear. Business suits are worn for daytime business meetings and women wear dresses or tailored suits to business appointments. Most people dress well for dinner at the better restaurants, although very few require a jacket and none to date requires a tie. During the day, lightweight sports clothes or casual dresses, slacks etc. In the resorts, casual sportswear and swimwear. Beachwear is not advisable if you leave the hotel or resort.

Departure Tax. There is a tax of US $10 for foreign citizens departing from the Dominican Republic. This money is used to improve and maintain the airport facilities and port terminals of the country.

Arrival at Las Americas International Airport

THE BASICS

WHERE IS THE DOMINICAN REPUBLIC?

The answer is simple: This small country is exactly where Christopher Columbus found it in 1492, on the eastern two-thirds of Hispaniola. The second largest of the Caribbean islands with an area just over 18,700 square miles, it is about the size of Vermont and New Hampshire put together and is, in fact, larger than Switzerland! The Dominican Republic is literally the "peak" experience of the Caribbean. Pico Duarte soars to 10,417 feet, while four rugged mountain ranges or *cordilleras* slash the length of the land. Between these lie rich, fertile valleys. One of the depressions in the southwestern region holds Lake Enriquillo, which is the lowest point of Dominican terrain at 144 feet below sea level. Thirty miles north of the island, in the Puerto Rico Trench, the sea plunges to a depth of 30,248 feet, an indication of the sharp geological contrasts in the area.

The northern coast is bound by the Atlantic Ocean, while the southern coast is washed by the Caribbean Sea. Its neighbor to the west is Haiti and to the east, just beyond the 70-mile stretch of the Mona Passage, is Puerto Rico. To define the special magic of this country is not a simple task. "Sensuous," "tropical," and "exotic" are words that come to mind. Do they capture the feeling of the country and its people? Words and pictures are never quite the same as the actual experience, but we'll give it a try. One thing is certain: Once you find the Dominican Republic, you'll never forget it. From cacti and rain forests to palm-laced beaches and cascading waterfalls, this land has the diversity that travelers love to discover. Here you'll find a nightlife that never ends in a capital city that never sleeps, all the sports that satisfy an active lifestyle, mountain retreats that are sometimes called the "Alps" of the Caribbean, and the tranquil waters of sheltered bays and coves preferred by the pirates and privateers of another century.

THE MELTING POT

The Dominican Republic has the second largest population of the countries in the Caribbean. As of July 1986, there were 6,380,973 inhabitants throughout the country, with 1,751,994 living in the greater Santo Domingo area, which extends as far as Boca Chica.

During the early days of the colony, Columbus left a group of thirty-nine settlers to hold the fort at Navidad while he went back to Spain completing his first voyage. Upon his return to the colony, Columbus found that the group had been slaughtered. By then, Columbus had a group of some 1,500 people, and with them he founded the first European settlement in the New World at Isabela, which lies on the northern coast of what is today the Dominican Republic. The year was 1494. Throughout the first decade of the 16th century, the Spanish population was maintained at a few thousand, with factors such as climate and disease keeping the population at a minimum. The population reached approximately 10,000 in 1512, which was the high point of Santo Domingo's prestige as the center of European interests in the New World.

The aborigine population was about 250,000 when the Spaniards arrived. The natives were virtually reduced to extinction in a 50-year period due partly to the introduction of heretofore unknown diseases and decimation by brutality. The conquistadors were not known for their humane sensitivity. Ferdinand and Isabel, the Catholic king and queen of Spain, although gravely concerned, were too far away to control the abuses effectively.

Dominican historian Frank Moya Pons points to the fact that in 1508 there were approximately 60,000 Indians on the island. By the year 1517, there were 11,000 and by 1520, there were only about 500. Not to be deterred by this, the colonizers soon found a substitute labor force and Governor Nicolas de Ovando (who ruled from 1502–1509) was the first to bring African slaves to the island. This slave trade, so essential to the development of the sugar industry in the country, was to have a fundamental effect on the racial makeup of the Dominican Republic. Both the influx of black slaves, as well as the later immigration of Haitians and freedmen during the years of the French annexation and the 20 years of Haitian occupation (1822–1844), brought about the predominantly mulatto society of modern times.

A reversal came in the mid–1930's, with Dictator Trujillo's open door policy to caucasian immigrants. In 1935, the population was 1,479,417, with a growth rate of 3.4% owing to the immigration of Western Europeans from Spain, Germany, Italy, and Austria during the pre-war years, as well as a substantial influx from the Middle East. These were mostly farmers or small merchants. Some were escaping religious or political persecution, while others were simply looking for a better life. This better life, from Trujillo's point of view, should allow for having large families of white babies. In his

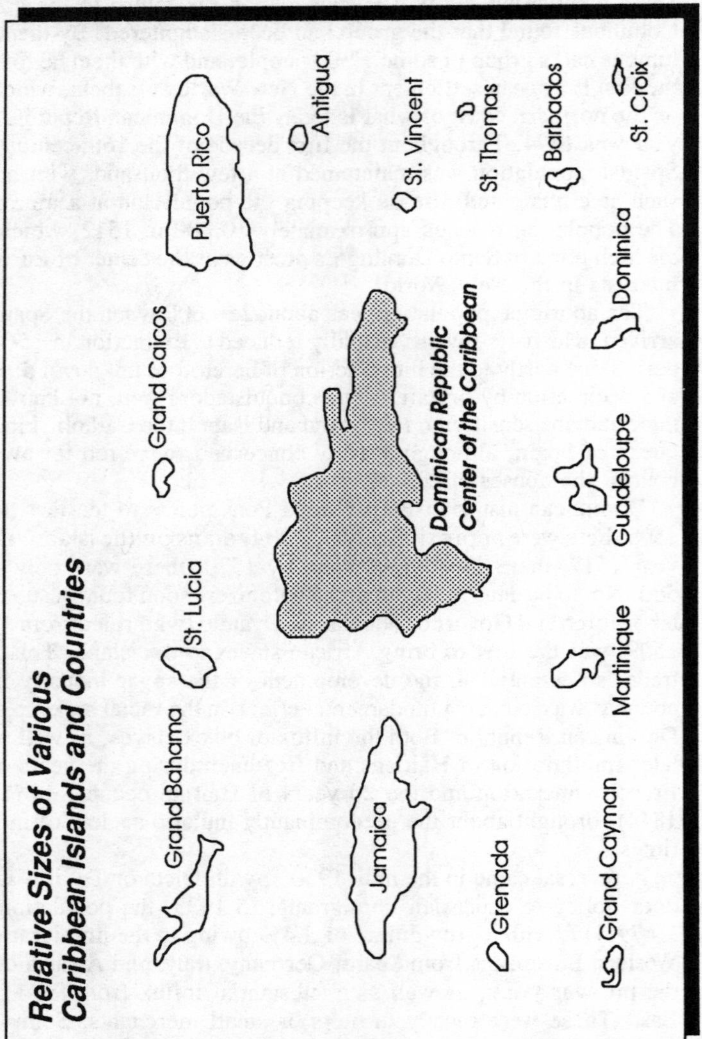

Relative Sizes of Various
Caribbean Islands and Countries

Grand Bahama

Grand Caicos

Puerto Rico

St. Lucia

Antigua

St. Vincent

St. Thomas

Jamaica

Dominican Republic
Center of the Caribbean

Dominica

Barbados

St. Croix

Grenada

Grand Cayman

Martinique

Guadeloupe

© Marc Paulsen Press

mind, white was not only beautiful, it was definitely preferable. Trujillo's racism, which was to culminate in the Haitian Massacre of 1937, was ironic in the fact that his maternal great-grandmother, Dyetta Chevalier, was among the Haitians that crossed over and settled in the Dominican Republic during the years of the Haitian occupation.

The mid–1960's saw a prosperous immigration of Chinese, mostly from Hong Kong, who made serious investments in real estate as well as the tourism industry.

This last decade has witnessed a substantial increase in U.S. and Canadian residents, many of whom are connected to multinational companies like IBM, Falconbridge, more than 140 Industrial Free Zone operations, or the numerous commercial banks with foreign capital that operate within the country. Others are involved in both large- and small-scale investments in tourism projects along the northern coast. These newcomers have become a part of the Dominican Republic and are integral to its development. They have also contributed to the country's cosmopolitan flavor.

With each new immigration, the country's ethnic and cultural heritage has become more interesting, and the country has become more of a melting pot. Perhaps because of the richness of their background, the Dominican people are considered the country's greatest resource. The lack of racial tension and the warm hospitality of the Dominicans have made the country a favorite destination among island-weary travelers. Plainly stated, its people have learned to coexist, and being a foreigner is neither a liability nor an advantage. You are simply accepted and welcomed along with everybody else. Another interesting point is that despite the dramatic increases in urban population since the 1960's, there is a relatively low crime rate.

POPULATION INFORMATION

Total population for 1985	6,242,729
Total population for July 1986	6,300,973
Growth Rate	2.21%
Total for urban centers throughout the country as of July 1986	3,316,830
Greater Santo Domingo as of July 1986	1,751,994
Greater Santiago as of July 1986	431,851
Greater Puerto Plata as of July 1986	96,484

City Proper as of July 1986

Santo Domingo	1,483,589
Santiago	314,819
Puerto Plata	51,233

These figures are based on analysis and projections of the Office of National Statistics (ONE) and Infratur, the Central Bank's department for the development of tourism infrastructure.

ACCESSIBILITY BY LAND

The Dominican Republic has an adequate network of roads, which is a way of saying it could be better but it's not bad. The highway leading out from the capital to the airport at Las Americas and the beaches beyond is in good condition. This is the same road that takes you to San Pedro de Macoris, La Romana, Higuey, and on to the resorts of the eastern coast. The roads are always transitable, but tend to require repairs after the rainy season. The road leading west from Santo Domingo to Barahona has an excellent surface as of this writing. All these roads, by the way, are scenically beautiful, with varied and exuberant vegetation.

Duarte Highway, the principal road connecting Santo Domingo to Santiago and Puerto Plata, was recently rebuilt and widened during the administration of President Jorge Blanco, and is probably the most highly transited road in the country. The surface is now in excellent condition, however, there are very few highway lights along the road, which makes it a real strain on the eyes for night driving. Adding to the problem, local drivers have a habit of leaving on their bright lights, which only makes night driving more hazardous. The drive to the central city of Santiago is about three hours, depending on traffic, with an additional hour to Puerto Plata on the northern coast. Daytime driving on this highway is much more interesting, and probably safer.

The coastal road that runs east from Puerto Plata is in good condition and leads you to the Playa Dorada resort area, Sosúa, Cabarete, Rio San Juan, Nagua, and Samana at the northeastern tip of the country. The International Airport of Puerto Plata is just before Sosua and about a 15-minute drive from Playa Dorada along the same road. An added bonus is the fact that this road is very scenic, leading through sugarcane fields, cattle-grazing land and densely vegetated coastal areas. You will also pass through many small villages that seem untouched by time.

Even though there are traffic regulations, Dominicans tend to drive at the speed of light. They also seem to improvise their own rules as they go along. They make Italian drivers and New York City cabs seem shy by comparison. In spite of this apparent chaos, there is radar control, usually just beyond the next curve, so for your own peace of mind, don't do as the locals do, and try to stay within the speed limits. If you are waved over, you should stop and inform the police of your willingness to obey the rules.

ACCESSIBILITY BY SEA

There are five large frequently used cargo ports in the country. Several shipping lines offer container service to North and South America, Europe, particularly the Mediterranean area, the Middle East and the Orient, as well as to the neighboring Caribbean islands.

Caribbean ports are exotic cruise destinations not only because of their golden beaches and the romantic images they evoke of colonial adventure and pirate fleets, but because of their heritage. There is, after all, the old English charm of Barbados and Jamaica, the Dutch confectionary flavor of Curaçao and the Parisian air of the French islands. The Caribbean offers it all. What is the special allure of the Dominican ports of call? Mostly, there's the fascination of knowing this is where it all started. To actually see the land as Columbus first saw it can be a thrilling experience for modern day explorers. A great climate, blue skies, palm trees, white sands, excellent shopping, restaurants, friendly people, and reasonable prices complete the offer.

Commodore Cruise Line, Carnival Cruise Line, Royal Caribbean, and Bahama Cruise Lines have traditionally sailed ships into Puerto Plata and Santo Domingo as part of their Caribbean itineraries. With Puerto Plata blossoming as a major tourist attraction, the cruise ship business in past seasons focused there. Of the 89,726 foreign arrivals by cruise ship registered for 1985, a total of 81,433 arrived via Puerto Plata. The industry, however, has suffered an overall decline in comparison to past years, due mainly to technical and service problems at the port facilities. These service problems are in the process of correction and cruise ship arrivals are expected to increase by over 300% for the 1987/88 season.

Another development has been the success of the ferry operation to Mayaguez, Puerto Rico. The route is operated by Dominican Ferries and offers daily (except Saturday) departures from San Pedro de Macoris, which lies halfway between Santo Domingo and La Romana. Passenger fares are RD$296 round-trip, at the time of this writing. For those taking a car on board, there is an additional fee of approximately US$75 or slightly more, depending on the size of the vehicle. Departures from San Pedro are at 10 a.m.

One current package which is a very attractive cruise offer is the *Atlas/Oceanus* cruises out of San Souci port in Santo Domingo. The operator and reservations center in Santo Domingo is Prieto Tours at 125 Avenue Francia (tel: (809) 685-0102/5715). The cruise itinerary covers the U.S. Virgin Islands, Puerto Rico, Guadeloupe, St. Martin, St. Lucia, Barbados (at this port you change to the sister ship for the second week of cruising), St. Vincent, Grenada, Caracas, Curacao, and Aruba. These two-week cruises sail out of the Dominican Republic at an average cost of US$1,700 to US$2,000 at the time of this writing, depending on the cabin location and the day of departure. Check with Prieto Tours in Santo Domingo.

Canadian tour operator Regent Holidays chartered the *TTS Atlas* and the *MTS Oceanus* from Epirotiki Cruise Lines of Greece in order to offer packages through April 1988 that include charter air fare from Toronto to Santo Domingo and two weeks of cruising in Caribbean waters with visits to 14 ports of call. The offer started in November of 1986, and is expected to continue with excellent all-inclusive rates being offered through Regent Holidays in Canada. Prieto Tours is the Dominican tour operator handling the groups in Santo Domingo.

ACCESSIBILITY BY AIR

The Dominican Republic is serviced by a number of international airlines: American Airlines, Eastern, Dominicana de Aviacion, and Pan American Airlines offer daily commercial flights from Miami, Puerto Rico, and New York. APA's small jets fly Miami/Puerto Plata. Iberia is currently flying in from Madrid four times a week. Eastern, Avianca, Viasa, COPA, ALM, as well as Dominicana de Aviacion, connect the country to other Central and South American destinations. Air Canada offers four frequencies a week out of Canada from Montreal and Toronto. Bal Air, a subsidiary of Swiss Air, is handling charter operations scheduled to bring tourists in from Italy and Switzerland. Air France, by the way, is currently negotiating the Santo Domingo-Paris route.

Service to neighboring islands has been further increased by the addition of three weekly Turks and Caicos National Airlines flights into Puerto Plata and a 30-passenger service offered by Air Puerto Rico which entails 32 flights per week out of San Juan and Mayaguez to Santo Domingo and 5 flights per week into La Romana.

There are two major international airport facilities: Las Americas International in Santo Domingo and Puerto Plata International, which services the northern coast. Punta Cana also boasts a remarkably beautiful international airport facility with a busy charter flight flow. A brand new international terminal is being constructed outside the town of Barahona. There are a number of small airfields located throughout the country to facilitate domestic travel. The most important of these is Herrera Airport in Santo Domingo. Flights are available on small craft from here to most of the tourism resorts. Charter services including private jets and helicopter rentals are also available.

The most beautiful of all the small air fields is the one located at Portillo on the northern coast. It services the resort at El Portillo and the adjacent Las Terrenas. You have to know where the airstrip is because the descent is in the middle of a coconut grove...talk about exotic!

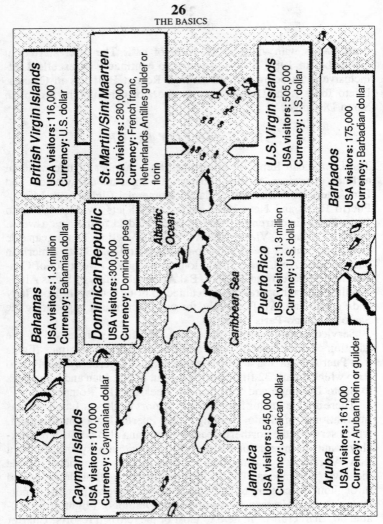

Our Vacation Fantasy Islands

British Virgin Islands
USA visitors: 116,000
Currency: U.S. dollar

St. Martin/Sint Maarten
USA visitors: 280,000
Currency: French franc, Netherlands Antilles guilder or florin

U.S. Virgin Islands
USA visitors: 505,000
Currency: U.S. dollar

Barbados
USA visitors: 175,000
Currency: Barbadian dollar

Bahamas
USA visitors: 1.3 million
Currency: Bahamian dollar

Dominican Republic
USA visitors: 300,000
Currency: Dominican peso

Puerto Rico
USA visitors: 1.3 million
Currency: U.S. dollar

Cayman Islands
USA visitors: 170,000
Currency: Caymanian dollar

Jamaica
USA visitors: 545,000
Currency: Jamaican dollar

Aruba
USA visitors: 161,000
Currency: Aruban florin or guilder

Atlantic Ocean

Caribbean Sea

FOREIGN ARRIVALS

Total foreign arrivals to Dominican Republic	1985	587,006
Total foreign arrivals by air	1985	497,200
Total foreign arrivals by sea	1985	89,726
In Puerto Plata: Total foreign arrivals	1985	100,405
Foreign arrivals by air	1985	98,972
Foreign arrivals by sea	1985	81,433
Foreign arrivals by air to Puerto Plata for the first 6 months	1985	53,293
Foreign arrivals by air to Puerto Plata for the first 6 months	1986*	65,016

*These figures supplied by Infratur, Central Bank indicate a 22% increase in the first 6 months of 1986 as compared with the same period of the previous year in Puerto Plata.

The North American market has shown a substantial increase in overall arrivals to the Dominican Republic. The first eight months of 1986 indicates a 70% increase in U.S. tourists visiting Puerto Plata; 42,033 U.S. citizens entered Puerto Plata by air from January to August of 1986. This is 16,569 tourists over and above the number registered for the same period in 1985. These figures have increased substantially during 1987–88. As for Canadians, the Caribbean Tourism Research Center recently reported that the Dominican Republic ranked third in Canadian choice for desirable vacation destinations.

Canadian tourism was up 20% in the first eight months of 1986, showing 40,181 arrivals as opposed to 34,838 tourist arrivals for the same period in 1985. Considering the limited promotional budget for tourism in the Dominican Republic, these results are an indication of what word of mouth can accomplish.

A recent Ministry of Tourism publication indicates that in tourism air arrivals during the period 1982–1985, there was an average growth rate of 11.4% yearly, which amounts to the highest in all of the Caribbean.

A Spanish courtyard

Average Monthly Temperatures in the Dominican Republic (in degrees Fahrenheit)

	Jan	Feb	Mar	Apr	May	Jun	Jul	Aug	Sep	Oct	Nov	Dec
Min.:	66	66	67	69	71	72	72	73	72	72	70	69
Max.:	84	85	84	85	86	87	88	88	88	87	86	85

Average Monthly Temperatures in the Dominican Republic (in degrees Celsius)

	Jan	Feb	Mar	Apr	May	Jun	Jul	Aug	Sep	Oct	Nov	Dec
Min.:	18.9	18.9	19.4	20.6	21.7	22.2	22.2	22.8	22.2	22.2	21.1	20.6
Max.:	28.9	29.4	28.9	29.4	30.0	30.6	31.1	31.1	31.1	30.6	30.0	29.4

CLIMATE

The Dominican Republic has a very pleasant climate. A tropical country, it is within the 70-to-80-degree Farenheit range on the northern coast and a bit warmer in Santo Domingo, particularly in July and August. On the northern coast, the tradewinds and the mountains combine to give the air a fresh, crystal clean quality.

Those who tell you there isn't a seasonal difference in weather are not very perceptive. From December through February you will probably need to sleep with a blanket and carry a sweater in the evenings. These months are significantly cooler, but the nice part is that it is always warm in the daytime, ideal for pool or beach. April-May and August-October are rainy seasons, which is not to say it is raining all the time. You might have a week of steady rain in this period. Usually, however, tropical showers are brief and there is a predictable time pattern. Don't be surprised if it rains at 7:30 p.m. every night for several days. These patterns seem to develop during the rainy spells. The good news is that even during these months, you can for the most part count on the morning sun, with the rain usually developing late in the day.

CLIMATIC CONDITIONS FOR PUERTO PLATA COMPARED WITH OTHER DESTINATIONS:

Destination	Maximum		Minimum		Mean	
Bahamas	82.9F	28.3C	69.9F	21.1C	76.5F	24.7C
Puerto Plata	80	26.7	72.1	22.3	76.5	24.7
San Juan	81	27.2	74.5	23.6	77.9	25.5
Ocho Rios	77	25	71.4	21.9	74.6	23.7
Acapulco	88.9	31.6	74.6	23.7	81.9	27.7
Honolulu	81.9	27.7	69.8	21.0	75.9	24.4

Chapter 2
GENERAL INFORMATION
TIPS FOR THE TRAVELER

Entry Requirements: Citizens of the United States and Canada need a Tourist Card, which may be purchased through the airline at your point of departure, through any Dominican Consulate, Dominican Tourism Office abroad, or upon arrival for US$5. The card is good for a maximum stay of 60 days, and either a valid passport, or proof of citizenship such as a birth certificate is needed to obtain a card. Legal residents of the United States require an Alien Registration Card in addition to their Tourist Card. Citizens of European countries, Central and South America, and the Far East have varying requirements, which makes it advisable to check with the nearest Consulate or Dominican Tourism Office. Germany, Great Britain, Italy, Switzerland, Spain and Sweden are among the list of countries that have a 90-day allowance without a visa requirement. Citizens must present their passports upon arrival. Citizens of France are required to purchase a Tourist card.

DIRECTORY OF DOMINICAN INFORMATION CENTERS AND TOURISM OFFICES ABROAD

UNITED STATES

485 Madison Avenue
New York, New York 10022
Tel. (212) 826–0750
Telex: 427051

2355 Salcedo Street, Suite 305
Coral Gables, Florida 33134
Tel. (305) 444–4592/93
Telex: 441126 TURIS UI

548 South Spring Street
Suite 309
Los Angeles, California 90013
Tel. (213) 627–3414

CANADA

29 Bellair Street
Toronto M5R 2C8
Canada
Tel. (416) 928–9188

PUERTO RICO

Edif. Miramar Plaza
Ponce de Leon 954
Santurce
Puerto Rico
Tel. (809) 725–4774
Telex: 3450434

ITALY

Via Serbelloni 7
Milan
Italy
Tel. 700290
Telex: 843–620452 GSI 1

UNITED KINGDOM

4 Braemar Mansions
Cornwall Gardens
London SW7
England
Tel. (01) 937–1921
Telex 919073 EMDOM-G

SWITZERLAND

Zollikerstrasse 141
CH–8034 Zurich
Switzerland
Tel. (01) 550242
Telex: 55412 ALPI CH

Via Roncheto 5
P.O. Box 63
CH–6904 Lugano
Switzerland
Tel. (091) 525–321
Telex: 843000

TOUR OPERATORS IN THE DOMINICAN REPUBLIC

CANADA

FIESTA HOLIDAYS
235 Yorkland Boulevard
Willowdell, Ontario M2J 4Y8
Tel. (416) 498–5533

ADVENTURE TOURS
162 Cumberland Street
Toronto, Ontario M5R 1A8
Tel. (416) 967–1510

MIRABELLE TOURS
277 St. Pierre
St. Constant, Quebec J0L 1X0
Tel. (514) 632–5330

REGENT HOLIDAYS
6205 Airport Road
Building A, Suite 300
Mississauga, Ontario LAV 1E1
Tel. (416) 673–0777
Telex: 06–968545

UNITED STATES

ADVENTURE TOURS
403 South Akard
Dallas, Texas 75202
(800) 527–9015
(800) 442–7212
(800) 268–7522 (New York only)
(416) 967–1122 (Toronto only)

A.O.T. TOURS
212–55 26th Avenue
Bayside, New York 11360
(800) 635–3637 (NY State only)
(800) 221–9350 (except NY State)

BERALDI TOURS
8150 S.W. Eighth Street
Majestic Plaza
Suite 216
Miami, Florida 33144
(305) 261–4242
(800) 221–1008

CARIBBEAN HOLIDAYS
711 Third Avenue
New York, New York 10017
(212) 573–8900

CAVALCADE TOURS
5 Penn Plaza
New York, New York 10001
(212) 695–6400

20 Third Street
South Orange, New Jersey 07079
(201) 761–1300
(800) 772–2225

410 Asylum Street
Hartford, Connecticut 06103
(203) 549–5100
(800) 842–0127

FLYFARE
300 East 42nd Street
New York, New York 10017
(212) 661–3100
(800) 367–1033
(800) 523–4116
(800) 825–7615

Sepulveda Boulevard
Suite 420
Los Angeles, California 90045
(213) 410–0278
(800) 237–4906

6600 N.W. 16th Street
Plantation, Florida 33313
(305) 581–4886
(800) 432–1187

FUNTASTIC TOURS
13613 Midway Road
Suite 190
Dallas, Texas 75244
(800) 527–0126

G.I.T. TOURS
2462 Coral Way
Miami, Florida 33145
(305) 854–0075
(800) 433–3977

GOGO TOURS
50 A & S Drive
Paramus, New Jersey 07652
(201) 967–3000
(800) 821–3731

432 Park Avenue South
Suite 1401
New York, New York 10016
(212) 683–7744

3051 Oak Grove Road
Suite 108
Downers Grove, Illinois 60515
(312) 960–4811

HOTELINK/TOURLINK
Box 27158
1712 E. Stop 11 Road
Indianapolis, Indiana 46227
(317) 887–9595
(800) 428–3088 (in U.S. and
        Canada)
(800) 382–3002 (Indiana only)

MARAZUL TOURS
250 West 57th Street
Room 1311
New York, New York 10107
(212) 582–9570
(800) 223–5334

MENA INTERNATIONAL
TRAVEL
2532 N.W. Seventh Street
Miami, Florida 33125
(305) 642–6362
(800) 327–4514

METROPOLIS TOURS
2540 N.W. 29th Avenue
Miami, Florida 33142
(305) 635–1047
(800) 228–4455

SUNBURST HOLIDAYS
4779 Broadway
New York, New York 10034
(212) 567–2900
(800) 223–1277

TRAILS TRAVEL AND
TOURISM
8792 S.W. Eighth Street
Miami, Florida 33174
(305) 227-2200
(800) 782-8687

TRAVEL CONSOLIDATORS
45 West 45th Street
New York, New York 10036
(212) 719-4882
(800) 223-9832

TRAVEL IMPRESSIONS
9 Northern Boulevard
Greenvale, New York 11548
(516) 484-5055
(800) 645-6311 (in the Northeast)

TRAVELOT, LTD.
23-25 Crest Avenue
Winthrop, Massachusetts 02152
(617) 846-5600
(800) 343-3258

Customs Regulations. One liter of alcohol, 200 cigarettes, and US $100 worth of gift items are allowed into the Dominican Republic free of duty. No duty is levied on personal belongings. Punishment for possession of any form of narcotic drug, even in small amounts, is severe and involves up to $50,000 in fines and up to 10 years of imprisonment. Diabetics and those who require prescription drugs should travel with a doctor's prescription.

Departure tax. Foreign residents visiting the Dominican Republic pay a departure tax of US $10.00 when leaving. The departure tax is paid at a designated window *after* departing passengers check in at airline counters. It must be paid before going through immigration. Tax revenues are used to augment costs of immigration processing and for airport facility improvement.

Driving. If you have either an international driver's license or a valid driver's license in your country of residence you may drive a motor vehicle in the Dominican Republic for 90 days. If you anticipate driving, please be aware of traffic regulations before going out. Be especially cautious of Dominican drivers, particularly if you see any large vehicle that says *onatrate* on it. Driving in the Dominican Republic can be confusing. Most of the car rental companies can give you a regulation manual upon request.

Traffic Policemen. As a visitor you have something of an advantage; you can smile and say you're a *turista*. This usually involves a pleasant conversation about your license, your nationality, your home town, and what you think of the Dominican Republic. A few "*muy bonito*'s" might get you through this first episode but don't press your luck, and never argue; it gets lost in translation.

Electric current. The electricity in the Dominican Republic is the same as in the United States, 110 volts, 60 cycles. Be prepared for occasional shutoffs of the power. The national electrical system is in need of improvement and is not quite up to catering to rapidly increasing business and residential demands. As a result, the power is sometimes shut off on a rotating basis that moves from area to area. This should present little or no problem if you are staying in a hotel. Most hotels have their own auxiliary power systems that automatically go on when the utility power goes off. However, if you are staying with friends, you may just have to put up with it.

Time (Atlantic Time). The Dominican Republic is in the same time zone as New York City in the summer. In winter, however, there is a one-hour time difference because Daylight Saving Time is maintained here all year round.

Travellers in the Dominican Republic should be aware that the country's attitudes toward time and punctuality are different from those in the United States. When you want something done for next week, you may want to say that you need it for this week. You may want to anticipate a laxness on punctuality and either relax about it yourself, or make sure that you tell people to show up or get a job done a bit earlier than you want it. Doublecheck things like airline reservations and arrangements for morning wake-up calls.

Language. The country's official language is Spanish. However, there has been a notable increase in the use of English and many people are bilingual, particularly in tourism-related industries.

Government. The government of the Dominican Republic is very similar to that of the United States. There are 29 provinces and the capital which is designated as the National District. Free elections are held every four years on May 16th, and the inauguration takes place on August 16th. There are many political parties, but only three major parties: the Partido Reformista, the Partido Revolucionario Dominicano and the Partido Liberacion Dominicano. The smaller parties throw their support to one or another of the leading parties at election time. There are three legislative bodies. They are the Congress, made up of the Senate and the Chamber of Deputies, the Executive Branch, and the Judicial Branch, with ordinary courts, courts of appeal, and the Supreme Court.

Dominican Holidays. Stores, banks, and most businesses close on the following days:

January 1	New Year's Day
January 21	Day of Our Lady of Altagracia
January 26	Duarte Day
February 27	Independence Day
May 1	Labor Day
June 17	Corpus Christi
August 16	Dominican Restoration Day
September 24	Day of Our Lady of Mercy
December 25	Christmas Day

Good Friday is also a holiday but the date varies. It is always the Friday before Easter. Very few places of entertainment operate on Good Friday, and all casinos are closed on this day.

Carnavál festivities correspond to the Catholic calendar, and usually start the week prior to Ash Wednesday, which begins Lent. The Merengue Festival is usually held the third week in July. Puerto Plata has a festival the second week of October. Easter week is the most crowded time of year at all Dominican beaches. Christmas festivities start early in December. On New Year's Eve, no matter where you are celebrating, the tradition is to meet on the Malecon in the wee hours and watch the sunrise. Most of the cafés and restaurants stay open to serve breakfast to early morning revelers. The Epiphany on January 6th marks the end of the Christmas season.

Clothing. If you are vacationing at a beach resort, casual is perfectly acceptable. In a place like Sosúa, for example, a pair of nice slacks or a summer dress is considered formal. This is a town where the norm is shorts and jeans. The resort hotels of Playa Dorada and Casa de Campo sometimes have activities at night for which you may want to bring casual but nice clothing. Many of the resort facilities have discothèques and one or two restaurants, so we suggest that men take a blazer and women pack a nice dress or pants outfit. For those staying in the city, it is wise to bring both casual pool clothing and sportswear for exploring the town in the daytime, as well as a couple of nice outfits for the evenings. It is not advisable for women to walk around the city in shorts. Shorts are also not allowed in certain restaurants, and are definitely not allowed in casinos. This rule also applies to landmark churches, where we advise conservative dress. We recommend packing comfortable walking shoes and sandals, as well as a sweater or jacket for the cool evenings and air-conditioned nightspots.

Communications. The Dominican Telephone Company, Codetel (a GTE subsidiary), offers domestic and international telephone service with direct distance dialing to the continental U.S., Canada, and Puerto Rico. Satellite three-way communications guarantee contact with any part of the world. Codetel also provides high-tech services, including feed-in to GTE Telenet for access to computerized data banks in over 50 countries. Conference calls and telefax electronic mail are among the available services. Codetel's international operators are all bilingual. Credit card calls operate in the same way as in the United States and all major cards are accepted. Many hotels add a surcharge for operator assistance. The Dominican Republic is the first Latin American country to be connected to the U.S. 800 line for promotion of its services and products. All numbers in the Dominican Republic can be dialed direct from Canada, Europe, and the U.S. by using the 809 area code. All-America Cable, RCA, and ITT provide 24-hour cable service worldwide. You can get *The New York Times* and *The Wall Street Journal* daily, and switch on NBC, CNN, or any of the other 18 cable television network stations which operate 24 hours a day. In addition, there are six local television stations, eight daily newspapers, over 200 radio stations, and one weekly newspaper in English, *The Santo Domingo News* (for local tourism and business news). Many of the hotels have installed television satellites as well.

Foreign Commercial Banks in the Dominican Republic. Please see section on investment for banking hours and addresses. The Chase Manhattan Bank, The Bank of Nova Scotia, and Citibank among others all maintain branches in Santo Domingo.

Currency and traveler's checks. The Dominican *peso*, written RD$, is the official monetary unit and fluctuates in value relative to the U.S. dolar. The *peso* symbol is the same as the dollar symbol, so if you become confused, stop and ask for further information. Coins resemble those of the U.S. and Canada. The rate of exchange has changed dramatically since 1987, and at this writing is in the neighborhood of RD$6.40 per US$1. You may exchange currency at the airport, commercial banks, and most large hotels and resorts. Avoid changing more than you need, as the banks are not permitted to convert *pesos* back into dollars (as of summer 1988). It can be *very* difficult to change Dominican money back into another currency, so we suggest that you buy Dominican *peso* only as you need them. Try to end your stay with almost **no pesos** if possible, then you will avoid last-minute problems with exchange. There are some street people frequenting high-density tourist areas who will attempt to sell you *pesos* at what appears to be an extremely favorable rate. **Beware.** Since they will take advantage of your limited knowledge of the monetary situation, you may either become a victim of a con game, or become party to a practice that has just recently been outlawed.

Traveler's checks are accepted by most gasoline stations, and most of the tourist hotels and facilities. You will also get fair exchange rates when exchanging travelers checks for *pesos* at typical Dominican exchange banks, such as Banco de Cambio.

Credit Cards. Most major credit cards are accepted here, and this can prove very convenient. Our experience has been that the exchange rates built into the credit card billing systems have worked out to be reasonably fair, so by all means use your cards. You will also get a favorable exchange rate with the use of credit cards. For business visitors, a credit card receipt is generally your best proof of purchase.

Tipping. Hotels, nightclubs, and restaurants include a 10% service charge on bills. It is customary, however, for patrons to leave an extra 10% gratuity for good service. A 5% government tax is added to all hotel bills. In addition, hotels, resorts, nightclubs, and restaurants are required to include a 6% value-added tax on all bills. Porters, taxi drivers, beach attendants, and housekeeping staff at the hotels should be tipped according to your usual custom and the quality of service offered.

TRANSPORTATION

Taxi. Whether you are staying in Santo Domingo, Puerto Plata, or one of the resort hotels, you will find taxi service readily available. Each hotel has a number of taxis—an average four to six per hotel—on duty throughout the day. The hotel doorman will summon the taxi driver up from the driveway or parking area. Many of the hotels have an extension number for their taxi service in case you wish to reserve in advance. The hotel taxis have a standard rate sheet which they can show you upon request. Some of the Playa Dorada resort hotels have started posting the rates at the entrance to the hotel. At the time of this writing, the Playa Dorada taxis charged 25 *pesos* round-trip, including waiting time, to drive you into town for lunch or dinner. The taxis operating out of the hotels tend to be comfortable, large eight cylinder cars, well maintained, and air-conditioned. If there isn't a taxi on duty at the moment you need it, the front desk can phone for one. You can arrange hourly fares or rates that include an entire morning or afternoon of service. Fares to Las Americas Airport from Santo Domingo average 20 to 25 *pesos* at present. If there is waiting time involved, there is an extra charge.

By law, taxi fares are in Dominican *pesos*. You are not required to pay U.S. or Canadian currency at any time, unless you wish to do so. Do not hesitate to confirm the fare before leaving your hotel. You will find the drivers polite and cooperative, and their vehicles in excellent condition. In addition to the hotel taxis, there are several services in Santo Domingo which you can call for a taxi. These companies work 24 hours a day for the most part, which makes them convenient, particularly if you require transportation late at night. The taxis are air-conditioned and in good shape. We have listed some of the better known companies. They offer single fare and hourly rates and the fares mentioned are current at the time of this writing.

TAXI RADIO: 562–1313, 562–1101

In addition to their single run fares, they offer an hourly rate of 17.50 *pesos* in the city. Trips to the airport cost 20.50 *pesos* during the day and 28.00 *pesos* at night. All the vehicles have a radio unit, so that when you phone in, they radio the car that is closest to your address.

TAXI RAFFI: 689–5468, 685–2268

Offers 24-hour service at the same rate as listed above.

MICROMOVIL: 689–2000

Service offered both in and outside the city limits during a 24-hour period. Micromovil uses air-conditioned vans, which are spacious, comfortable, and ideal for family transportation. Their rate in the city is currently 20 *pesos* an hour.

TAXI LA PALOMA: 567–1412, 567–1437

Operates between 6 a.m. and 12 p.m. and is currently offering a special hourly rate of 15 *pesos* inside the city. Airport runs have a fare of 19.50 *pesos* between early morning and 4 p.m. changing to 24.00 *pesos* between 4 p.m. and 12 p.m.

All these taxi services have reliable, registered drivers, full insurance and are perfectly safe. They will also quote rates over the telephone for driving you outside Santo Domingo to destinations in the interior and coastal areas of the country. Tipping the driver is not required, but is customary.

Public Taxis (*Público*). In Puerto Plata you will always find taxis around the central square that encases the Victorian gazebo. Be clear on the fare before you get in. " *¿ Cuánto cuesta?* " is the key phrase for finding out how much this is going to cost you. The small towns of the interior all have public taxis or *públicos* as they are known. The cars are generally in varying stages of dilapidation, but the drivers are usually very pleasant and for those with a sense of adventure this can be a very entertaining experience.

In Santo Domingo, we only advise you to take *públicos* along busy thoroughfares. For example, if you are going from the Santo Domingo Hotel to Calle El Conde, a *público* ride down Independencia will only cost you 40 *centavos*. It's an inexpensive and rapid way of getting around but has its drawbacks. The cars are not usually in good condition, the drivers speed, and you are subject to having other passengers pile in on top of you since they sometimes cram up to five passengers in the back seat. Generally speaking, we really don't encourage you to experiment with *público* transportation unless you are very gregarious by nature and don't mind roughing it a bit. If you are determined, stand by the side of the principal avenues, Independencia, Bolívar, or Abraham Lincoln, and wait for one to come along. When a driver signals straight ahead, you'll know that is his direction; if he signals left, for example, it means he will make a left turn in his route. Once you are in, don't wait for him to ask you for the fare. Have your money ready; a *peso* will more than cover you, and the driver will give you the change. Most runs average 40 *centavos*. When you want to get off, just say "*aquí por favor*" or "*la próxima*," which indicates the next corner. The driver will stop constantly along his route to let passengers on or off.

These *públicos* also do *carreras*, or private passenger runs to a specific address, and will cost less than the cab companies and the hotel taxis. It's a trade on comfort for savings, but they will get you where you want to go. You can just hail one as you normally would any taxi and say "*carrera*." The fare from colonial Santo Domingo to one of the uptown hotels can run from five to eight *pesos*.

Car Rentals. Renting a vehicle in the Dominican Republic is never a problem. Agencies such as Avis, Hertz, and Budget service the airport terminals and have offices in both Santo Domingo and Puerto Plata. Rates are about comparable to those in the States, although they may be higher. The reason for this is that no automobiles are manufactured in the country. As a result, imported autos are charged a very high import tariff by the government, resulting in high operating costs for cars when averaged out by the mile. This is a very understandable problem for the Dominicans, so bear with it, and go with the flow when it seems prices are somewhat high. A pleasing effect of the high gasoline prices in the country is that most of the rental cars have engines that get extremely high mileage. Most companies require a deposit of approximately $100 or a major credit card in order to rent.

There are more than 50 car rental companies registered with the Ministry of Tourism. Several dozen operate out of Las Americas Airport alone. A driver's license from your country of residence or an international driver's license is required.

Many of the companies have a minimum rental requirement of two to three days. Insurance coverage plans are available for an additional charge of approximately 15 to 35 *pesos*, depending on the type of coverage. Some of the companies offer a basic insurance plan as part of the rental fee. Most of the large hotels have rental agencies in the lobby. A partial listing of the most popular companies follows.

Maps offered by the auto rental companies are only so-so. We recommend your buying *Mapa Turistico*, a very good road map of the country privately published and sold in most major hotel gift shops for about 10 *pesos*.

DIRECTORY OF AUTO RENTAL COMPANIES

Auto Rental	34 Ortega y Gasset	565–7873
Avis	Abraham Lincoln Ave.	533–3530
Budget	John F. Kennedy Ave.	567–0173
Econo Car	George Washington Ave.	682–6242
Fama	27th of February Ave.	688–0707
Hertz	Independencia Ave.	688–2277
Jomi	27th of February Ave.	567–5956
Marlon	27th of February Ave.	566–3435
McDeal	George Washington Ave.	688–6518
National	Abraham Lincoln Ave.	562–1444
Nelly	139 Jose Contreras	532–7346
Pueblo	Independencia Avenue	689–2000
Quality	George Washington Ave.	687–8727
Rentauto	27th of February Ave.	566–7221
Roma	Independencia Ave.	532–0505
Rentauto Puerto Plata	Puerto Plata Intl.	(800) 631–0058
Puerto Plata Rent Car	Puerto Plata Intl.	586–0215
Abby Puerto Plata	John F. Kennedy Ave.	586–2516/ 586–3995

We took a random sample so as to see what you can expect from some of the more popular rental companies. All of these have a large selection of air-conditioned vehicles, both automatic and standard shift, ranging from economy compact cars to luxury sedan models. Average rental runs approximately the equivalent of US$50 per day. This is expensive by international standards, but cab fares add up too, and there is no question that having a car at your disposal allows you maximum freedom of movement.

AVIS: 533–3530, 533–9295

Santo Domingo: Offices at the Sheraton, Hotel Santo Domingo, and Las Americas Airport.
Puerto Plata: 586–3988; Puerto Plata Intl. Airport: 586–0214

Free mileage. 24-hour minimum rental period. Repairs until 9 p.m. Large selection with average cost of 150 *pesos* per day. 30% discount on weekly rentals.

AUTO RENTAL: 565–7873, 687–0640

Offices at Ortega y Gasset 34 and at Las Americas Airport.

Free mileage. Minimum three-day rental. Average rental cost of 138 *pesos* per day. 18 *pesos* per day discount if you rent weekly or monthly. Also rent vans with or without drivers.

BUDGET: 567–0173/74/75/76 in Santo Domingo
               586–2685 in Puerto Plata

Offices on John F. Kennedy Avenue and at Las Americas Airport. Free mileage. Average rental of 128 *pesos* daily. If you rent for a week, you get one day free. They have minibuses and jeeps as well.

EXPRESS: 687–9369
Bolivár Avenue

Free mileage. Two-day minimum. Average 150 *pesos* per day with insurance included. Free day if you rent on weekly contract.

HERTZ: 688–2277
Avenue Independencia

Limited mileage. Minimum one-day rental. Average cost between 100 and 200 *pesos* per day.

TOYOTA RENT CAR: 566–4221
27th of February Avenue

Free mileage. Two-day minimum rental. One day free on weekly rentals. Average rental of 180 *pesos* plus insurance. Minibus, jeeps, and limousines available. Limousines are chauffeur-driven and cost 50 *pesos* an hour. They must be rented for a two-hour minimum.

NATIONAL RENT CAR: 562–1444
Abraham Lincoln Avenue and Las Americas Airport

Free mileage after three days. No minimum number of days required. Average rental 132 to 159 *pesos* plus insurance.

GENERAL RENT CAR:

Las Americas Airport	687–0528
Embajador Hotel	533–2131
Continental Hotel	689–1151
Caribe Hotel	688–8141
Montemar Hotel	586–2800
Sosúa	571–2683

Automatic, air-conditioned cars. Can hire with driver. Average US$45 per day rentals.

RENT AUTO: 1(800) 631–0058, 567–7128/7146
Located 27th of February Avenue in Santo Domingo

Santiago	582–3130
La Romana	556–4181
Puerto Plata Intl. Airport	568–0240
Las Americas Intl. Airport	687–0655

Free mileage. Can rent by the day, week, or month. Average rental 148 *pesos* including insurance. Limousines available with drivers on an hourly basis at 50 *pesos*.

A newcomer to the Puerto Plata region is RENT-A-WRECK, with offices at the rotunda on the road to Playa Dorado. Here, you can rent a canvas-topped vehicle that looks like a converted motorized tricycle for 45 *pesos* including insurance. Sturdier transportation goes for 92 *pesos* including insurance. Another popular mode of transport in Puerto Plata and the resort areas of Playa Dorada and Sosúa is the motorbike. Small 80cc motorbikes rent for an average of 30 *pesos* a day at the resorts, but are available for weekly rental at about 150 *pesos* per week by the port.

Bus Travel. There is excellent daily bus service to the major tourist spots and towns of the interior. The buses are air-conditioned, comfortable, and well cared-for. They run on reliable schedules. Most, however, are driven at breakneck speed. The principal companies all seem to operate on a one-way fare system; you buy your ticket when you arrive at the terminal sales desk. Advance telephone reservations are advisable however, particularly if you are traveling on the weekend. Call the day before or very early on the morning of your trip. A few of the best companies are listed below. Rates are current at the time of this writing.

METRO:
Santo Domingo: 566–6590
566–6587

Puerto Plata: 586–3736

In addition to the many interior towns on its itinerary, Metro offers three daily trips to and from Puerto Plata and five trips daily to and from Santiago. One-way fares are 15 *pesos* for Puerto Plata and 12 *pesos* for Santiago.

TERRABUS:
Santo Domingo: 565–2333
Santiago: 582–4554
Puerto Plata: 586–4202

Terrabus travels eight times a day to and from Santiago, and four times daily to Puerto Plata. You'll think you're on a plane when you see the uniformed stewardesses serving free coffee and snacks. Uses the same one-way fare system and rates as Metro. Box lunches are available for an additional 2 *pesos*. They use brand new Mercedes-Benz buses. Registered baggage handling and medical services available. Magazines and newspapers on board. Buses leave from Plaza Criolla. Their Puerto Plata terminal is part of a new shopping mall, Centro Comercial La Plaza, which includes a restaurant and boutiques.

CARIBE TOURS:
Santo Domingo: 687–3171/76, 685–6215
Puerto Plata: 586–0282

Currently, this is the only company with service to and from Sosúa with two trips a day at a one-way fare of 14 *pesos*. They run several times a day to Puerto Plata at a one-way fare of 12 *pesos*. Also covers Santiago, Rio San Juan, and Samana. All of the above are also available for charter service and group ground operations as are Transporte Tanya (565–5691) and Expresos Dominicanos (682–6610).

INTERNAL TOUR COMPANIES

There are many. Almost every hotel has a tour desk and an operator in residence. Tours can be tailor-made, or you can select one of the available scheduled trips. Santo Domingo's city tours are standard. They involve the principal landmarks of the colonial city, the Malecon, the modern city, and Plaza de la Cultura. Tours allow time for shopping, as well as visits to nightclubs and casinos. From what we've been able to determine, the going rate is about US$10 for the basic city tour with a duration of approximately three hours.

In Puerto Plata, the city tours include shopping and a visit to Mt. Isabel de Torres, with a cable car ride. There are also trips available to Sosua, and to Santiago at night for dinner and casino.

DIRECTORY OF TOUR OPERATORS

BIBI TRAVEL:
Santo Domingo 532–7141

DIMARGO TOURS:
Santo Domingo 562–5656/6952

MAGNA TOURS:
Santo Domingo 532–8267/7141

OMNI TOURS:
Santo Domingo 566–4228

DORADO TRAVEL:
Santo Domingo 688–6661

PRIETO TOURS:
Santo Domingo 688–5715
Puerto Plata 586–3988

SANTO DOMINGO TOURS:
Santo Domingo 562–4865/4870

TANYA TOURS:
Santo Domingo 565–5691

TURINTER:
Santo Domingo 685–4020

THOMAS TOURS:
Santo Domingo 687–8645

VIMENCA TOURS:
Santo Domingo 533–9362
Puerto Plata 586–3883

METRO TOURS:
Santo Domingo 567–3138

PUERTO PLATA TOURS
Puerto Plata 586–3858

VIAJES CONTINENTES:
Santo Domingo 532–0825

TROPICAL TOURS:
La Romana 556–2636

Light Airplane Charter. Cessna, twin- and single-engine planes and helicopters are all available for rental complete with pilot. There are several small craft charter companies operating out of Herrera Airport in Santo Domingo. Available for charter are LearJets, Cessna Citation, Cessna 400 series twins, Piper Navajo, Cessna 206, 172, 182, Bell Jetranger, and a number of other possibilities. The principal companies are:

FAXA AIR TAXI: 567–1195

SERVICIOS AEREOS PROFESIONALES: 565–2448

SERVICIOS AEREOS TURISTICOS: 566–1696, 567–7406

TRANSPORTE AEREO: 566–2141

UNI CHARTER: 567–0481, 567–0818

Round-trip charter costs run from approximately 400 *pesos* to 1,050 *pesos*, depending upon the destination within the country, size of plane, and number of passengers. There are no scheduled flights; it's all done on a charter basis. Helicopters run 700 *pesos* per hour. These companies also provide ambulance service.

Prieto Tours operates an air taxi service to Portillo costing 290 *pesos* one way. Just phone and reserve the day and time you wish to go (685–0102/688–5715).

Airborne Ambulance Service (52 Tiradentes Avenue, tel. 567–1101/4171, or their beeper at 567–9551 ext. 884), a division of National Jets, rents executive jets. In addition to business services, they offer complete ambulance services, 24 hours a day.

STREET ENTERTAINMENT

Windshield Cleaners and Street Vendors. Sometimes these are a convenience and sometimes a total nuisance. It is always wise to have a *peso* on hand in case you see some attractive fruit. Most vendors will rush up to your car with a bunch of bananas or a bag of oranges for about one *peso*. One hundred oranges at one of the sidewalk fruit stands go for about seven *pesos*! Also, keep some small change on hand for the window washers, who are usually children trying to make a living. Some of us have our windows done about ten times a day.

Strolling Musicians and "the Monkey Man." The towns of the interior have their own variation of this, but in Santo Domingo it is the "monkey man" and a number of strolling guitarists, portable steel bands, singers, art peddlers, flower people, and roasted peanut vendors. They are all quite harmless and part of the local folklore. You are either interested or you are not. If not, a firm *"no gracias"* should do it. You haven't really completed your tour of Santo Domingo, unless you sit through one of the monkey man's bilingual acrobatic performances. They usually take place on the Malecon, in front of Vesuvio or any one of several outdoor dining facilities.

Fresh coconut juice is a popular drink

Chapter 3

EARLY HISTORY

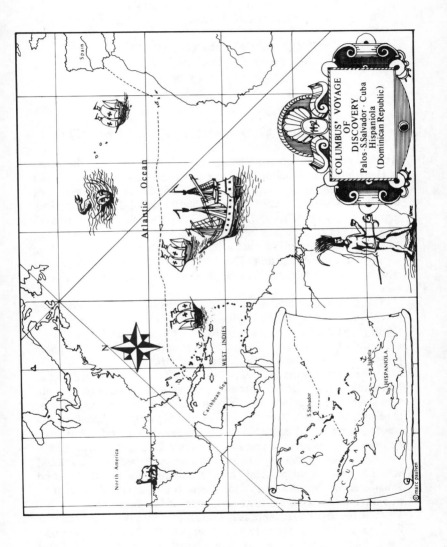

COLUMBUS' VOYAGE
OF
DISCOVERY
Palos-S.Salvador - Cuba
Hispaniola
(Dominican Republic)

Spain

Atlantic Ocean

North America

Caribbean Sea

WEST INDIES

S.Salvador

Isabela

CUBA

HISPANIOLA

© marc paulsen

"Behold the island of Espaniola,
The most beautiful land human eyes have ever seen"

CHRISTOPHER COLUMBUS,
"ADMIRAL OF THE OCEAN SEA"
Diary of first voyage
December 5, 1492

DISCOVERY AND EARLY SETTLEMENTS

At the time of discovery by Christopher Columbus in 1492, the island of Hispaniola was inhabited by descendants of Arawak Indians. Some of these tribes, unlike the Caribes who were the most belligerent of the island warriors, were of a noble and peaceful disposition. This gentle society came to be known as *Taino*, which means "good." However, not all the tribes were equally gentle. The Ciguayos and the Macorixes were more like the Caribes in their methods of waging war against the early colonizers. The natives called the island *Quisqueya* which means "greatness," or *Haiti* which signifies "rugged mountain."

There were five *cacicazgos* or realms, presided over by *caciques* or rulers. Jaragua, for example, was the name of one *cacicazgo*. Higuey was the name of another. Many of these same Indian names are familiar to us today because they have been used to designate provinces, cities, tourism facilities, and parks.

On his first voyage in 1492, Columbus built a provisional fort at Navidad (which means Christmas), a name he chose because the date was December 25th. He had his men build the fort with wood from the *Santa Maria*, which hit the reefs as the ships approached the north coast. As he sailed eastward along the coast from Fort Navidad,

Columbus discovered and named Monte Cristi, the Yaqui River, which he named Rio de Oro or river of gold because you could actually gather gold particles by the handful, and finally reached Samana Bay, where he set sail for Spain. It is understandable that he was anxious to tell the King and Queen of his discoveries.

After his departure, there is historical evidence that the settlers at Fort Navidad became greedy, hoarding gold for themselves and taking as many Indian women as they fancied. This latter practice did not endear them to some of the local *caciques*. Caonabo, Cacique of

Maguana and a mean-tempered Caribe, decided a massacre was in order. So much for the original 39 settlers.

The second voyage of the Admiral saw the creation of Isabela, named for Queen Isabel of Castile, the Catholic Queen of Spain. The town of Isabela was founded on January 2, 1494 by a small group of settlers who quickly constructed housing, a small plaza, church and hospital. This was for these men a true beginning.

From Isabela, explorers set out to look for gold. They found considerable amounts in the Cibao mountains, the region of Constanza and the area of La Vega. It was from the mountains of the Cibao that the first shipments of gold were sent from the New World to the King of Spain. There are many interesting anecdotes connected to the quest for gold. One favorite is the story of Miguel Diaz, who fled Isabela on criminal charges. He headed south and became romantically involved with a beautiful Indian princess from the Ozama area. She told him of gold deposits near the Haina River. Being a clever man he traded on this for his pardon. Thanks to this early form of plea bargaining, the Spaniards headed south. Lured by the prospect of gold, they came to Santo Domingo, a settlement founded by Bartholomew, brother of Christopher Columbus, in 1496. As for Miguel and his lady, they were married, had children, and she was baptized Catalina.

In those early years, while Columbus was busy colonizing and traveling back and forth four times, the gossip at the Court of Spain was raging. On his third voyage, he was actually sent home in irons. The intrigue was an attempt by other explorers to discredit the Admiral with King Ferdinand of Aragon and his Queen, Isabel, and thereby break the Columbus monopoly.

Meanwhile, back on Hispaniola, everything was going as well as could be expected, although this was not true for the Indians, who were being ''pacified'' into the role of vassals of Spain. Caonabo had been arrested for his part in the destruction of Fort Navidad and subsequently died while being shipped to Spain as a sort of exhibition piece. Caonabo was regarded as the most valiant *cacique* of his time. After his death, the subjugation of the others was achieved with relative ease and unabashed brutality, a well-chronicled trait of the Conquistadores.

In the year 1502, Nicolas de Ovando became governor of the island. He was convinced that the Indians were planning an uprising and that the best way to deal with the problem was to find a ''final solution'' for their leaders. Ovando completely ignored the admonitions of Queen Isabel about the mistreatment of the Indians and he set out to Jaragua to round up and slaughter as many *caciques* as possible. One victim of the massacre was the widow of Caonabo. Her name was Anacaona and she was considered to be the most beautiful and intelligent woman on the island. She received the Ovando contingent in peace with a celebration of music and dance. She was hanged for her efforts, although there is some debate as to whether her execution took place in Jaragua or whether she was brought to Santo Domingo and publicly executed in what is today Duarte Park. Many of the other *caciques* and tribesmen were massacred during the siege of Jaragua.

In spite of his cruelty to the Indian population, Ovando was considered a capable governor. He centralized all systems and built up the city of Santo Domingo. He fully exploited the potential of the mines, which kept the court of Spain happy. After the forced labor of the mines virtually destroyed the Indians, Ovando, ever inventive, brought the first African slaves in. His administration was also the first to introduce the production of sugarcane, which had been brought in from the Canary islands. By 1509, when Ovando handed the government to Diego Columbus, son of the Admiral and newly appointed Viceroy of Spain, the colony was well-organized and prosperous.

By all indications, the court of Diego was one of political intrigue, constant scheming, religious fervor, and privileged extravagance. Diego was a despot, even by colonial standards, and the Indians suffered worse abuse during his administration. As for the ostentation of the court, news of silk clothing embroidered in gold, silver, brocade, and jewels, reached the disapproving monarch of Spain. Worse still, these excesses were not limited to the court, but to all the prosperous colonists as well. Diego was not deterred by Spain's disapproval. Armies of servants, grand houses, and pomp aplenty were all part of the role he had assumed. His *Alcazar* was a fortress and palace befitting a king and consort. His wife, Maria de Toledo, fit the role, too. She was a niece of the Duke of Alba and a favorite of the court of Spain. Rumors were rampant that perhaps being viceroy was not quite enough for the headstrong ruler. Such accusations plagued Diego throughout his career in Santo Domingo. Much of the gossip originated among influential members of his colonial court, such as Miguel Pasamonte, who directed the treasury and enjoyed King Ferdinand's favor.

THE ADMIRAL AND THE PRIVATEER: CHRISTOPHER COLUMBUS

Most likely born in Genoa around the year 1446 (some historians believe his date of birth was actually closer to 1450), Columbus started sailing at the age of fourteen. As a youth, he studied geometry and astronomy at the University of Pavia, but his first love was always the sea.

In 1476, he was bound for England with four ships when he was attacked off the coast of Cape St. Vincent by a privateer whose name was Guillaume de Casenove. Two of the four ships escaped with him to Lisbon and subsequently he resumed his voyage to England, where he is said to have spent some time traveling around the British Isles as far as the northern coast of Scotland. For a time, he is said to have made navigational maps and charts for a living, while living in Porto Santo, where his wife's family were prestigious merchants in the community. At this time he became fascinated by the tales of the local seamen about their voyages and the mysterious legends of the western seas. He conceived the idea of reaching Asia by sailing west in the early 1480s. This was to be called his "Western Enterprise." He was greatly influenced in his geographic concepts by the work of past navigators like Marco Polo and Leif Ericson, as well as by reports of ancient mariners.

But this is not to suggest that Columbus was a dreamer. He loved the sea above all else and was as moved as any youth of his day by the stories of exploits on the high seas. He was also practical and ambitious. From all accounts, he had very definite ideas on the course he would follow and his need for backing from one of the courts of Europe. He was not particularly patriotic, but he was determined to go with the sovereign who was most sympathetic to his project and would support his trip. To outfit ships and a crew for such a venture was costly, and Columbus was pragmatic enough to know that he could not approach the kings of Europe with an attitude of humility and a modest proposal.

He initially sought the protection of King John II of Portugal and presented his plan of sailing a western route across the ocean to reach Asia. Columbus believed the world to be round and much smaller in proportion than he later realized. By the same token, he completely overestimated the size of the Asian continent.

King John submitted the Columbus plan to a council of advisors who were opposed to the scheme. But King John secretly tried to put the plan into effect with his own navigators. Discovering this betrayal, Columbus packed his bags and left Lisbon for Spain in 1484. His departure for Spain was hasty and secretive, presumably to give the slip to King John but more than likely because he had considerable debts in Lisbon. Among many of the early explorers and conquistadors bad debts were commonplace and a number of them were to leave Santo Domingo in later years under similar circumstances. This does not take away from Columbus' grandeur, it simply indicates that he was as human as his colleagues: he was not only ambitious and shrewd, but also expedient and pragmatic.

He spent the next twelve years trying to enlist support for his project at the courts of Spain, France, and Portugal. He settled in the south of Spain while preparing his proposal to the court of France. During this period, he applied to Queen Isabela of Spain and was ultimately summoned to her court at Cordova in 1486. The time he chose was not the best. Castile and Leon were in the middle of conflict with the Moors, who were advancing from Granada, and the King and Queen were too preoccupied with the Moorish threat to listen to his farfetched plans of exploration. He used the time at court well, making many friends and winning important supporters for his cause. One of these admiring supporters was Beatrice Enriquez, who was to be his second wife and mother of his son, Fernando.

He was not successful in gaining the support he sought as he followed the Spanish sovereigns around from court to court. While they were situated in Salamanca, he left for Lisbon to try and patch up his differences with King John. Again frustrated in his attempts at obtaining tangible support, he returned to Spain, where he finally received a promise from the court that they would consider his plan once the Granada war was over. After the surrender of Granada in January of 1492 he saw his opportunity in an audience set up by the Queen's confessor, Juan Perez.

He felt a modest approach would not make much of an impression on the monarch, so he presented his requirements on a grand scale. Columbus first asked for the rank of Admiral of the Ocean in all the seas, islands, and continents he might discover, along with the Vice Royalty of everything he discovered. He also asked for a tenth of all the precious metals found within the domain of his admiralty. At first the conditions were rejected, but ultimately an agreement was signed in April 1492 between Columbus and the Catholic Kings. Men, ships, and supplies were made ready for him. Columbus was also given a royal letter of introduction to the Grand Khan of Cathay from Isabel and Ferdinand. The expedition set sail on Friday, August 3, 1492, with three ships: the *Nina*, a 40-ton ship manned with a crew of 18, the *Pinta*, a 50-ton ship also manned with a crew of 18 men, and the *Santa Maria*, the largest of the three ships and a decked ship of 100 tons with a crew of 52 men commanded by the Admiral himself.

After a brief stop at the Canary Islands, they set sail again for what must have seemed endless days at sea, until at 2 a.m. on Friday, October 12, 1492, Rodrigo de Triana, a sailor aboard the *Pinta*, sighted land—the first glimpse of the New World. Columbus called this first sighting the island of San Salvador but it was later known as Watling Island. This first voyage resulted in the discovery of islands today known as Rum Cay, Crooked Island, Cuba, and Hispaniola, which is now comprised of Haiti and the Dominican Republic.

The *Santa Maria* ran aground on the northern coast off Hispaniola. The ship had to be abandoned and Columbus had his men use the materials from the ship to build the first fort in the New World, Fort Navidad. He left behind the bulk of the crew while the Nina and Pinta sailed back to Spain. Because of storms at sea, it was mid-March before he finally reached Portugal.

Columbus enjoyed a triumphal return, received in full court with a great deal of pomp. While he exhibited riches and spoils from the first voyage, he was seated with the King and Queen of Spain. In addition to gold, he brought back cotton, parrots and rare birds, Indian weapons, medicinal plants, and a few Indian natives brought back for baptism. As a result of his accomplishments and the bounty from his maiden trip, Columbus was conferred with full honors: the title of ''Don'' was affixed to his name, bestowing upon him the position of aristocrat in the Spanish court, and a magnificent scutcheon was blazoned for him in May 1493 in which the royal castle and lion of Castile and Leon were combined with five anchors. All of this excitement whetted the Admiral's appetite for a second voyage, and plans were immediately started for the expedition of late 1493.

THE SECOND VOYAGE

Three galleons and 14 caravels (light frigate) left on September 25, 1493. This time, they carried over 1,500 men along with provisions, personal belongings, and cattle for the first settlement. The expedition left with orders to christianize the islanders and to treat the Indian population of the islands well, under threat of punishment. On this voyage, Dominica, Guadeloupe, and Puerto Rico were discovered, as were the Virgin Islands.

Columbus arrived at Hispanola in late November, only to find Fort Navidad destroyed. He founded La Isabela on the coast between Monte Cristi and what is now Puerto Plata. During this expedition he discovered Jamaica and explored the islands of the Caribbean as well as the Mona Passage. In his diary, he claimed that during this exhausting period, he went for 33 days with hardly any sleep. He became very ill and, upon returning to La Isabela, had to remain convalescing for five months. There was a great deal of sickness in the colony because of poor nutrition, heat, tropical disease, problems of hygiene, and overall conditions that were drastically different from what the settlers were accustomed to. Greed for gold and disrespect for the native population compounded the problems of colonization faced by the Admiral.

Meanwhile, back at the Spanish court, intrigue was rampant. Because of negative reports reaching the monarchs, Juan Aguado was dispatched to Hispaniola with a royal commission to report on the state of the colony. He arrived with the attitude of a judge and this was irritating to the Admiral. Columbus decided it was time to journey home to Spain in order to clear things up. He arrived by June 1496 at the port of Cadiz. The King and Queen unexpectedly welcomed him and put a fleet of eight vessels at his disposal. He was also offered a tract of land and the title of Duke. For three years he received up to 10% of net profits from each voyage. His sons were received at court as pages to the Queen.

THE THIRD VOYAGE FROM SPAIN

Columbus set sail again in May 1498. On this journey, he discovered Trinidad and, by August, was sailing along the coast of South America. He apparently underestimated the size of the continent, at first thinking it to be another island. By late August 1498, he entered the harbor of Santo Domingo, by now the capital city of Hispaniola and the first city of the New World.

Back in Spain, gossip prevailed. There were many negative reports on excesses in the colony and on the abuse of the Indian tribes. To put this in perspective, it is important to recall that Columbus had maneuvered himself into a position of monopoly on exploration, a fact that irritated many potential explorers who would have liked to cash in on the riches of New World exploits. By May 1499, Columbus was out of favor at court and Francisco Bobadilla was appointed Governor of Hispaniola. Bobadilla arrived in August 1500, took possession of the Admiral's residence, put Columbus in irons, and sent him in disgrace back to Spain.

According to historical accounts, on the journey back to Spain the captain of the vessel, Alonso Vallejo, an admirer of Columbus, ordered the chains removed but the Admiral refused, saying he would wear them until the King and Queen ordered their removal and that even afterwards he would keep them to remind him of his reward for service to the crown. His younger son, Fernando, later recalled seeing these chains kept as a sort of relic by his father and claimed his father wanted them to be buried with him. There is no evidence that this wish was carried out when he died.

Royal feeling in those days was volatile at best and, before Bobadilla could do further harm, Columbus admirers at court convinced the Queen he had been wronged. He regained his good standing and, by the time he made his appearance in court, all was well and he was received with honors. The Queen is said in some accounts to have been moved to tears at the thought of how this great man had been wronged. Columbus promptly requested and received compensation for the losses and damage done him. A new governor, Nicolas de Ovando, was sent along with a fleet of 30 ships to take over from Bobadilla and restore the Admiral's property.

FOURTH AND LAST VOYAGE FROM SPAIN

Determined to please the Queen by finding a strait that would lead through to Asia, Columbus set sail once more in 1502. He weathered a hurricane off the coast of Hispaniola during which many galleons en route to Spain perished, including the one carrying his enemy, Bobadilla. After refitting his ships near what is now Azua, he left the coast of Hispaniola and sailed for the coast of Honduras.

On a small coastal island near Honduras, an old Indian chief told him of rich lands to the east which he assumed must be the empire of the great Khan. After enduring hardships and near mutiny, he resolved to turn around and abandon further exploration for the moment, but not without first attempting to form a colony on the border of the river Veragua. (The name Veragua was subsequently given as title to his descendants and the current Duke of Veragua was instrumental in the restoration and refurbishing of the Columbus fortress-palace in Santo Domingo, the "Alcazar," which is described in the section on colonial landmarks).

Colonization attempts were aborted at this point, and the Navigator headed back for Cuba in search of rest and provisions. Unfortunately, he ran his ships aground in Jamaica, in the harbor of St. Ann's Bay. This small inlet is still called Don Christopher's Cove. The year was 1503. Columbus remained here for a year, during which time his men did their best to alienate the natives and he, in turn, kept them in a cooperative frame of mind by convincing them that he had supernatural powers by predicting an eclipse and playing on their superstitions. Governor Ovando sent ships to his aid, and Columbus was finally able to set sail in 1504. He arrived briefly in Hispaniola and then continued on to Spain, which he reached in November of that year, almost twelve years to the date of the start of his great adventure.

This time, he was too ill to go to court. He suffered from gout and was exhausted from the years of constant strain, threat of rebellion, ignorant crews, problems with the Indians, disease, storms at sea, and intrigue at court. Some historians have claimed that he was a broken man at this stage. He was not broken in spirit, and was convinced to the end that he could still do extraordinary service to the King and Queen.

Aside from the diary he kept as a journal of his explorations, Columbus left a will which is believed to be his last extant document. It is very typical of its time in that he leaves everything to his sons and male heirs, with instructions for them to look after his widow and female descendants. The head of the house in each subsequent generation is to sign letters and all documents with the title "Admiral." Not without generosity, he instructed that 10% of his income be distributed among the poor.

Columbus died May 20, 1506, a broken and tired man, three years before his son became Viceroy, and was first buried in the Carthusian Monastery of Santa Maria of the Caves in Seville, Spain. In view of his will, it is perhaps an irony that the Columbus line continued through the female descendants of the family. The present heir holds the title of Admiral and Duke of Veragua. There is said to be one existing portrait of the great explorer owned by the de Orchi family in Como, Italy. The likeness of a strong, tall, and well-built man is softened by his sad, thoughtful eyes. A man who lived intensely and fought well for all the honors he received, he is said to have had one weakness, his love for one Caribbean island towards which he was determined to sail his last sunset, the Isle of Hispanola.

THE COLUMBUS CONTROVERSY

In his last testament, the navigator willed his burial place to be Santo Domingo. In 1544, Maria de Toledo, now widowed, embarked from Spain with the Admiral's remains. The ship she sailed on was one of 27 vessels that arrived in Santo Domingo on September 9, 1544 and came to port in the Ozama River. The Admiral's ashes were then buried in the Cathedral of Santo Domingo, alongside the remains of his son Diego, who had died in 1526. In later years, Luis Columbus, son of Diego, would also be buried there.

The will to remain in Santo Domingo must have been stronger than death itself for Christopher Columbus. In the year 1795, when the Treaty of Basle ceded the colony to France, the Lieutenant General of the Spanish Armada decided to take Columbus' remains to Cuba so that he could be buried on Spanish soil. So, in December of 1795, three centuries after he had first sighted the island of Hispaniola, Columbus was to leave it for the last time. Once again, his burial supposedly took place in a solemn ceremony in the Cathedral of Havana in January of 1796. On an uneventful morning some 82 years later, Padre Francisco Billini was supervising the repair of the Cathedral floor in Santo Domingo. It was September 10, 1877, and the tedious job of maintenance must have seemed endless to both workers and pastor. Suddenly, one of the workers discovered a small crypt, unmarked and just 16 centimeters from the one emptied in the year of the French occupation. Inside, he found the urn with the mortal remains of Christopher Columbus. A few days later, his grandson's remains were also located. The Bishop of Santo Domingo, Haiti, and Venezuela proclaimed the discovery of Padre Billini and his workers and the findings were recorded in notarized documents. Diego Columbus still lies in the Cathedral of Havana.

In the annals of the colonial period there is one exceptional figure: Enriquillo. His story proves there was nobility as well as brutality in the history of the first colony. The son of one of the *caciques* who perished at Jaragua, he was educated by the friars of the Monastery of Saint Francis in Santo Domingo.

Enriquillo and his wife, Mencia, were "assigned" to the Spaniard Valenzuela, whose son tried repeatedly to seduce Mencia. Filled with resentment, Enriquillo took to the mountains where he and his followers fought off any attempt on the part of the Spaniards to put down their revolt. He was the victor in confrontation after confrontation. Enriquillo would not kill his captives, as Ovando had done with his tribesmen. Instead, he would confiscate their weapons and send them packing! The Spaniards would send more men and again they would be vanquished. Once more Enriquillo would claim that all he wanted was peaceful coexistence. Enriquillo became a legend in his own time and left behind a legacy of dignity rarely matched in Dominican history.

Hearing of this remarkable Indian leader, Charles I of Spain, the grandson of Ferdinand and Isabel, sent a personal emissary to Enriquillo. Francisco de Barrionuevo searched for two months before he finally located him on the isle of Cabrito, right in the middle of what today is known as Lake Enriquillo. Barrionuevo had power from the King to confer knighthood upon Enriquillo and allow him to choose land for a settlement, where he could live among his own people as long as their community did not make war on Spain. Enriquillo chose the mountains of Baoruco, where he ruled as Don Enriquillo, *Cacique*, and Knight of the Spanish Court until his death in 1533.

The early 1500s were exceptional years on Hispaniola, not only because of the excitement of discovery and the material wealth to be had, but also because Hispaniola became the seat of Spanish rule in the New World, its most important settlement, and the crossroads to the high adventures still ahead. When you consider the breed of men who lived in the colony during those years, who spoke together, plotted and drank together, it had to be a period of great excitement. It was a time when palace corridors and taverns were filled with conspiracy and plans for further conquest. There were many conquistadors: Velazquez of Cuba, Ojeda of Panama, Bastidas of Colombia were but a few. From the port of Santo Domingo, they set sail on countless expeditions. Vasco Nuñez de Balboa lived in Santo Domingo until his debts started making his life span a matter of some doubt. The story says that he finally managed to escape in a "cask of victuals" destined for a ship. He was after the gold of Peru and the adrenalin of adventure. What he found for certain was the Pacific Ocean. Alonso Martin, who had also lived in Hispaniola, was on the same expedition with Balboa and Pizarro and was the first European to actually embark on the Pacific in the Gulf of St. Michael.

Francisco Pizarro came through Santo Domingo in 1510, before going on to Panama and to the discovery and conquest of Peru. Hernan Cortes settled in Azua, on the Dominican southern coast, where he worked as a farmer and notary public—uneventful professions for a man who was itching for a taste of conquest. He later sailed from Hispaniola to Cuba and on to the conquest of Mexico. Juan Ponce de Leon arrived on the northern coast with Columbus' second voyage. From Santo Domingo, he eventually went on to be governor of Puerto Rico in 1509. Four years later, in his search for the fountain of youth, he discovered Florida. These were the sort of men who gave Santo Domingo a special vitality. There were no boy scouts in those ruthless days of exploit. Of Pizarro, Balboa, Ponce de Leon, and Cortes, only the latter died a natural death. They passed through this island on the way to their own destinies, but their personal histories are woven into the fabric of Hispaniola.

Among the many "firsts" of this island during the colonial period were Santo Domingo, the first city of the Americas; the first university in the Americas founded in 1538; the first commercial center of La Atarazana, which included everything from ironsmiths and tailors to blacksmiths and ship suppliers; the first convents and monasteries;

the first schools; the first Cathedral of America, constructed from 1523 to 1547; the first palace, which was the Alcazar; the first fortresses and the first coat of arms assigned by the King of Spain to the New World. Even the first cigar to be had in the New World was allegedly smoked here by Rodrigo de Xeres, who traveled with Columbus on the maiden voyage!

Of the most important historic "firsts" for the Dominican Republic was the first court of law, the royal court of appeals or *La Real Audiencia*. It was constituted in 1511 to encompass Veragua, Nicaragua, Guatemala, Honduras, Venezuela, Cuba, Puerto Rico, Florida, and the other possessions of the New World. This royal court of appeals of Santo Domingo had jurisdiction over each colony in the hemisphere until 1549. From that point on, Mexico, Sante Fe, and Panama formed their own courts and the concentration of Spanish power shifted from its former headquarters, Santo Domingo, to the continent. The discovery of vast treasures in these new lands resulted in a loss of interest in the original colony and there was an exodus from Hispaniola which made it increasingly vulnerable to pirates and privateers operating in the Caribbean.

SIR FRANCIS DRAKE

Just as negotiations to transport the remains of the Great Discoverer back to Hispaniola were being conducted, the wife of an ardent Protestant preacher gave birth to a boy in England. The year was 1541 and the boy was Francis Drake. One thing is certain. At that time and place no one suspected that he too would have enormous and fateful impact on the same Caribbean island Columbus so loved.

As a young man, Drake made several slaving voyages to South America, and these evidently were responsible for his love of adventure on the high seas and for his early negative experiences with the Spanish. In 1567, on a slaving voyage with his kinsman, Sir John Hawkins, Drake experienced a brutal attack off the coast of Vera Cruz by Spanish ships, which both he and Hawkins survived. This experience apparently solidified his intense hatred for Spaniards.

Drake first saw the Pacific in 1572. A man of resolute will, he vowed to sail an English ship there. Between 1577 and 1580, he was the first Englishman to sail around the world. Drake was a privateer who was sponsored in his ventures by a Welshman and court favorite, Kit Hatton. Hatton's manor house, Radnorshire Arms in Presteigne, Wales, is worth visiting; it has been restored as a charming hotel in the Trusthouse Forte collection. Within its panelled walls, one can easily imagine Drake planning his most daring exploits.

Largely through Hatton's influence, Drake was favored by Queen Elizabeth I, who approved of his activities and secretly supported his expeditions and siege of wealthy Caribbean ports. Under commission to the queen, his ship, the *Golden Hind*, sacked towns along the coast of South America and plundered Spanish ships sailing from Chile and Peru and the other ports under Spanish rule carrying treasure back to the court of Spanish King Philip. In 1586, he sacked Santo Domingo, burning much of the city and seizing the Cathedral treasure, the silver and gold ornaments found in the city and the jewels of the wealthy residents. In exchange for a handsome ransom of golden ducats, he finally left Santo Domingo only to pillage Cartagena and St. Augustine, Florida, on the same expedition.

Drake was said to be a ruthless man. He was not cruel on a whim, but certainly was capable of cruelty. Once, he had a fellow sea captain who disagreed with him executed, on the pretext that the captain was a conjurer. He excommunicated his chaplain for writing an unfavorable account of one of his expeditions. But never did he vent his wrath more intensely than on the Spanish settlers of Santo Domingo.

He made fortunes with his share of spoils and bought Buckland Abbey in South Devon, England, as his home and that of his heirs. Today, the Abbey is the Drake Museum. Knighted by the queen on board his ship, by 1500 Drake was a Vice-Admiral. He was by then an established challenger of the Spanish Armada, having attacked them on their own territory in the Port of Cadiz. The latter part of his career at sea was distinguished by his service to England in the war against the Armada. When the Spanish entered the English Channel in June 1588, he was said to be busy playing a game of "bowls" with other commanders and is reputed to have exclaimed that there was time for his game first and then time enough to beat the Spanish afterwards. He played a leading role in the attack off Gravelines on July 29, which finally shattered the Armada.

In 1595, Drake and Hawkins sailed with a fleet to the Caribbean to try and recapture the adventures of their youth and repeat the successful sackings of 1585–86. Since Porto Bello was Panama's most important Caribbean port, Spanish defense of it proved strong enough to fend off his attack. Hawkins died off the coast of Puerto Rico, and Drake died off the coast of Porto Bello on the night of January 27, 1596. Later, many galleons would leave Porto Bello laden with shipments of gold bound for Spain.

A man of medium height, fair coloring, and penetrating eyes, Drake was considered shrewd and imperious. In many ways, he embodied the Elizabethan spirit of his time: no adventure was too great and no difficulty was insurmountable. Although he is regarded as an evil pirate in Dominican history, it is important to recall that he was not a pirate, but rather, was commissioned by the queen and therefore sailed within the conventions of law. The British see him as a glamorous and daring figure of the British naval tradition. He was in any event not a man to have as an enemy. Ironically, he was buried at sea, in the same waters of the Caribbean that fascinated him as a youth.

Cathedral in Moca

Chapter 4

ERA OF OCCUPATION AND POLITICAL DEVELOPMENT

THE ERA OF OCCUPATION

As the once flourishing colony started to decline, the French began to extend their sphere of influence in the New World. By the Treaty of Ryswick in 1697, Spain was forced to cede the western portion of Hispaniola to France. Less than one hundred years later, France gained control of the entire island under the provisions of the Treaty of Basle.

Toussaint L'Ouverture, the Black Spartacus of Saint Domingue, occupied the Spanish colony in the name of the French Republic. Soon after L'Ouverture's death, Henri Christophe and Jean Jacques Dessalines tried to dominate the eastern part of Hispaniola under the flag of a newly independent Haiti. These were years of incredible turmoil, with the French, Haitians, and Spaniards all competing for settlement of the colony while other factions were negotiating for annexation to Gran Colombia. Haiti took advantage of the state of instability in those years of transition to unify the island under the Haitian flag from 1822 to 1844.

In 1844 the Dominicans, under the leadership of Juan Pablo Duarte—who in Dominican history occupies a place similar to that of Simon Bolivar in South American annals—regained their freedom and formed the first constitutional republic. In that campaign, Duarte was ably assisted by Francisco del Rosario Sanchez and General Matias Ramon Mella. Together, they are the Fathers of the country. These three men had great hopes for their republic, but the road ahead was not to be a smooth one. From 1844 on, the Dominican nation was to have 51 leaders and 36 constitutions. The fact that it has achieved a stable democracy in modern times is very much to its credit in light of its turbulent history.

RULE OF THE DESPOTS

The Dominican Republic has had its share of dictators, too. Pedro Santana ruled as president of the newly independent republic intermittently from 1844 through to the Spanish annexation. The country had experienced a great deal of economic instability and Santana had an obsessive fear of another Haitian occupation. Both of these factors contributed to the theory that the only solution to the problems facing the young republic was to seek the protection of a European power. Santana literally gave the country back to Spain in 1861. During his term in office, the constitution was rewritten to sanction dictatorial powers. Being cast once again in the role of a colony did not evoke much popular support from within the country and a war of restoration resulted in an abrupt end to the colonial interlude in 1865. Santana may have handed the republic back to Spain on a platter, but Buenaventura Baez, who also rewrote the constitution to suit his own autocratic style, has the distinction of having tried to sell it. At his prompting, a treaty of annexation was prepared which would incorporate the republic into the United States. All Dominicans would become U.S. citizens and all government lands were to become property of the Union. The price tag for this transaction was $1,500,000, to be paid to the Baez government. Baez, who had a flair for the theatrical, staged an overwhelming plebiscite to show the American public just how eager everyone was to be annexed. President Ulysses S. Grant, however, found the U.S. Senate less receptive. The treaty was rejected by 10 votes in 1870.

You will find a street in Santo Domingo named Avenue Charles Sumner. Senator Sumner led the opposition to the annexation from the U.S. Senate floor, suspecting the entire project to be a scam designed by Buenaventura Baez for profit, supported by President Grant, who was interested in securing Samana Bay as a naval base for the United States. For the Dominican people, who had struggled so hard to achieve independence, Senator Sumner is something of a hero. He had taken a stand at the risk of antagonizing Grant, and he paid for his decision for he was removed shortly afterwards from his post as head of the Foreign Relations Committee of the Senate.

Undaunted by this setback, Baez signed a contract the following year with the Samana Bay Company of Santo Domingo for a 99-year lease of the Samana peninsula and bay for $150,000 a year as of January 1, 1873. With President Baez determined to auction off the Dominican Republic one way or another, the citizens of the country decided enough was enough. A group of distinguished generals, headed by Gregorio Luperon, accused Baez of treason. Baez was subsequently deposed and the contract on the Samana venture was filed and forgotten.

Ulises Heureaux came to power ten years later (1882–1884). He again secured the presidency in 1887, the start of yet another dictatorship which was to last 12 more years. "Lilis," as he was called, didn't lose sleep over the country's fiscal mess. He simply issued paper currency with no backing. With the exception of his regime, presidents followed in rapid succession and the country remained economically unsound.

U.S. MARINES AND THE ERA OF TRUJILLO

The inability of the Dominican Republic to meet payments and resolve its foreign debt, together with the suspicious presence of European ships in coastal waters, resulted in the U.S. Marine occupation from 1916 to 1922. The intervention was decided upon for the expressed purpose of forestalling possible German intrusion and protecting American investments. The U.S. also assumed control of the Dominican customs to try to counteract the fiscal crisis. All military and civilian firearms were confiscated, and a National Guard was formed, comprised of Dominicans under American officers, for the purpose of maintaining order. Rafael Trujillo, who was very much a product of the National Guard, came to power in 1930 for what was to be three decades of absolute rule.

Trujillo was a man of contradictions. He was capable of generosity, yet could be absolutely ruthless on a whim. He was an excellent father to his own children, yet completely insensitive to the children of the men he persecuted. He was brilliant, callous in his ambition and had an inordinate capacity for evil. He would never forget a slight, and had a way of seeing through people that was very unsettling. Trujillo was both intimidating and assertive in his style, yet he had a very high-pitched voice that was almost feminine in quality. He was extremely macho, yet he evidenced an exaggerated preoccupation with his appearance, from his finely cut clothes to his taste for perfumes and powders. He was a nationalist, no matter what his motivation, and yet he expertly courted foreign powers.

As an administrator, Trujillo introduced an era of fiscal stability. He balanced the budget and paid off the foreign debt. He regained the administration of the customs and their revenues and established the Central Bank in 1949. None of these fiscal improvements should come as a complete surprise, since what was good for business was obviously good for him.

During his regime, the country was run as a corporation, with Trujillo the self-appointed chairman. His business interests included hotels, the cement factory, textiles, the shoe factory, the paint factory (a monopoly), banks, air cargo, maritime freight, salt production (another monopoly), cattle feed, construction materials, 80% of the sugar mills throughout the country, wood for export and local furniture production, the marble industry and a monopoly of the country's minerals, insurance, soft drinks, publishing, and so on.

Trujillo decreed laws which were beneficial to businesses, particularly his own. One such law made it illegal to walk along roads without shoes. Another decree required property owners to paint their houses every year. Between the private and the public sectors of his domain, it is safe to say that 80% of the population was directly or indirectly employed by the Generalissimo.

Throughout his years in power, Trujillo's extravagances and those of his family were legendary. In keeping with that image, he bought the fabulous yacht *Sea Cloud* from Mrs. Joseph Davies, the Post Toasties heiress, and rechristened the yacht *Angelita* in honor of his daughter. It was a luxury yacht fit for a king, and both royalty and international dignitaries were frequently entertained on board. Trujillo's son, Ramfis, was a favorite subject of gossip columnists throughout the U.S. for his playboy activities and lavish gifts to film stars.

It is estimated that Trujillo's personal fortune ran into the hundreds of millions of pesos and that his foreign accounts totaled upwards of US$200,000,000 at the time of his death. His holdings in assets and real estate, which were confiscated after his assassination on May 30, 1961, are simply incalculable.

Trujillo's administration made advances in health care, road construction, education, and communication systems. However, these contributions, and the fact that by 1951 he had increased the GNP to ten times what it was when he took power, were marred by the political tortures, the atrocities and a consuming fear which became the hallmark of life in his era, condemning him in the court of world opinion.

When he finally fell, Trujillo was leaving the city on a deserted sea-front avenue. His assassins were a mixed bunch: some were outraged men of conscience, some were part of his inner circle, some had experienced public humiliations at his hands, and some acted out of ambition. In death as in life, Trujillo still inspires a combination of terror and fascination among his people.

THE LAST TWO DECADES AND THE BIRTH OF A STABLE DEMOCRACY

The first free elections, after the death of the Generalissimo, were held in 1962. Juan Bosch was elected president and took office on February 27, 1963, only to be overthrown by a military coup seven months later. A triumvirate was formed to govern and was presided over by Emilio de los Santos and subsequently by Donald Reid Cabral, both highly respected citizens. The triumvirate's administration came to a turbulent end on April 24, 1965 with another putsch, this time by Bosch supporters trying to reinstate their president. Civil war erupted and President Lyndon Johnson sent U.S. Marines in to restore order. Between American and other O.A.S. troops, over

30,000 men intervened. A provisional president, Hector Garcia Godoy, was ultimately assigned the task of preparing the country for free elections in 1966.

In the 1966 election, Joaquin Balaguer and his *Partido Reformista* won a victory which led to three consecutive terms in office. Balaguer's administration made significant strides in urban development, housing projects, cultural programs and the tourism industry. During this period, most of the colonial city of Santo Domingo was restored. The museums and the National Theater at Plaza de la Cultura were constructed. It was also during this period that the development of Puerto Plata as a touristic center was initiated, and the economic growth rate rose to one of the highest in Latin America.

Balaguer's years were followed by the election of President Antonio Guzman, a respected leader of the PRD Party, who came from Santiago with one of the most distinguished first ladies the Dominican Republic has ever known. Renee K. de Guzman was particularly noted for her work with Dominican children through the Conani organization which she directed. President Guzman's death, just prior to the end of his term, brought his vice president, Jacobo Majluta to the presidency.

The 1982 elections were won by President Salvador Jorge Blanco, a lawyer by profession. His administration has been haunted by charges of corruption. It did, however, witness the ascent of tourism to the position of the number one industry in the country.

Since the First Republic of 1844 was constituted, the Dominican people have had a succession of leaders, from archbishops and soldiers to statesmen and poets. Some were outstanding, others incompetent. For the past two decades, however, the democratic process has been faithfully upheld with each election. One interesting aspect of the last election, held in May of 1986, is that it brought together three former presidents in contention for the number one spot: Juan Bosch, Joaquin Balaguer, and Jacobo Majluta. Balaguer, now 79, was elected to what will be his fifth term in the presidency. The "Doctor" as he is fondly called by his followers, selected as his running mate Carlos Morales Troncoso, a specialist in the sugar industry, former Chief Executive of Gulf and Western Americas Corporation, and a pillar of the tourist industry in the Dominican Republic.

WHAT LIES AHEAD

The Dominican Republic shows every promise of being discovered again. The tourism industry should reach a new high in the next few years as a result of the many factors contributing to a positive growth rate.

Prices in the Dominican Republic are among the lowest of the major Caribbean resorts. You can dine on lobster for the equivalent of US$10, order custom-made shirts for about US$15, and buy leather sandals for approximately US$8.

More importantly, the Dominican people are friendly and kind, and have a wonderful sense of humor.

In the last five years, the development of Puerto Plata on the northern coast as a resort has progressed in measured steps. One of the problems holding it back was the limited number of commercial flights formerly connecting Puerto Plata to the U.S. mainland and other destinations. Fortunately, a bilateral aviation treaty was signed in July of 1986, opening the skies of Puerto Plata as an unrestricted entry port for U.S. airlines from all points in the United States. Puerto Plata is not the only zone slated for development now, as both the eastern and the southern coasts are getting a great deal of attention, mostly from private investors. Generally speaking, there seems to be a lot of construction going on, and if that's an indication of a country's potential, it looks as if the Dominican Republic is becoming a major tourist destination.

In the cruise ship industry, a 300% increase in traffic is expected in the next few years. There were 28 visits scheduled for the first four months of 1987 by such cruise ship notables as the *Stella Solaris*, *Berlin*, *Ocean Princess*, *Vista Fjord*, *Europa*, and *Caribe I*. Sans Souci terminal in Santo Domingo is currently a base from which two ships, the *Oceanus* and the *Atlas*, offer regular departures on two-week Caribbean cruises through Regent Holidays of Toronto. This program is expected to bring more than 16,000 Canadians through the Dominican Republic en route to other ports of call. The Ministry of Tourism also has plans for developing the potential of Samana as an attractive port of call.

The stability of the country's democracy has encouraged foreign investment, particularly in tourism-related industries, but also in agribusiness and off-shore manufacturing. Incentive laws, such as Law 153, have been designed to motivate foreign investment in the country, while international lending organizations such as the World Bank and the Interamerican Development Bank have committed millions over recent years to the development of the Dominican Republic. An Interamerican Development Bank loan of $50 million is currently being reactivated for the purpose of financing new tourism projects throughout the country, and a World Bank loan for improving existing roads and constructing new highways is currently under study.

The people of the Dominican Republic have a strong sense of national identity. This identity sets the country apart from others in the Caribbean as it approaches its 500-year anniversary celebration. It is a country steeped in history, and in looking ahead to a brighter future, it is never out of touch with its past.

Along Anacaona Boulevard

Chapter 5

THE DOMINICAN REPUBLIC TOUR

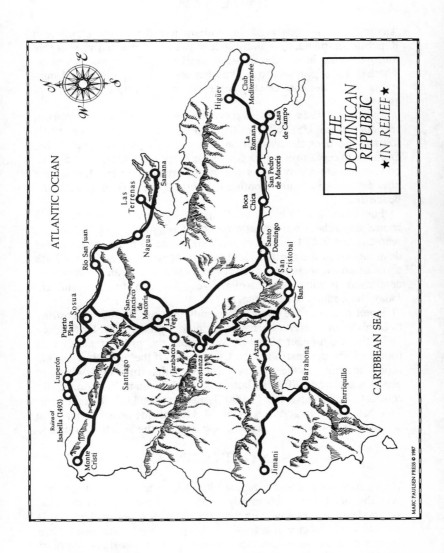

THE DOMINICAN REPUBLIC
★ IN RELIEF ★

ATLANTIC OCEAN

CARIBBEAN SEA

Higüey
Club Mediterranée
Casa de Campo
La Romana
San Pedro de Macoris
Boca Chica
Santo Domingo
San Cristobal
Baní
Azua
Barahona
Enriquillo
Jimani
Constanza
Jarabacoa
La Vega
San Francisco de Macoris
Santiago
Luperón
Ruins of Isabella (1493)
Monte Cristi
Puerto Plata
Sosua
Rio San Juan
Nagua
Las Terrenas
Samaná

MARC PAULSEN PRESS © 1987

THE DEVELOPING TOURISM INDUSTRY

Anyone who has observed the tourism industry in the Dominican Republic firsthand over the last few years has noticed remarkable improvements in all the existing tourism facilities and services. There is still a long way to go, but that does not discount the substantial accomplishments already achieved, particularly in the last five years.

In a recent study, the Ministry of Tourism pointed out that tourism revenues were US$368.2 million in 1985. In fact, since 1984, tourism has been the number one earner of foreign exchange in the Dominican economy. This accounts for the priority tourism and related services are receiving, as well as the attention to building all the new facilities in Santo Domingo, Puerto Plata, and mountain and beach resorts.

For 1985, the Ministry of Tourism registered a total of 8,562 rooms throughout the country. Santo Domingo claimed 33% of the whole, while 2,430 of these rooms were located throughout the resort destinations of the northern and eastern coast. Figures for 1987–88 show dramatic increases in hotel room estimates, with a heavy concentration in what were formerly very low-density areas and are today the country's new resorts.

Hotel rooms in the country currently number 10,300. According to Minister of Tourism Fernando Rainieri's predictions, by October 1988 the Dominican Republic will offer the greatest number of rooms of any destination in the Caribbean. Of the more than 14,300 rooms he estimates the country will have at that time, 60% will be at beach resorts and 70% in hotels with more than 100 rooms. By contrast, the Bahamas has 12,000, Jamaica offers 11,000, and Puerto Rico has 7,000. In addition to the 14,300 definite projections, there are another 3,400 rooms pending approval by the Tourism Ministry.

SANTO DOMINGO

What can you say about a capital city? Like capital cities the world over, this one is noisy, has unruly traffic, and too many people. Now, the good part. Compared with most big cities, it is reasonably safe. It also has an abundance of activities to keep you well entertained, such as a great variety in restaurants, discothèques, and casinos that offer Las Vegas odds. If nightlife is not your primary interest, there are great shopping arcades, marketplaces, boutiques, and craft centers. You will also find spectator sports like baseball and the canodrome, and everything from tennis to dance classes and spas. It's a 24-hour town. About the only thing Santo Domingo doesn't have is a beach; the closest beaches are half an hour out of town. It does, however, have a very attractive seafront boulevard, bursting with round-the-clock activity.

Santo Domingo has culture. Symphony performances and ballet, chamber music and solo recitals. It has elegant nightclubs. It also has striptease clubs and massage parlors, the other side of midnight. Everywhere you go, there's the sound that sets the pace, the sound of Merengue. The first week of October 1986, *Time* magazine featured an article on Dominican Merengue which started out: "Sweet deliverance! Finally, a dance anyone can do...a fast dance, a hot dance...a little flame and no shame." That "little flame" goes on burning all day and all night in Santo Domingo.

This Caribbean capital also has a unique historical past and enough colonial landmarks to sweep you back to the 16th century with all the romance of colonial nights! History buffs and anyone with a little adventure will find enough galleon treasure, antiques, and art masterpieces to keep them coming back. It has parks for jogging and bicycling, amusement parks for the kids, and secret caves with Indian hieroglyphics. Santo Domingo has modern residential areas and houses of the very wealthy that could hold their own alongside the Newport mansions. Then, there is the other side of survival for the thousands who barely get by in the city's ghettos. Santo Domingo is a study in contrasts. A Caribbean story. But the one thing that seems to stand out in the memory of visitors to the capital, is not so much the quality of life as the quality of its people. No matter the level of society, Dominicans are warm, and have an exceptional sense of humor. Santo Domingo's people are what you are likely to remember the most!

WALKING TOUR OF SANTO DOMINGO'S COLONIAL SECTOR

Nowhere is the Dominican Republic's heritage more alive than in the colonial city of Santo Domingo, and no trip to Santo Domingo would be complete without a visit to its colonial sector, which was designed by Governor Nicolas de Ovando in 1502. Ideally, a walking tour of old Santo Domingo would be a week-long project. Assuming you may not have the time, allow at least two full days for ambling around this fascinating first city of the Americas. The following itinerary covers most of the essential points of interest.

© Marc Paulsen Press

Mileage Quick Reference Table

	Azua	Bani	Barahona	Boca Chica	Constanza	Higüey	Jarabacoa	La Romana	La Vega	Monte Cristi	Puerto Plata	Punta Cana	Samaná	San Cristóbal	Santiago	Santo Domingo
Bani	55															
Barahona	80	135														
Boca Chica	151	96	231													
Constanza	180	115	205	179												
Higüey	260	210	355	130	285											
Jarabacoa	170	158	355	186	43	290										
La Romana	230	175	355	79	255	35	265									
La Vega	200	150	355	156	70	265	30	225								
Monte Cristi	285	295	355	308	210	415	165	375	145							
Puerto Plata	290	250	355	255	140	355	95	320	90	135						
Punta Cana	330	270	355	169	350	60	365	105	335	480	425					
Samaná	325	270	355	276	235	385	205	355	175	305	210	455				
San Cristóbal	90	35	355	61	168	175	140	115	290	210	200	235	145			
Santiago	230	202	355	186	90	175	50	255	36	200	240	190	145	145		
Santo Domingo	120	65	355	31	140	290	155	110	270	69	365	245		30	155	
Sosúa	304	275	355	213	410	143	350	124	139	25	450	155	285		94	240

A good place to start your tour is at Parque Duarte (Duarte Park) and Padre Billini Street. Legend has it that this park is the site where the beautiful Anacaona was hanged. Presumably, it was also here that Sir Francis Drake ordered the hanging of two Dominican friars in the center of the square. Facing the park is the Convent and Church of the Order of Preachers, known as El Convento.

The Convent was established in 1510, although construction was not begun until 1524, and it was not completed until 1532. The first Chair of Theology was established that same year, and in 1538 the University of Saint Thomas Aquinas was founded. This was the first univeristy in the New World, offering courses in philosophy, theology, law, and medicine. Today, this colonial landmark is again the site of a progressive university. The Church is regarded as the oldest standing church in all of the Americas. From its pulpit the orators of the Dominican order helped to shape the history of the colony with sermons that vehemently condemned the abuses of slave labor.

El Convento is a very impressive building made of squared stone, brick facing and decorated with 16th-century Spanish tiles. Although it is much in keeping with the Gothic style preferred by the Catholic King and Queen, there are decorative elements which are Plateresque and early Renaissance. The rose motif around the window, the decorative vines, and the beautiful interiors all soften the austerity of the building. In the 16th century, the central nave was a university classroom. The altar was a gift of the Emperor Charles V, grandson of Ferdinand and Isabel. The Hapsburg eagle appears on the altar piece because Charles I of Spain was simultaneously Charles V of Germany.

The Rosary Chapel is particularly interesting because of the astrological signs painted on its vaulted roof. The zodiac does not typically appear in churches of the Spanish colonial period, and the presence of the signs still remains somewhat of an enigma. The four seasons are represented by Jupiter, Mars, Saturn, and Mercury portrayed revolving around the sun. The 12 signs of the zodiac and an array of stars complete the composition. It has been suggested that the zodiac signs represent the 12 apostles. Whatever the metaphor, it is an interesting and surprising feature, and those intrigued by astrology will have an unusual start to their tour.

If you walk a block east along Padre Billini to the corner of Merino Street, you will find three of Santo Domingo's most popular small restaurants: El Buren, for typical Dominican specialties; El Bodegon, for the flavor of Spain; and Il Buco, a long and narrow Italian restaurant that also happens to be long on style.

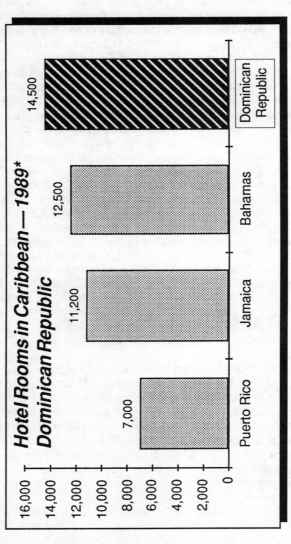

Hotel Rooms in Caribbean — 1989
Dominican Republic

*Estimated

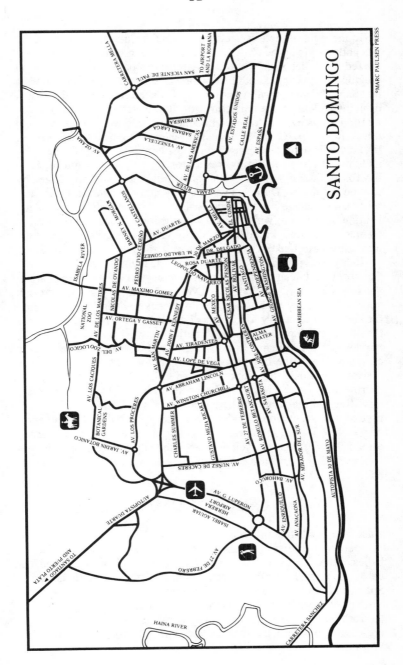

SANTO DOMINGO

©MARC PAULSEN PRESS

To the right of the intersection, stands the Casa de Tostado, in the late gothic style of the Catholic King and Queen. This style is characterized by a flat stone façade and repeated patterns of doors and windows on the upper and lower stories. It is important to remember that Santo Domingo was months away from the court of Spain, which explains why Gothic architecture still dominated the design of colonial buildings even as new architectural trends were being put into effect in Spain. Casa de Tostado, which belonged to the scribe, Francisco Tostado, was one of the most gracious homes of the colonial era. The Tostado family was a prominent, yet unfortunate, family. Tostado's son, a professor at the nearby university, was killed by cannon fire during Drake's invasion. Another descendant of the family is said to have had a tragic love affair during the years of the Haitian occupation, which ended with the lover's death in the well of the interior garden, killed by militia looking for deserters. Part of the local lore is to make a wish at this well for good fortune in love.

Today, Casa de Tostado houses the Museum of the Nineteenth-Century Dominican Family, and has been restored with loving care to the style of a more gracious era. Don't miss the display of Victorian wicker furniture, mahogany period pieces and antiques gathered throughout the country for this special collection. The architecture of the house itself, with its beautiful patio, fretwork and Gothic double window (this geminated window is one-of-a-kind in America), is certainly one of the most appealing of the old city.

Halfway along this same block of Billini Street, you'll spot a narrow alley known as the "Way of the Priests." In colonial times, this alley led the friars to the courtyard of the Cathedral. It is still used as a shortcut along a narrow cobbled walk to the first Cathedral of the New World. If instead of turning into the alley, you proceed directly down the street, you will reach the city wall. Santo Domingo was a walled city because of its strategic importance and its vulnerability.

CALLE LAS DAMAS

Once you reach the city wall, you are on Calle Las Damas, or the "Street of the Ladies," so called because it provided lodgings for the ladies of the viceroy's court. The street has recently been restored to a cobblestone surface which, combined with the dimly-lit lanterns, Spanish archways, enormous mahogany portals and an intricate network of courtyards, transports modern day visitors to the romance of the 16th century. The street was originally known as Fortaleza Street, because it runs past the Ozama Fort, the first fortress of the New World.

COLONIAL
SANTO
DOMINGO

©MARC PAULSEN PRESS

PLACES OF INTEREST
COLONIAL SANTO DOMINGO

1. Puerta de la Misericordia (Door of Mercy)
2. Church of San Andrés
3. Churt of Nuestra Señora del Carmen
4. Square of Los Trinitarios
5. Regina Angelorum Convent
6. Chapel of the Third Dominican Order
7. Los Dominicos Convent
8. Plaza Fray Bartolomé de Las Casas
9. Casa del Tostado and Museum of the Dominican Family (XIX Century)
10. Casa de Teatro
11. Casa de Hernando Gorjón
12. Santa Clara Convent
13. Callejón de los Curas (Alley of the Priests)
14. Cathedral Santa María La Menor
15. Parque Colón (Columbus Park)
16. Palace of Borguellá
17. Callejón de los Nichos
18. Ozama Fortress and Tower of Homage
19. Casa de Rodrigo de Bastidas
20. Casa de Nicolas de Ovando
21. Jusuit Convent
22. Nathional Pantheon
23. Nuestra Señora de Los Remedios Chapel
24. Del Rosario Chapel
25. Las Casas Reales Museum
26. Puerta de San Diego (San Diego Door)
27. Columbus' Alcazar
28. Puerta de la Atarazana (Atarazana Door)
29. Casa del Cordón (House of the Cord)
30. San Francisco Mónastery Ruins
31. Casa de La Moneda (House of the Cord)
32. Nicolas de Bari Hospital Ruins
33. Nuestra Señora de las Mercedes Monastery
34. San Lázaro Temple and Hospital
35. Puerta del Conde (Conde Door)

A tall statue of Gonzalo Fernandez de Oviedo stands in the inner square of the fortress. Oviedo, warden of the military enclave during colonial times and the first historian of the New World, wrote the Chronicles of the Indies. It is said that when he died, it was necessary to pry open his hands to remove the keys of the keep.

THE TOWER OF HOMAGE

The Tower of Homage with its two-meter thick walls, still stands as it stood in the early 1500's, keeping a silent vigil over the entrance to the River Ozama. From atop the tower, homage was traditionally rendered to ships entering port. The Tower of Homage was the tallest structure of the colonial city, built on a site chosen by Governor Ovando. The warden's lodge within the tower was actually the first residence for Diego Columbus and his queen, Maria de Toledo, when they arrived in Santo Domingo.

Adjacent to the Fortress, is the house of Rodrigo de Bastidas, who was one of the early conquistadors and explorers, as well as governor of Santa Maria, which is now Colombia. The house has a series of graceful Romanesque arches surrounding a breathtaking interior patio, which consists of about 2,000 square meters of lush, verdant vegetation, and makes you feel far from the noise and bustle of city streets.

The Bastides house also boasts an art gallery that often has special exhibits of painting, photography, and furnishings. Following the gallery, you'll find Planarte, a craft center which could easily be the high point of your shopping trip! Planarte is sponsored by the Dominican Development Foundation and here you can purchase crafts directly from the artisan. There are attractive displays of gift items from pottery and hand-painted glazed tiles, leather goods and rag dolls in all sizes and shades to hand-carved birds, silver jewelry and baskets. Planarte is a must for anyone interested in handicrafts at good prices.

Continuing along Las Damas Street, you'll pass Casa de Francia on the left. It is a French cultural institute and was traditionally known as the house of Hernan Cortes, who is said to have planned some of his exploits here.

HOSTAL NICOLAS DE OVANDO

On the right hand side of Las Damas, you will find the Hostal Nicolas de Ovando, easily one of the most romantic hotels in the world! It consists of two houses, the colonial residence of Governor Ovando himself, and the home of the wealthy Davila family. In the restoration process, both houses were united around a central pool area, overlooking the Ozama River and port. This is an ideal place to stop for lunch or a beverage, and a walk around the various courtyards with their Andalusian fountains, archways, lanterns, flowers, and balconies.

The Davila house was the only residence in the colonial sector to have its own private church and fort. The watch tower of the house overlooks the hotel's pool area. This tranquil complex is one of the most treasured landmarks of the city; it is beautifully restored, recently refurbished, and decorated with period-style furniture, tapestries and antiques. On the second level of the Hostal, before and after photographs of the elaborate restoration process are displayed.

When you sit in the serenity of the Spanish patios of Davila house, let yourself imagine what life must have been like here in the 1500's. The intrigue and sense of adventure these colonial men and women must have experienced seems easily within your reach. You can visualize Las Damas Street outside, teeming with life in a world populated by court ladies and soldiers, monks and noblemen.

NATIONAL PANTHEON

In front of the Hostal, you'll see a small plaza named after Maria de Toledo, and immediately next to this, is the massive stone building that was an 18th-century Jesuit church, and is today the National Pantheon. It's a dimly lit, evocative place. A friend once observed that its interior would make a perfect set for Romeo and Juliet! It manages to be awesome and romantic at the same time. The austere structure has been through a series of interesting transformations throughout its history. Construction of the church started in the early 1700's, and according to a date inscribed over the baptismal font, it was completed in 1748 as the church of the Jesuit order. It was subsequently a tobacco warehouse, a theater, and for a time, it housed the ministry of culture. In 1955, during the Trujillo regime, it was restored and decorated with many of the gifts sent to Trujillo to commemorate its restoration. The grand copper chandelier which hangs down from the cupola was a gift from the Spanish dictator, General Francisco Franco, in 1955. The marble tiles surrounding the eternal flame were a present from the government of Italy. The second floor iron grill was a present from the government of Germany, in honor of the restoration effort. This last is decorated with Latin crosses which are rumored to be swastikas taken after the war from a Nazi prison. National heroes and men of letters are buried here and their names are inscribed on the walls of the Pantheon.

The Ozama Fortress, Santo Domingo, which was begun in the first decade of the sixteenth century

MUSEUM OF THE ROYAL HOUSES

The next corner, at the intersection of Las Damas and Las Mercedes Streets, holds the Museum of the Royal Houses (*Casas Reales*). The building has an anchor from a salvaged Spanish galleon leaning against the exterior wall. The Museum covers three centuries of life in Santo Domingo, from its construction in the early 1500's, to the independence from Spain in 1821.

In colonial times, the building housed the Palace of Governors and Captains General, the Royal Audience and Court of Appeals, the Royal Counting House and the Treasury. The fully restored museum building was inaugurated in 1976 by President Balaguer in the presence of King Juan Carlos I and Queen Sofia of Spain. There are many worthwhile permanent exhibits which include a remarkable collection of weapons, such as antique hunting daggers, crossbows and swords, many with elaborately carved and jeweled handles; a monolith milestone that once separated the Spanish and French parts of the island; an apothecary exhibit; and, as befits the colonial governor's official residence, a richly appointed reception room.

The museum's main attraction, featured in *National Geographic* magazine (see the December 1979 issue, "Graveyard of the Quicksilver Galleons") and honored by television documentaries for CBS and ABC as well as special exhibit tours in major U.S. cities, is the permanent exhibit of galleon treasure retrieved from two areas of important salvage operations. The first part of the exhibit offers treasures and artifacts salvaged by Captain Tracy Bowden from the *Guadeloupe* and the *Conde de Tolosa* galleons, both wrecked during a hurricane in Samana Bay in 1724. Whoever said that children don't enjoy museums has never taken his own to see this exhibit! From military paraphernalia to priceless gold chains, the treasure from the galleons is most impressive. These galleons were en route to colonial settlements with a valuable cargo of mercury, which is why they came to be known as the "quicksilver" galleons. Of the 600 passengers, only about 40 survived. As for the others, their belongings and valuables perished with them. These wrecks are regarded as major archaeological finds because of the variety of artifacts found in them.

The silver bank galleon, *Concepción*, was salvaged by Burt Webber, and involves a much earlier wreck dated 1641. It too went down in a hurricane. This ship was on its return trip to Spain with a precious cargo of silver bars and minted coins. The treasure of the *Concepción* never reached its intended destination, and it now forms the second part of this extraordinary exhibit. Tracy Bowden once observed that there are more than 400 wrecks around the island of Hispaniola. It's

The Alcazar, a sixteenth-century palace which served as the home of Columbus and his family for three generations

no wonder that Santo Domingo's colonial haunts still pulsate with tales of galleon treasure and swashbuckling exploits. There is no better place to get a taste of this than at the Museum of the Royal Houses, where you can see the bounty firsthand. The sundial opposite the museum was built in 1753, and positioned so that the judges seated in chambers across the way in the royal court could always tell the time.

THE ALCAZAR

The Alcazar palace is the high point of any tour of the colonial sector and you'll see it next, as it looms up before you at the end of Las Damas Street. It is open for tours in several languages both mornings and afternoons. But perhaps the most dramatic view of the Alcazar is at night, when specially designed lights set the palace magically ablaze.

There is still a lot to see, so this might be the best point to call it a night and resume your tour the next morning. If you still have some energy left, then by all means explore the delightful Atarazana Street that runs down alongside the Alcazar, and stop for a drink at one of the taverns located here. The Atarazana is filled with lovely restored houses from the early 1500's now converted into galleries, gift shops, pubs and restaurants. In colonial days, this was the site of the royal arsenals, warehouses and customs. Along this same street were the early commercial establishments which included everything from ironsmiths to ship suppliers. Innkeepers did well here too from all accounts. It is believed that the first tavern in America was located in one of these houses.

Drake's Pub is a necessary stop along this street. This landmark building is a masterpiece of privately-done restoration that kept uncovering secret doorways, arches, and a staircase. Owners Gary Hampton and John Gillam (a former Bozo the Clown) will gladly talk about the restoration process and their many discoveries. Fortunately, much of the original wood was salvaged, and the leftover ceiling wood was used to make table tops; these are now boasted to be the oldest tables in the New World. The pub will provide you with a corner full of history and good conversation.

Further down the street, there's the Fonda of the Atarazana, with a great atmosphere for dinner or a snack. Cross through to its interior courtyard which runs along the network of galleries and shops on this street. Nader's is full of the canvases of Dominican and Haitian masters, and the gift shops here have their own treasure trove of amber, black coral, larimar, and Dominican gold and silver jewelry at reasonable prices.

The "Hill in the Atarazana"

Sundays on the Atarazana are of special interest to bargain-lovers because of the flea market sponsored by the office of Cultural Patrimony at the Atarazana parking lot. Here you will be likely to find everything from junk to antiques, including many fine silver and pewter objects.

TOUR OF THE ALCAZAR

Next morning's tour should resume at the Alcazar. It was built by Diego Columbus between 1509 and 1512, as a home suitable for a viceroy and his consort. It brought him untold aggravation and criticism from his enemies, and certainly provided the stage for a great deal of colonial back-stabbing! Years later, in 1533, the Alcazar served as a general headquarters for the Spanish troops that came to stifle the rebellion of the Indian leader, Enriquillo. This is particularly ironic, as Enriquillo's wedding to Mencia had been celebrated in this house at a time when he still enjoyed the protection of his court patrons. Still, through the years of the colony, it was very much the "Columbus house," both in moments of celebration and of sadness; Bartholomew, Christopher Columbus' brother, died here in 1544 and the queen, his daughter-in-law, died here in 1549.

The Alcazar fortress-palace was restored twice in the 20th century. Its interiors are fully furnished and recreate the style of the period. There are hand-carved antiques, desks with ivory and gold inlay, cabinets with secret compartments for storing state documents and valuables, musical instruments including a beautiful 15th-century clavichord, and rich tapestries. One in particular bears the coat of arms of the Columbus clan and was donated by his direct descendant, the Duke of Veragua. There is also a remarkably restored 16th-century Flemish woodcarving of the dying virgin that was shattered into approximately 40 pieces by gunfire during the revolution of 1965 and subsequently took 10 years for restoration experts to put back together!

You can visit the kitchens, dining room, reception rooms, and bedrooms of Bartholomew, Diego, and Maria, and see Maria's private chapel. You can sit on the windowseats from which she and her court ladies watched and waited tor their men to return from distant expeditions. No matter what else you sacrifice, don't leave Santo Domingo without a visit to the Alcazar and the Viceroyal Museum of religious and colonial art objects situated in the Alcazar square. This is where it all began, and with the 500-year celebration upon us, it has a very special significance.

If after touring the Alcazar and Atarazana area, you head past the post office building along Emilio Tejera Street, you will find Isabel La Catolica Street, named after the Spanish queen. Almost at the corner, you will find the Casa del Cordon, so-called because the entrance is framed with the cord of St. Francis. The first stone house built in America, it was constructed in 1503 as the home of an aristocrat, Don Francisco de Garay. He was one of the early colonizers of Santo Domingo, a man made wealthy by the early explorations and search for gold. He later became governor of Jamaica.

Beyond its coat of arms and impressive façade, this is a house alive with history. It was here that Diego Columbus and Maria de Toledo lived as they supervised the construction of their Alcazar. In 1586, the ladies of Santo Domingo gathered in this house to give up their jewels to Sir Francis Drake as ransom for the freedom of their city and their men. This wonderful old house is today the main office of the Banco Popular Dominicano, one of the country's most solid banking institutions, which financed the restoration project.

Also on this street at number 308 in the house of Juan Pablo Duarte, the founding father of the country and intellectual leader of the independence movement. He started a revolutionary cell group called *La Trinitaria* in this same house. The idea behind his trinity was that each member who was chosen then secretly chose another, so that in the event of capture or torture, each could only reveal two names. After Duarte's exile, his sister, Rosa Duarte, continued to gather friends here to melt lead into bullets. In her garden, she grew jasmine, the flower that was to become the symbol for the group and their ideals. It was also in this house, that the first Dominican flag was made by another patriot, Maria Trinidad Sanchez. This was the flag that was unfurled over the bastion of Conde Gate on February 27, 1844, the day of Dominican independence from Haitian rule.

SAINT FRANCIS MONASTERY

At the end of Emilio Tejera Street are the imposing ruins of Saint Francis Monastery, the oldest in the New World, with sections of the sanctuary dating back to 1508. The monastery was set on fire during the siege of Sir Francis Drake. Through the centuries that followed, it experienced serious deterioration, and a large part of the structure collapsed during the St. Zenon hurricane of 1930. The monastery is said to have an underground passageway that connects it to the Alcazar and port. Most of the principal buildings from the colonial era

Facade of the Casa del Cordon (house of the Cord), Calle Emiliano Tejera, Colonial Santo Domingo

have these subterranean passageways, but they have been sealed off for security reasons.

Like all of Santo Domingo's colonial landmarks, this one has its share of legends. In 1881, Father Billini founded an insane asylum here. You can still find vestiges of the cells and the chains with which the inmates were held down. Local residents say that at night the laments of the madmen are sometimes heard, an eerie echo from the past. Despite this, the ruins are not regarded as a sinister place. On warm summer nights, you'll find students preparing their lessons and couples out for a quiet stroll. At the monastery lie the remains of Bartholomew Columbus, a number of governors and captains general, and Alonso Ojeda, conqueror of Panama. Ojeda's remains mysteriously disappeared, however, and legend has it that the conquistador asked to be buried a few steps from the main entrance, so that all those entering would step on his grave. It was intended as a form of atonement for a lifetime of sin. Not all of the monastery's stories are tragic or mysterious. It was here that the Franciscan friars educated Enriquillo. The great Indian leader sat under these archways, looked out upon these gardens, meditated, and learned to be a man of rare nobility. The colonial days saw many of the great conquerors pass through here offering prayers of hope for the New World. These walls were later a refuge for artists who fled to Santo Domingo seeking political asylum during the Spanish Civil War. Today, the monastery is sometimes used as a set for concerts or ballets. A performance in the dramatic shadows of the ruins is an unforgettable experience!

As you leave the monastery, make a right on Hostos Street and follow until you reach the ruins of Saint Nicholas of Bari Hospital. This was the first stone hospital in the New World. It is said that it was built on the site where a black woman had generously cared for the poor sick in a small shack that was her home. During Drake's invasion, the hospital suffered damages and about 6,000 ducats worth of valuables were taken. Its chapel still stands, now part of the Church of Our Lady of Altagracia, the Dominican patroness.

Across from the hospital ruins are two houses dating back to the early 1500's. The corner house is the Village Pub and next door to this is Raffles, a popular and imaginatively decorated bar. Up the block from here, on the corner of Luperón and Duarte, is the newly restored Hostal Nicolas Nader, a colonial house turned into a "mini" hostal, with about 10 ample guest rooms and a lovely interior courtyard.

CATHEDRAL OF SANTO DOMINGO

If you head back toward Conde Street and to the Parque Colon, the square that has the imposing statue of Columbus, you are back at the Cathedral of Santo Domingo. The Cathedral, with its 14 chapels, is an unusual blend of design elements which include Romanesque arches, Gothic vaults, and a Renaissance façade. Part of the reason for this is that the Cathedral was begun in 1523 and construction continued until 1540. Much more than just a place of worship, the Cathedral was a symbol of ecclesiastical power. As of 1542, when Pope Paul III declared it the "Primate Cathedral of the Indies," it assumed ecclesiastical superiority over all the churches in this hemisphere. Its importance in the colonies of the New World has never again been equaled by any one religious institution outside of the Vatican.

Although started by the first Bishop to preside here, Alexandro Geraldini, the construction of the Cathedral was completed by the son and heir of Rodrigo de Bastidas, who, equipped with his father's name and fortune, used part of his inheritance to see the project finished. In his role as bishop, he is said to have placed the last stone in the north door of the Cathedral in 1540. When Drake took over the Cathedral as his headquarters, he decided in one of his drunken rages to cut off the hand and nose of Bishop Rodrigo de Bastidas' statue. Fortunately, however, Sir Francis saw fit to leave the Bishop's chair unharmed. This is the oldest piece of mahogany in the colonial city and is thought to have been carved by Indian artisans. The chapel of St. Peter was used by Drake as a jail. On the wall, you will see the names of the bishops and archbishops whose successive administration of the Cathedral spanned over four centuries.

Near the main door of the cathedral is a marble plaque that commemorates the decree of Pope Benedict XV, in which he raised the Cathedral to the rank of a Basilica dedicated to Santa Maria la Menor. Above the door, you will again see the eagle of the Hapsburgs, the imperial coat of arms of Charles V. For such an austere place of worship, the frieze which decorates the main entrance is surprisingly festive with horns of plenty and mythical figures.

The Cathedral has its share of beautiful oil paintings, baroque altarpieces, and carved mahogany. Its treasury still holds some of the fabulous jewels that were donated by the great-grandfather of Simon Bolivar, as well as a large number of religious objects and jewelry given to the church over the centuries by its faithful congregation. The most outstanding of these is a processional tabernacle made of silver and first used on Corpus Christi in 1542. There are gold chains,

Santo Domingo Cathedral bell tower, begun in 1543

jeweled lizards, filigree silver, and crosses inlaid with rubies and amethyst. Most of the treasure will be exhibited during the 500-year anniversary celebration in a museum of religious artifacts. But the Cathedral's star attraction is the elaborate monument of marble and bronze done in 1898 during the time of President Heureaux to serve as the burial place and memorial for Christopher Columbus. It is here that the "Admiral of The Ocean Sea" found a permanent resting place, despite a great deal of international controversy on this subject, when his remains and those of his son were brought here in 1544 by the viceroy's widow, Maria de Toledo. She is herself buried in an unmarked tomb in the Cathedral floor. Although time and successive occupations of the city have taken their toll on the great Cathedral, it still has an air of grandeur. Its symmetry and elegance are a living monument that testifies to the greatness of colonial Santo Domingo.

When you walk out to the courtyard of the Cathedral known as the priest's square, you can see that the Ozama Fortress is only a short block away. This connecting walkway is the shortest block in the city and was known as Calle Los Nichos in colonial times. Today, as Pellerano Alfau Street, it has been converted into a lovely pedestrian walk, joining the Cathedral and the fort. The house with the two-tower balconies has always been known as the House of the Blessed Sacrament. In the 1500's, the house was owned by the Garay family. Don Luis Garay and his wife, Librada, had an infant son. They also had exotic tastes in house pets. It seems their pet orangutan carried the baby up to the roof of the house with the apparent intention of hurling it to the ground like a discarded banana peel. The frantic mother vowed to donate her home to the church in honor of the blessed sacrament if the ape returned her child unharmed. Miraculously, this is exactly the outcome of the story, and for generations the legal owner of the house was listed as the Blessed Sacrament. There are completely different styles of houses and different periods of architecture along this small block. An interesting house is number 2, which was the home of four Dominican Presidents. It is a 19th-century house constructed on the site of a colonial mansion, and is today the official residence of the Cardinal of Santo Domingo. It seems we're right back where we started, so now it's time to leave the colonial city for more modern sectors of town.

Cathedral of Santa Maria de la Encarnación, the first cathedral in the Western hemisphere

A WALKING TOUR OF CALLE EL CONDE: SANTO DOMINGO'S "OLDEST" PEDESTRIAN SHOPPING STREET

The Cathedral Square known as Parque Colon has a sculpture of Columbus which you may recognize. It is a 19th-century work by the French artist Gilbert, and it depicts the Admiral with the Indian princess Anacaona at his feet. Taking El Conde Street from the square in the direction of Independence Park is a short walk that will give you plenty of opportunity for shopping in the downtown commercial sector.

The very first corner is the intersection of Conde Street and Arz. Merino. Here, you will notice a lovely old building which used to be the town hall of Santo Domingo. The original structure was remodeled at the turn of the century and currently houses the Worker's Bank. The building boasts some beautiful murals by Vela Zanetti, the Spanish artist who went into exile during the Spanish Civil War, and whose work can be found in many of Santo Domingo's public buildings. El Conde Street, which means the "Street of the Count," has had other names. It was called Imperial Street during the years of French occupation. At another time it was called Separation Street, in celebration of the republic's independence. It has been El Conde Street since 1934.

The street has its share of bars and informal café-restaurants, where you can find good local cooking at fair prices. These places have a vitality all their own. Much the same can be said for shopping along El Conde. The area is a bustling array of stores, large and small, which carry everything from clothing, fabrics, furniture, shoes, and housewares to toys, jewelry, records, and art supplies. You'll find some excellent buys in shoes along here. Dominican shoe stores work mostly with leather for everything including soles and inner soles. The use of synthetic materials is limited because they are imported and custom duties make the use of leather preferable, as it is less costly and readily available. There are also some lovely shops that sell fine gift articles made of Dominican silver and gold. Jewelers offer reliable work at very reasonable prices here. Generally speaking, the prices tend to be lower than those at the more exclusive uptown shopping malls. Another good buy is children's clothing. Hand-embroidered clothing for infants and handmade linen and cotton clothing for children are excellent here.

The recent designation of El Conde Street as a pedestrian walkway has converted the entire length of the street into a comfortable, traffic-free and safe shopping mall. Conde Street really begins at the point where it meets Independence Park. The Conde Gate used to the western limit of the city. It was converted by the Count of Penalva, who was Captain General of Hispaniola, into a bastion commemorating the Spanish victory over the English intruders. The year was 1655, and the defeated invasion was led by Penn and Venables. The Latin inscription upon the Conde Gate roughly translates: "To die for one's country is sweet and dignified."

The gate's more recent history is tied in with the country's national identity perhaps more closely than any other site in the city. It was here that on the night of February 27, 1844, the Trinitarians raised the first Dominican flag and proclaimed their freedom from Haitian domination. The gate is used as the point from which all distances to and from Santo Domingo are measured.

The remains of the founding fathers, Juan Pablo Duarte, Francisco del Rosario Sanchez, and Matias Ramon Mella, were buried here until 1976, when their ashes were transferred to the mausoleum built in Independence Park, across from the gate. The massive monument of contemporary design is now the altar of the fatherland and an eternal flame burns here. There is always a military guard standing at attention, but you are free to visit the memorial.

WALKING TOUR OF GASCUE, NATIONAL PALACE, AND PLAZA DE LA CULTURA

Follow the direction of the traffic up from the park, and you will find yourself on Bolivár Avenue. If you make a righthand turn on Doctor Delgado Street it's a short walk to the National Palace. The palace sprawls along 18,000 sq. meters of beautifully landscaped grounds, and is clearly visible from the street. The National Palace is not used as a presidential residence. Each of the country's presidents has maintained his own private residence. The palace is used for executive and administrative offices, and as lodgings for visiting dignitaries. The luxurious suite of rooms on the third level was used to house the King and Queen of Spain during their state visit in 1976. These accommodations were refurbished for that occasion. An elegant grand staircase and majestic columns lead into the Renaissance-style castle that was designed by Italian architect Guido D'Alessandro. It took two years to complete, and was officially inaugurated in 1947. The use of centennial mahogany, gold inlay, marble from Samana in various shades, fine mirrors, and crystal has made the Palace one of the most beautiful in the hemisphere. Probably its most famous room is the grand reception ballroom known as the "room of the caryatids,'' which are 44 elegantly draped female sculptures that rise as columns around a hall that glitters with Baccarat chandeliers and the reflection of mirrors. Here you feel transported to the opulent courts of Europe, in a setting fit for royalty! Guided tours of the interior rooms are available by appointment only.

Cesar Nicolas Penson Avenue leads away from the Palace sector along shady quiet streets that contain some of the most graceful private residences of the city. This entire area is known as Gascue. The homes, most of which were constructed in the 1930's and 1940's, are solidly built and draw from different styles from the Spanish to the Republican and Victorian periods. With a flair for the eclectic, this area even boasts examples of Tudor, and you are likely to see everything from wrought iron fretwork to bay windows. The nice thing about strolling along here is that the homes are visible, not hidden behind forbidding fences and walls. There's a welcoming, friendly, neighborhood feeling, which not always present in the more modern parts of the city. This is an area where people still recognize each other and family names go back to the last century.

Past the modern Central Bank buildings and the gracious manor house of the American Embassy, lie the enclosed grounds of the Plaza de la Cultura. This cultural complex includes the National Library, Museum of Natural History and Geography, the Museum of the Dominican Man, the Gallery of Modern Art, and the National Theater. The grounds of the cultural complex are very well maintained, and the plaza is notably reminiscent of New York City's Lincoln Center both in appearance and concept. The Museum of Natural History and Geography offers permanent exhibits on the flora and fauna of the island and recreations of the amazing changes the topography and vegetation have undergone through the centuries. This facility is open to the public from 10 a.m. to 5 p.m., Tuesday through Sunday. The Museum of the Dominican Man offers a panoramic view of Dominican folklore and history. It houses a remarkable collection of pre-Columbian *cemies* (gods) and artifacts for ceremonial and household purposes. Fabulous costumes used in Carnaval and other Dominican celebrations are on display. You can also see the Popemobile at this museum. Hours are Tuesday through Sunday from 10 a.m. to 5 p.m. The Gallery of Modern Art houses paintings and sculptures by noted contemporary Dominican artists. There are also regular individual showings and photography exhibits. The Gallery is open from 9 a.m. to 5 p.m., Tuesdays through Sunday.

The National Theater offers daily tours of its facilities, and advance sale of tickets is available at box office. The theater has an audience capacity of 1,600 in its main hall for opera, ballet and

National Library building, Santo Domingo

symphonic presentations, and 170 people in the Sala Ravelo for chamber music and recitals. Native mahogany, marble, and onyx are used in the entire complex. Since its completion in 1973, the theater has presented major international companies like the New York Philharmonic, the New York City Ballet, The Royal Danish, the London Chamber Orchestra, the National Theater Group of Spain, as well as performances by local artists. It currently houses the National Symphony Orchestra, which was founded in 1941. The orchestra is made up of Dominican and foreign musicians of the highest musical standards and is presently under the musical and artistic direction of Maestro Carlos Piantini.

THE MALECON

The "Malecon," as George Washington Avenue is called, is a seafront boulevard that runs alongside the jagged southern coast in Santo Domingo for approximately 30 kilometers. For the residents of the capital city, however, it is a great deal more than just a pretty avenue; it is a hub of activity day and night.

The avenue starts at the old cargo port and winds uptown past the statue of Friar Anton de Montesinos, who was a champion of human rights in the colonial period. It stretches alongside the seafront passing two obelisks. The first, smaller obelisk commemorates the payment of the Dominican debt to United States banking institutions in negotiations between Trujillo and U.S. Secretary of State Cordell Hull. The second obelisk, the larger of the two, was erected in 1952 to commemorate the naming of the city as Ciudad Trujillo during the height of the dictatorship. By the second obelisk, you will see balloons and inflatable beach toys on sale, horse and buggy stand, street vendors offering everything from cashews to meat pies and the recently inaugurated offices of the Ministry of Tourism, formerly the Music Conservatory. The Malecon is where Carnaval and Mardi Gras festivals take place every year, but the avenue is much like a carnival all year round. It is lined with movie theaters, bars and clubs, sidewalk cafes, and seafront eateries. Several major hotels are located in the Malecon, as well as Vesuvio's Restaurant, a classic spot for people-watching. Past the elegant Santo Domingo Hotel, which boasts interiors by the Dominican-born and internationally acclaimed designer Oscar de la Renta, you will spot the fair grounds and buildings of the 1955 International Exposition.

The Malecon is always alive with activity. It is enjoyed by joggers and cyclists as well as those who prefer to ride in horse-drawn carriages. You will find many handicrafts on sale, and a variety of

The Malecon by the sea, Santo Domingo

goods that ranges from pizza to crêpes. Try some of the national beers, which many tourists say taste better on the Malecon.

RECREATIONAL PARKS AND ZOO

The **Paseo de los Indios** or Mirador Park as it is commonly called, is a seven-kilometer (five-mile) paradise for joggers, cyclists, lazy strollers, picnic enthusiasts, and children of all ages! It has wonderful caves with hieroglyphics and echoes everywhere, playgrounds for kids, and quiet walks for a little meditation. There is also a small lake for boat rentals and a restaurant overlooking the lake. The variety of trees in the part ranges from pine to floral. The park borders beautiful Anacaona Avenue, with its breathtaking private residences and modern condominium apartments. Many embassies are now located along this modern residential avenue, prompting many to call it "embassy row."

The **Botanical Garden** is one of the largest and most luxuriant in the world. It covers an area of almost 2 million square meters. The garden features pavilion exhibits of the natural flora of the island, its exotic plants, and native orchids. The Japanese garden is one of the most spectacular areas of the park. The exhibition of aquatic plants and the orchid pavilion are also noteworthy. The Dominican Republic produces 300 varieties of orchid. The garden also boasts the largest floral clock in the world! It's a great setting for walking, but the best way to see the entire facility is by carriage ride or train. It is open from 9 a.m. to 5 p.m., every day except Monday.

The **National Zoo** covers about 10 square kilometers of natural habitats maintained for a wide variety of animals. These include those native to the tropics and those that have been brought in from all parts of the world, such as elephants, camels, tigers, zebras, lions, and antelope. The "African Plain," surrounded by a moat, is a big attraction. There is also an aviary that covers 135,000 square feet and a collection of snakes. Take the train ride, but pause on your way out to watch the crocodiles, flamingos, and the colorful exotic birds that like to perch high in their cages. The zoo is open seven days a week, from 8:30 a.m. to 5:30 p.m.

PARQUE LOS TRES OJOS (THE THREE EYES)

Sound ominous? There are no three-eyed monsters in this park, but a visit is worth the ride out on Las Americas Avenue, on the way to the airport. The park consists of a very unusual cave formation over

Birdhouse in a Santo Domingo park

three lagoons, or circular lakes of waters, that run deep and cold and are fed by an underground river. The lakes are surrounded by lush vegetation and a cool, eerie beauty that seems frozen in time. The third of the ''eyes'' is the largest. Set inside a crater, it can be crossed on a small makeshift boat. There are stalagmites and stalactites as well as other interesting rock formations in this spectacular natural setting. It is open daily until 6 p.m. Wear sneakers for this excursion. By the way, the steps leading down into the cave are steep, so if you have vertigo problems this may not be the place for you.

Quisqueya Children's Park (Parque de Diversiones) is an amusement park and playground on Alma Mater Avenue with plenty of rides and activities for children. The entrance fee and charges for each ride are minimal (under one *peso*). Most rides are 50 *centavos*. Operates every day, including holidays.

PUERTO PLATA

Puerto Plata was founded in 1502 by Nicolas de Ovando by personal-decree of Christopher Columbus, who gave the settlement its name for the shades of silver that enveloped its coast at dusk. The region is as visually stunning today as it must have been in colonial times. Puerto Plata is the name of both the region and its urban center.

The coastline of the province of Puerto Plata is known as Costa de Ambar (amber coast) because of the rich amber deposits found in the mountains between Santiago and Puerto Plata. The golden hues of amber and the sun-drenched beaches of Puerto Plata's coastline have made this area the Dominican Republic's golden offering to the tourism industry. The town itself is comfortably cradled between an awesome natural harbor and a looming mountain backdrop, Mt. Isabel de Torres. There is no argument that Puerto Plata City and its surroundings provide some of the most appealing vegetation and scenic beauty of the island. All of a sudden, this quiet town of gingerbread architecture, colonial landmarks, and easy charm has been propelled into an awareness of its own potential. It is the hottest new tourist attraction of the country and its people seem to have a ''lookout, here we come'' enthusiasm about Puerto Plata's special offerings as compared to other Caribbean vacation spots.

FORT SAN FELIPE

Still standing in silent testimony to Puerto Plata's colonial past is the Fort of San Felipe. The history of the fort is a long and labored one.

PUERTO PLATA
©MARC PAULSEN PRESS
ATLANTIC OCEAN
LONG BEACH PARK
HERMANAS MIRABAL
TO AIRPORT
AV. CIRCUNVALACION SUR
AV. 27 DE AGOSTO
CIRCUNVALACION NORTE
CALLE 1
CALLE 2
CALLE 3
JUAN LAFITTE
PRESIDENTE VASQUEZ
AV. 27 DE FEBRERO
EL MORRO
FRANCISCO PEYNADO
16 DE AGOSTO
VIRGINIA ORTEA
AV. ISABEL DE TORRES
20 DE DICIEMBRE
MARGARITA MEARS
12 DE JULIO
JOHN F. KENNEDY
BELLER
DUARTE
ANTERA MOTA
SALOME UREÑA
LA ALTAGRACIA
SAN JOSE
F. KUNHART
SEPARACION
TEREZA SANCHEZ
MELLA
SAN FELIPE
EDUARDO BRITO
30 DE MARZO
AV. PENETRACION PORTUARIA
CALLE ANTIGUA VIA FERREA
TO SANTIAGO
TO CABLE CAR

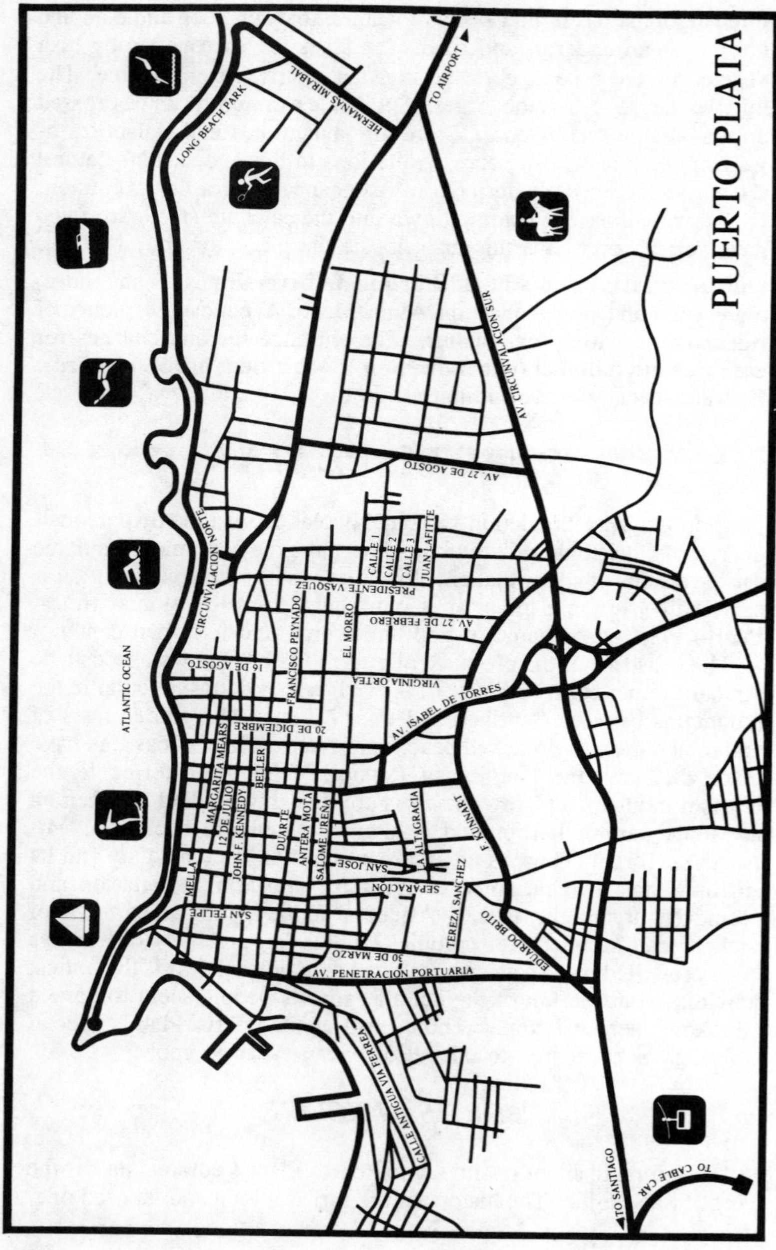

Construction started in 1541, at a time when there was the constant threat of intrusion in a harbor that provided a natural refuge for profiteers. If the intention of the fort was to defend the port against French pirates and other foreign menace, the reality is that it was never put to the test. By the time it was completed in 1577, Puerto Plata's importance as a port had diminished and the island's strategic value to Spain had declined with the conquest of richer lands on the continent. Puerto Plata flourished again at the turn of this century. It still preserves much of the Victorian graciousness of a quiet seaport city of pastel-shaded houses, tree-lined boulevards, carriage rides, and park concerts. Many of the gingerbreads have been carefully restored, and the gazebo on the central square was recreated from period drawings of the original design. Modern hotels like the Puerto Plata Beach Resort in town and the Playa Dorada Holiday Inn at the nearby resort, borrow some of the Victorian charm of the town in details on doors and windows, balconies with fretwork, and the hand-carved woodwork of their interiors.

MT. ISABEL DE TORRES

Mt. Isabel de Torres remains a dramatic backdrop to the story of contemporary Puerto Plata. The mountain stands at 2,565 feet and is crowned with a sculptured Christ figure similar to the one we identify with Rio de Janeiro. Horseback riding up the mountain trail is another popular activity that takes you through some lush vegetation to the summit. Cablecar rides up to the recreational park atop the mountain are a main attraction, particularly in the early morning for breathtaking views of the Atlantic coast below. The cablecar was built a few years ago as an attraction for nationals as well as tourists. It was built by a well-known Dominican engineer in collaboration with Italian engineers who had built many of the prominent systems around the world. It is fully computerized, and is considered to be a state-of-the art installation.

WEST OF PUERTO PLATA

Is there life beyond Puerto Plata? The area stretching from Puerto Plata west along the northern coast, including Luperón, Monte Cristi, and Manzanillo is as beautiful as it is remote. One vacation paradise that must be included in any section on destinations off the beaten path is Punta Rucia. Punta Rucia is only 12 miles from La Isabela which was the site of Columbus' first settlement on the island.

A delicacy captured—a torchlight hunt for landcrabs

The ruins are still there for the curious and the history buffs. The Punta Rucia beach is certainly one of the most beautiful in this region of lovely vegetation, quaint fishing villages and quiet countryside. Located here is the resort of La Orquidea del Sol ("sun orchid"). A charmingly rustic beachfront resort, Orquidia del Sol is tops on the list for a restful getaway vacation. While you are in the area, try and arrange boat trips (preferably with Bazooka, a local boatsman who works for the resort property) to some of the more secluded cove beaches nearby such as Playa Goya and La Encenada. Also on the agenda should be a boat trip to "La Laguna," a mangrove rich in birdlife and fish. We've even spotted eagles here. A place where the rest of the world just doesn't matter. Look for the pink seashells!

PLAYA DORADA

Five minutes from Puerto Plata or a fifteen-minute ride from Puerto Plata International Airport is Playa Dorada. This resort complex is destined to hold 14 projects of which six are already in operation and three more are under construction. Playa Dorada currently offers 3,800 rooms, with another 1,800 planned for the next 18 months. (More information on these resorts can be found in the section on hotel listings.) Fifteen years ago, the land site of the Playa Dorada resort area was little more than sugar cane. Had you seen it then, it would have been difficult to imagine a network of access roads joining sophisticated hotel properties with beautifully landscaped lawns and a magnificent 18-hole championship golf course designed by Robert Trent Jones. A windy course of very subtle design, the golf course doesn't appear to be as difficult as it really is. The decade of the 1970s brought the creation of the Tourism Infrastructure Department of the Central Bank of the Dominican Republic (Infratur) to prepare the groundwork for the development of the Puerto Plata region. The financing for large scale tourism projects like those at Playa Dorada was channeled through Infratur with a World Bank loan designated for that purpose. Playa Dorada is phase one of the operation and Playa Grande, further along the north coast, will be phase two. By 1979, the infrastructure of roads, electric power, water purification systems and a modern airport facility were ready to operate. The first of the resort properties (today's Jack Tar Village) at Playa Dorada was inaugurated in 1980. It was inaugurated in 1979 and is equipped to handle the largest aircraft in operation. This excellent facility services the entire northern coast. Transportation within Playa Dorada is handled by horse-drawn carriages, a Puerto

Plata tradition that dates back to Victorian times. There is always taxi service at the hotels for those who wish to venture into town or visit nearby Sosúa, which is well worth a trip.

SOSÚA

Three miles beyond Puerta Plata International Airport and just 25 kilometers east of Puerto Plata is the town of Sosúa. It may once have been a sleepy fishing village, but no more. Sosúa, divided into two distinctly appealing sectors named El Batey and Los Charamicos, has blossomed into a special tourist spot with its many guesthouses, apart-hotels, luxury vacation homes, pubs, restaurants, boutiques, and craft shops. It is situated on a sheltered cove and boasts one of the finest, some will argue *the* finest, beaches in the country. Many wealthy Dominicans maintain homes here, and the El Batey sector at the end of the beach offers many fine guest houses, apart-hotels, and restaurants with an international flavor. Somehow, it has managed to retain much of its small town charm. It is still a place where neighbors stop to chat on corners, people amble along at a relaxed pace, and where nothing is ever done in a hurry. As for Sosúa's perfect u-shaped beach, well, that's where everybody ends up!

If Sosúa has a decidedly European flavor, don't be surprised. In 1940 it became home for about 600 European Jewish refugees of World War II. Although only about 100 of the original colony remained, these settlers did much to give Sosúa its special character. They developed the dairy and sausage industries Sosúa is famous for. The original synagogue still stands and English, German, and French are widely spoken in the town. Despite the fact that Sosúa seems to have new hotel and apartment projects coming up every day, it is a town with respect for traditions. The old synagogue still holds service every week and the original United Fruit Company warehouse, a landmark building, was renovated into a restaurant and club (La Roca), rather than being torn down to make way for the new, as in so many other resort towns.

Just outside Sosúa, Sea Horse Ranch is a very exclusive private development along 250 acres of seafront, woods, and countryside that will hold both hotel and private residential projects. Residential lots for a total of 167 homes are between 1,500 and 4,000 square meters. The property enjoys two kilometers of seafront, and will include its own equestrian center.

Sosúa is serviced by taxis from the North Shore Office in El Batey and the Caribe Tours bus line, also located at the entrance to El Batey.

Taxis in Puerto Plata and Playa Dorada offer set fares for rides to Sosúa.

For general information on Sosúa, contact Servicios Turisticos (tel. (809) 571–2665; telex: ITT 3462005).

CABARETE

Located 14 kilometers to the east of Sosúa, Cabarete has developed from a tiny seaside settlement into a desirable spot for vacation homes. It is only 15 minutes from Puerto Plata International Airport. Cabarete's proximity to Sosúa results in its being regarded as part of the same offer, even though it is a separate community. Cabarete boasts six kilometers of excellent beach, particularly noted for its windsurfing. It offers a fully equipped center for windsurfing and rentals. Just one of its latest new hotel projects is the Pelican Beach Resort, a multi-million dollar private investment.

RIO SAN JUAN

The further east you travel along the northern coast, the more luxurious the vegetation becomes. Rio San Juan, with its beautiful Gri Gri lagoon and its proximity to some of the loveliest beaches like Caleton and Playa Grande, is another very special seacoast town.

Along with beautiful local beaches, Rio San Juan has some of the most striking rocky coastline with crystal clear blue waters. Here a boat ride can be taken through mangrove thickets and along the coastline. The trip includes entry to a watery cave in rocks. As the boat turns in the cave, the ocean swells rush in, making the boat rise and fall dramatically. The boat ride is a very pleasant and inexpensive excursion, which lasts a bit over an hour.

Two World Bank loans totaling over $40 million financed the development of the northern coast infrastructure and tourism projects and served as a catalyst for the flow of foreign investment in this region. It is here, more than anywhere else in the Dominican Republic, that U.S. and Canadian investors have wanted to own a piece of the most coveted real estate. Before the development frenzy is over, a second is scheduled to begin at Playa Grande. When it gets off the ground, this site will provide the region with yet another 2,000 hotel rooms.

PLAYA GRANDE

Located about an hour's drive from Puerto Plata International Airport, Playa Grande offers 300 hectares of coconut groves and a 1,600-meter-long beach, which is white and powdery. The Playa Grande projects will include luxury villa hotels, apart-hotels, tennis courts, equestrian stables, and another 18-hole championship golf course designed by Robert Trent Jones for those who can't get enough of a good thing! Until this happens, you can still call the virgin beach your own and, particularly on weekdays, walk the length of it without seeing another soul.

Beyond Playa Grande, the lighthouse of Cabo Frances Viejo (Old Cape France) followed by the bay and cliffs of Cabo Breton (Cape Brittainy) reveal an area that has become an exclusive haven for private residential investments. These homes, secluded and luxurious, are sometimes available for vacation rentals. The next interesting stop along the northern coast road is Nagua, the urban center for the province of Maria Trinidad Sanchez. In Nagua you'll see a beautiful stretch of palm-laced beaches which is bound to be a prime choice for development in the next few years.

EL PORTILLO AND LAS TERRENAS

Between Sanchez and Samana, there is a turn off the road for those driving to El Portillo and Las Terrenas. The road goes for 15 kilometers over the sierra before winding down to the coast again. El Portillo Beach Club is today a thriving complex of cabanas, apartments, and vacation villas with some of the most memorable beaches along the northern coast. Las Terrenas is the continuation of the same stretch of beach, but the ambiance is simpler and more rustic. It boasts some of the finest seafood restaurants in the country. To the west of Las Terrenas, is the El Cozon Beach near the "Key of the Whales," so-called because in the winter months, you are likely to see the humpbacked whales that come here to breed and escape the cold currents of the North Atlantic. Although the access road through the mountains can be hazardous, the area of Las Terrenas and El Portillo can be easily reached by small plane. There is a landing strip at El Portillo Beach Club that services this region. It is only about a 30-minute flight from Santo Domingo and there is air taxi service from Herrera Airport through the El Portillo Beach Club offices in Santo Domingo.

SAMANA

The Samana peninsula is a place of exuberant vegetation that is an explosion of tropical colors. When you see paintings for sale along the streets of Santo Domingo, you might think the canvases are an exaggeration of the artist's mind. Come to Samana and you'll see for yourself that those canvases are not the wild imaginings of some Caribbean Gauguin. Samana is proof that places like that do in fact exist. There are hills rich in marble deposits, covered with coconut trees. Vibrant vegetation surrounds a turquoise bay dotted with small islets. The most famous of these keys is Cayo Levantado, a self-contained paradise of vacation villas known as Club Carousel, which has 50 meters of private beach complete with silky sand and a proliferation of palm trees.

The town of Samana has an interesting history. It was founded in 1756 by the governor of the island, Francisco Rubio y Peñaranda, with settlers brought in from the Canary Islands to avoid the intrusion of French adventurers from Tortuga interested in controlling the bay. The entire coastline was vulnerable to smugglers and pirates. Because of its isolation, Samana developed slowly, having very little contact with the rest of the settlements itself. Santo Domingo is 245 kilometers away. The 1820's witnessed an underground immigration of freedmen and black slaves from the United States. At that time the island was under Haitian rule and the Haitian president negotiated with American abolitionists to relocate a settlement of American blacks, about 6,000 of them, many of whom settled in Samana. Even today, surnames like Smith, Johnson, and Williams are not unusual in this area and the English language spoken locally is rich with the idioms of the Old South.

Although much of the 19th-century gingerbread architecture of Samana was torn down during the last Balaguer administration to make way for modern concrete buildings, the original "churcha" as the small evangelist church is called, still stands keeping vigil over town and bay. The church dates back to 1823 and was founded by an English missionary, Narcissus Miller, who brought Methodist teachings to the Samana community. In the 1870's, there was an all-out effort to annex Samana to the United States because of its strategic importance, and had it not been for ten votes in the U.S. Senate, Uncle Sam would be in residence there today! History has it that Hitler coveted the bay for its control of the Mona Passage and the immediate pre-war years actually saw the visits of at least three German warships to Samana.

Desired by many and neglected by all seems to be the plight of Samana, as it has not yet been the site of any major tourism development. Its beaches are unsurpassed. Anadel, Rincon, and Miches all have an untouched quality, a remote kind of beauty. In many ways, Samana has not been in the least affected by the passage of time. Still a quiet fishing village, it has great potential as a cruise ship port of call.

THE EASTERN SHORE

The beaches of the eastern coast from Macao to Punta Cana are truly places of almost savage beauty. Crystalline white sand beaches, every variety of palm, coconut groves, and an abundance of seafood all form part of the eastern coastline's special offer. Macao is as yet undeveloped, except for a few small cabaña-type projects. It is close to the city of Higuey, a center for spiritual pilgrimage and the site of the Basilica of La Altagracia, which honors the country's patroness. Bavaro and Punta Cana, on the other hand, have been the site of a great deal of activity in private sector investment. In fact, the area has been developed entirely with private funding. It boasts an international airport of remarkable architectural design (you think you've arrived at some magical south sea destination) and, to date has three major tourism projects at Bavaro Beach, Club Mediterranée and Punta Cana Yacht Club, which collectively provide the region with over 1,100 hotel rooms.

The Rio Yuma flows to the south of Higuey and empties out at Boca de Yuma, on the southeastern tip of the island. Every year the renowned Boca de Yuma tournament attracts fishermen from all parts of the world. Sport fishing in this part of the island where the Caribbean meets the Mona Passage is said to be among the best in all of the islands for blue marlin. Although the eastern coast is accessible by road (about a three-hour drive from the capital), the flight from Herrera Airport to Punta Cana International is only 30 minutes. Charters run about 700 *pesos* and will give you an extraordinary aerial view of the vibrant beauty of the eastern region.

THE ROAD TO THE EAST

Boca Chica is 30 kilometers east of Santo Domingo and just a five-minute drive from Las Americas International Airport. Boca Chica used to be the status beach for people from the capital. Its famous Hamaca Hotel has stood in dilapidated ruin for over a decade as testimony to what once was. The beach itself has always been exceptional. A natural reef barrier, transparently clean waters, a sandy bottom, and slow currents make Boca Chica seem like a big swimming pool. Not only does it give the impression of an oversize swimming pool, but you can literally walk out to the reef at low tide! Boca Chica boasts two lovely little islands on that reef: La Matica (the little tree), to which you can walk at low ebb, and Los Pinos (the pines), the larger of the two, which can really only be reached by swimming out or by boat. No matter, it's well worth the extra effort, and has a secluded little beach of its own called La Escondida (the hidden beach).

Boca Chica actually developed in the early part of the century as a busy port because of its sugar mill. By the 1930's, the town started evolving around a central square. Since 1967, it has been the site of the Santo Domingo Club Nautico, the yacht club and marina. Deep sea fishing charters leave from here for marlin, bonito, sailfish, and dorado. Major tournaments and regattas are also organized by the club, a favorite with the residents of nearby Santo Domingo. Despite the many efforts of the club, Boca Chica suffered a sharp decline in the 1970's, when all the attention and financing of new tourism-related projects were focused on the Puerto Plata region. In the past two years, however, Boca Chica has truly enjoyed a renaissance. Today, there are those who call Boca Chica's beachfront which extends from Lindomar terrace to Piccolo Italia, *Playa St. Tropez*. Chaise-lounges dot the shore, while pedal boats, catamarans, jet skis, windsurfers, as well as snorkeling and scuba equipment are all available for rental. Scuba divers may be interested in the sunken ship at La Caleta. The "face-lift" has resulted from the amount of small-scale foreign and local investment in Italian, French, German, and Creole restaurants, inns, clubs, activities services, and rentals. The results have been nothing less than dramatic. Guest houses like El Paraiso and Romagna Mia, restaurants like L'Horizon, Le St. Trop, and Don Mike, late bars like Willy's, El Fortin, and Café Chocolate, and discos like Golden Beach and Playero have all combined to make this a popular and relatively inexpensive place for an uncomplicated vacation. Its casual style is very popular with Europeans and French Canadians.

The nostalgic days of the *Hamaca* are long gone, but in its place Boca Chica boasts a large and recently inaugurated project, the Don Juan apart-hotel project with 70 junior suites. There is also the promise of a new complex, the Boca Chica Beach Resort, with a projected 220 apartments. Meanwhile, Boca Chica is still a place for simple

The beach at Boca Chica

pleasures, such as barbecues and bonfires on the beach, secluded picnics at La Escondida, or charter cruising from Club Nautico. These are the reasons Boca Chica has come back, more popular than we ever thought possible!

COSTA CARIBE

Going east from Boca Chica, Guayacanes and Juan Dolio are also thriving as "low profile" vacation spots where the emphasis is more on relaxation than on glamour. Ranging from existing projects like the 300-room Tumbacoco Beach Resort, and the smaller and traditionally popular Playa Real and Talanquera Beach resorts, to new projects under construction like the 174-room Metro Hotel and a brand new 200-room Eurotel, this area is enjoying a boom similar to that of the Puerto Plata region in the early 1980's. The area is popular because of its affordable prices, excellent all-inclusive packages, and accessibility to the capital city, which is less than an hour's drive from the Costa Caribe area.

SAN PEDRO DE MACORIS

San Pedro de Macoris was only founded in the late 19th century, but by the 1930's it was a thriving community, in many ways more cosmopolitan than the capital of Santo Domingo was at the time. It was founded by Europeans and had a real cultural mix of Italian, German, and Arab residents, who had reason to take pride in their pretty seaport town. Some called it the "Sultan of the East" because of the prosperity it enjoyed in the days when its sugar production went for high international market prices. It was so important a city in those days, that Pan American Airlines used to fly its hydroplanes in and out of San Pedro de Macoris to the United States. But the town of San Pedro is notable for many other reasons. For one thing, it is the city that has reputedly supplied the greatest number of baseball players to the major leagues! Joaquin Andujar, Alfredo Griffin, Pedro Guerrero, Mariano Duncan, and the great Rico Carty all hailed from San Pedro, and winter league ball is still played with the same tradition of excellence at the Tetelo Vargas Stadium with its home team the "Estrellas Orientales" (Eastern Stars). San Pedro is also a thriving center of education. Its university, the Central University of the East, is considered to have one of the finest medical schools in the country, and has many U.S. students enrolled in its medical programs. Its large sugar mill still produces, although the decline in the world market affected San Pedro severely. Today it also holds one of the country's large Industrial Free Zones. Past San Pedro lies the resort area of La Romana.

LA ROMANA AND CASA DE CAMPO

La Romana was also a thriving sugar port at the turn of the century, but its current fame came in the decade of the 1970's, when Gulf and Western Corporation entered the resort business and launched the resort darling of the jet set: Casa de Campo. Today it is operated by Premier Hotel Corporation, owned by the Fanjul brothers, José Pepe Fanjul and Alfonso Fanjul. In the February 1986 issue of *Town and Country* magazine, the Fanjuls were quoted as remarking, ''Where else in the world can you walk from your jet to your house?'' Where else indeed? Casa de Campo is a 7,000-acre playground with 14 pools, nine restaurants, approximately 900 hotel rooms and villas distributed alongside the golf and tennis facilities. It has 17 tennis courts (13 of which are clay courts), two famous Pete Dye Championship golf courses, both offering 18 holes worth of challenge. The *''dientes de perro''* (dog's teeth) course is a magnificent seafront course regarded as very difficult with high winds; the inland ''links'' course is considered to be a tight course with awesome rough. There are also two polo fields, equestrian facilities for adults and children, luxury hotel rooms, and the Altos de Chavon artist village.

There are some new developments at Casa de Campo worth noting. There are plans for expansion, including a new 18-hole championship golf course, a new 150-room hotel, additional recreational facilities, and a conference center for 800 people which is planned for the end of 1988.

ACTIVITIES TO ENJOY AT CASA DE CAMPO

Water sports at Minitas Beach, Hobie cats, windsurfing, sailing, and snorkeling are available at Minitas Beach daily. Lessons are also available. Sturdy sunfloats are popular for drifting in the calm protected waters. Beach snorkeling is also a favorite, particularly for beginners and children.

MARINA ACTIVITIES

Deep Sea Fishing. The crafts used for deep sea fishing are two 31-foot Bertrams, holding a maximum of eight persons, four of which

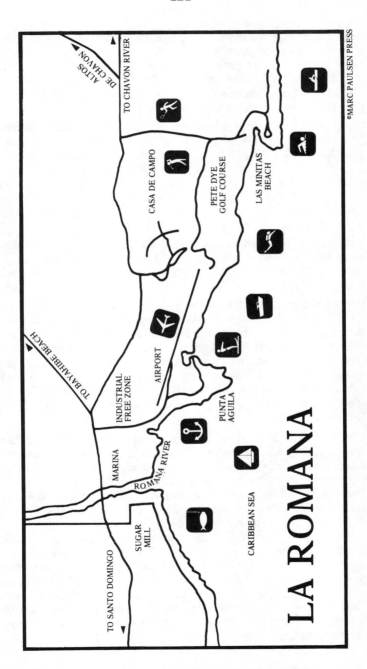

LA ROMANA

©MARC PAULSEN PRESS

can be fishing at one time. Trolling is the method used to catch the plentiful wahoo, dolphins, tuna, kingfish, sailfish, marlin, and barracuda. Casa de Campo provides the boat, captain, mate, tackle, and soft drinks. Box lunches may be ordered separately. The cost is US$250–350, depending on the duration, which can be a half-day or full day. The fee is per boat, not per person.

Snorkeling at Catalina. Catalina is an uninhabited island with some of the most beautiful beaches and coral reefs in the country. The cost includes snorkeling equipment, towels, soft drinks, and instruction if required. The half-day excursion on a 44-foot Bertram requires a minimum of six persons. It takes approximately half an hour to reach the island. Charges per person for a half-day are US$20; for an entire day, US$26.50. If the boat is being taken by a group, charges are US$450 per half-day and US$600 for a full day.

Sunset Sail. This romantic voyage on the Merengue Schooner sails along the southeastern coast into the sunset. The ship can hold 25 persons, but a minimum of eight are required for the trip. Charge per person is US$18.50.

River Fishing. Light tackle fishing is one of the most popular watersports at Casa de Campo. It takes place on the spectacular Chavon River, where almost world-record snook have been caught. There are three boats available for this excursion with out- board engines that will hold two persons and a guide. A half-day trip costs US$16.80 per person; US$28.50 for the full day. There is also a spectacular river tour for those who just want to relax and enjoy the scenery of tall cliffs and exuberant palm trees. The river tour per person costs US$13.50.

Charters. All the boats at Casa de Campo may be chartered for special excursions. In addition to the flagship *Merengue* and the others mentioned, there is the additional choice of *La Nina*, a 24-foot sloop sailboat with a maximum capacity of four persons, and *La Pinta*, a 26-foot sloop with capacity for six. These smaller sailboats are a favorite with experienced sailors and cost around US$100 per day for the boat. The *Merengue* costs US$300 per day.

One highly recommended excursion is a visit to the Isle of Saona, which is part of the "National Park of the East." Special charter arrangements are necessary. Beautiful beaches are found here, comparable to the best in the Caribbean. Columbus once had to seek refuge in these waters when caught in a storm during his voyage of 1494 (when he was returning after his discovery of Jamaica). On his way back to Hispaniola, he was caught in a tempest and had to remain on Saona for eight days.

Golf. *Golf* magazine has called Casa de Campo's two 18-hole courses designed by Pete Dye the finest in the world. Players come from all parts of the world to find out if this assessment is correct. The courses have been the sites for many international championships. The "Teeth of the Dog" runs along the coast with seven holes directly over the coral reefs; "The Links" go inland, with panoramic views of the entire property. Green fees for "Teeth of the Dog": US$33.50 per person for 18 holes and US$20 per person for nine holes. For "The Links": US$23.50 per person for 18 holes and US$20.00 per person for nine holes. Rentals of clubs are US$13.50 for 18 holes and US$8.50 for nine. Golf carts are US$10.00.

Tennis. La Terraza tennis club offers 13 competition clay courts, six of which are illuminated for night play. The club includes pro shop, bar, snack bar, swimming pool, and spectator deck. Rackets are available for rental and tennis accessories are for sale, including the materials for stringing rackets. The charges are US$13.50 for day-time and US$16.50 for night play. Racket rentals are US$4.00 and pro lessons US$30.00.

Equestrian Center. Hundreds of very fine horses are available for all levels of riding ability with both Western and English saddles. There are one-hour trail rides for beginners and for those who are out of practice. This trail goes as far as Minitas Beach and back to the Dude Ranch. A three-hour ride is available for the experienced rider and includes a ride through the sugarcane fields and the various scattered villages of the cane cutters. All riders whether experienced or not are required to wear helmets, and guides are mandatory at all times. These trail rides range from US$15 to $30 per person, depending on the length of the ride. Riding lessons are US$24.00 per hour.

Shooting Range. Trap and skeet shooting are available at Casa de Campo. Wing shooting is also available for the avid marksman.

Fitness Center. Right across from the main entrance to Reception at Casa de Campo is the fitness center. Racquetball, squash, sauna, whirlpool, and a fully-equipped gym are part of their facilities. Aerobic classes are scheduled throughout the week.

ALTOS DE CHAVON

Altos de Chavon is a magnificent recreation of hillside villages like those in the south of France (the medieval charm of Eze Village comes to mind). It has been said that the total investment eclipsed US$40 million. In certain ways, it is reminiscent of an elaborate stage set. It was sculpted out of stone with no specific plan in mind, it just evolved. Today, it is a successful and thriving artist community that includes a museum of pre-Columbian artifacts, a 5,000-seat amphitheater where artists like Julio Iglesias and Frank Sinatra and musical groups like Air Supply and Miami Sound Machine have held sold-out concerts, its own hotel facility (La Posada Inn), a number of excellent restaurants, art galleries, and jewelry and craft shops. It offers a self-contained little world with a very broad scope of activities ranging from silkscreen to photography and painting exhibits. Parsons School of Design recently displayed a fabulous collection of Dominican Carnival Masks at their exhibition hall in New York, to celebrate their five-year affiliation with the Altos de Chavon School of Design. The program at Altos de Chavon includes illustration, graphic design, fashion, and interior design.

Altos de Chavon was the brainchild of Charles Bluhdorn, the late founder and chairman of Gulf and Western Industries, who had a special feeling for the Dominican Republic and its culture, and believed that the potential for an artist village in this magnificent setting was enormous. Today, his daughter, Dominique Bluhdorn, is administrator of the Altos de Chavon Center and Foundation, and continues to be very involved in the cultural activities of the village. His widow, Yvette Bluhdorn, still maintains her magnificent home at Casa de Campo.

The central "piazza" at Altos de Chavon boasts the Church of St. Stanislaus, carved in stone. It gives the impression that it has stood vigil for centuries, overlooking the breathtaking cliffs that border the Chavon River. Much of the stonework was deliberately chipped to create the illusion of age, as were the obelisks in the central square. Altos de Chavon is all cobblestone and lantern-lit magic, particularly in the evening. This is a must on any itinerary to the east, and could well be the high point to your Casa de Campo sojourn.

A "Caribbean Charmer," as *Town and Country* magazine defined it, it's no wonder that Casa de Campo and the town of La Romana regularly host celebrities like Dominican-born designer Oscar de la Renta (who built his own residence "Casa de Madera") in the exclusive Punta Aguila area of the resort), Fiat Chairman Gianni Agnelli, Guy de Rothschild, Henry Kissinger, Placido Domingo, and many other notables from the world of industry, politics, and the arts. Dino de Laurentis and Dru Montague have fabulous homes here.

THE MUSEUM AT ALTOS DE CHAVON

The Archaeological Museum of Altos de Chavon is devoted to teaching tourists and Dominicans alike the cultural history of the island. Altos de Chavon is an appropriate location for this museum devoted to the Indian aborginies of Hispaniola. The Indians of the island believed that when they died, good souls would go to a paradise rich with fertile land, running streams, and lush vegetation, where they would be reunited with their ancestors and enjoy all the riches of the material world. The Altos de Chavon artist colony and the surrounding area with its palm groves sweeping either side of the cliffs down to the river is just such a place, as close as an earthly paradise as any spirit could want.

In this special place, the Tainos, as the native tribe was called, are surrounded by both nature and art. They would be very familiar with the museum vicinity, since they settled these very heights overlooking the river, and many of the relics and artifacts displayed were found nearby and throughout the southeastern region.

Most of the archaeological treasures exhibited here are from the collection of Dr. Samuel Pion, who dedicated half a century to the investigation of this Dominican heritage. Robert Dunphy of *The New York Times* once referred to this collection as "one of the richest collections of Taino Indian pieces in the world."

The Tainos were a gentle people, repeatedly called "noble" in the early colonial history books. Columbus himself praised them in a letter dated June 7, 1503, to Queen Isabela of Spain:

> They are not vulgar. On the contrary, they are spiritual. Their stories contain amazing deeds and their imagination is fantastic. Some invited us to eat, others to drink. This solicitude gives us the impression of incredible love and benevolence.

In tracing this special legacy, the museum devotes sections to the preceramic tribes that came before the Tainos. The public is given a view of the early cultures that evolved to the advanced artistic levels of the Tainos through colorful murals and exquisite engravings.

It is presumed that the Taino civilization descended from the Arawak, who came from the Orinoco-Amazonic zones of South America in the first century of the Christian era and migrated from island to island. The museum focuses mostly on the Taino heritage. At the time of the arrival of Christopher Columbus, the Taino Indians populated Puerto Rico, Santo Domingo, part of Haiti, and eastern Cuba. Santo Domingo had the largest settlement.

The Pion collection includes all types of utensils that might have been found in a normal pre-Columbian Taino home. There are stone hatchets, heart-shaped vases, clay pots, elaborately carved decorative items, clay cooking items, and utensils, such as the griddles used to bake the casabe bread made from Yuca, which are still eaten today.

Taino society was based on agriculture. They cultivated yuca, corn, tobacco, and peppers. These agricultural activities were supplemented by fishing and hunting. Large illustrations of the Tainos in their canoes or hunting serve to underscore the functional nature of the items displayed in the museum. The artifacts on exhibit are mostly objects used in everyday life or used in rites and special ceremonies. Sports were also very important to them. The equipment for their ballgames can be seen at the museum. *Batey* was their favorite sport and the teams would be supported by crowds of fans, just as in contemporary sports events. They also entertained themselves at the *areyto* ceremony with dance and song, dressing their bodies with festive beads and necklaces made of delicate shells. Beads and shells are still an intrinsic part of the crafting of jewelry in the Dominican Republic.

The Mythology and Art section of the museum holds some of its most interesting pieces, such as the *trigonolitos*. These were considered to be the most important *cemi* (idol) of the Tainos, since it was the god of agriculture and was believed to make crops grow. Indian chieftains usually possessed three of these stone *cemies*: one to grant them crops, one to allow painless childbirth, and one to provide sun and rain. The *trigonolitos* were three-pointed forms, usually a head at one end, flexed feet at the other, and a rising projection of a woman's breast. This mammary form symbolized nutrition and the sustenance of the human body. Sexual organs were often represented in Taino artwork. They were a very erotic people, but never in a vulgar sense. Sex was thought to be something mystical and divine. Phallic shapes were frequently used, for example, as a symbol of respect and celebration of male virility.

One showcase at the museum explains the principal religious ceremony called the *cahoba*. During this ritual the chieftain or *cacique* inhaled the hallucinatory powder which was also called *cahoba*. It was a practice also used by the tribe's medicine man. The Tainos believed that this powder would put their leaders in a trance-like state during which they could speak to the gods. Anthropologists believe the powder came from a mimosacea called *Acacianiopo*, still used by tribes in South America. While under its influence, the Tainos experienced visions of the future happiness or fate of their people. The occasional inhaling of *cahoba* may have been the inspiration of their expressive and imaginative art, much of which is animated, visionary, sensual, and mystical.

The exhibit includes a valuable *cemi* with a plate on its head which held the powder. The collection also includes the spatulas used to cleanse the system and help participants prepare their bodies for this special communion with their *cemies*. *Dujos*, the engraved seats used during the rite, are also on exhibit.

Since the museum opened in 1981, thousands of people fascinated by this art have made a pilgrimage to Altos de Chavon. The museum's designers were the talented Patricia Reid and archaeologist Manuel Garcia Arevalo.

For visitors with an interest in pre-Columbian cultures and their art, Santo Domingo also offers the Museum of Dominican Man, Museo del Hombre Dominicano, and the Prehispanic Art Hall, at the Sala de Arte Prehispanico of the Garcia Arevalo Foundation located at the Seven-Up building in Santo Domingo.

THE SOUTHWEST

BARAHONA

Barahona is located on the southern stretch of the Dominican Republic's Caribbean coast, 130 miles from the capital. The name Barahona suggests an Indian origin, particularly in a region which is rich with traces of its Indian heritage. However, it is not. It is the name of one of the early colonizers, who was the first to settle that province. Today, both the province and its principal town have been christened Barahona. This region represents one of the last unspoiled horizons of the Caribbean. It sounds like it might be remote, but Barahona is only about a 20-minute flight by small craft from Santo Domingo, and just under three hours by car, along an excellent and scenic road that runs southwest from Santo Domingo through Haina, San Cristobal, Bani, and Azua (watch for the goats) on to Barahona city.

The road through Bani will lead you southwest to Palmar de Ocoa, just a few kilometers away. This seafront town is populated by fishermen. Many city residents maintain weekend homes here because the fishing is excellent: kingfish, sea bass, grouper, octopus, and squid. You can arrange a fishing trip with one of the local boatsmen or just enjoy the beach here as a day trip from Rancho Francisco.

Barahona's landscape is etched in mountain streams, waterfalls, and dense vegetation, and is bordered by endless beaches. Some of the most beautiful beaches, like Paraiso, are totally virgin and provide a dramatically beautiful coastline of mountains sloping down to kiss the sea. There is only one drawback to this breathtaking beauty: most of the beaches have a rocky surface. At least Barahona makes up for it in scenic beauty and crystalline waters. Both hunting and fishing are said to be excellent.

The town has a number of small guest houses and a state-operated hotel, the Guarocuya, which although not in the best of conditions, is clean and functional, and has a lovely sandy beach that forms a small cove adjacent to the hotel's terrace. To date, the only major tourism project under construction in the area is the Bahoruco Beach Club and Resort, which includes a 90-suite hotel and 34 apartments destined to be part of a time-sharing facility, which will ultimately involve over 100 apartments. The project site is located between the villages of Bahoruco and Cienega, and faces an excellent beachfront.

The province of Barahona is one of the country's greatest natural attractions. Just by the beach of Los Patos, for example, are the rarely visited caves (Las Cuevas de los Patos) which take you back in time to a noble Indian civilization. Going in the opposite direction through Cabral, Duverge, Jimani, and on to La Descubierta, you will discover some more of the noteworthy attractions of Barahona. Here, for example, lies Lake Enriquillo, the largest of all in the Antilles, with Isla Cabritos right in the center of the lake. This island serves as home to at least 50 resident and migratory birds, including the American flamingo. It is also the natural haven for the American crocodile, an endangered species. This natural shelter was also the domain of Enriquillo, the Indian chieftain of legendary fame from the colonial period. The Sierra de Bahoruco was his playground and domain. Evidence of the country's Indian past can also be found at Las Caritas Cave (cave of the little faces), another highlight of the area of La Descubierta. Here, you enter through what appears to be stone faces coming together in a timeless embrace into caves full of the petroglyphs of an ancient civilization. La Descubierta is also known for its sulfur baths and its cold water baths at Las Barias.

Barahona province will have its own fullscale international airport facility, currently under construction, just 14 miles from the Bahoruco project site. When completed, the facility will greatly increase the tourism potential of this province rich in natural wonders, parks, preserves, mountain rivers, and reef-protected beaches. Barahona may always have a "world apart" quality, but once its international airport is ready to operate, this special hideaway province will not be a secret for very long.

THE CENTRAL VALLEY

SANTIAGO: HEARTLAND OF THE CIBAO

Santiago is the second most important city of the Dominican Republic, although many locals would argue that in spirit it is way ahead of the capital! It was founded in 1495 on the banks of the River Yaque by Bartholomew Columbus, the Admiral's brother. The original settlement was destroyed by an earthquake in 1562. The following year, Santiago de los Caballeros (of the gentlemen) was rebuilt on the site it holds today.

Santiago is an interesting town, and a very proud one. It has reason to be. Santiago has given the country its greatest number of presidents. In fine arts and literature it also boasts some outstanding names. Its women are said to be beautiful, and its folklore is one of the richest. Santiago is the cradle of the Merengue, the national rhythm, part and parcel of the cultural patrimony. This is the sound that *Time* magazine recently claimed is taking the United States' club scene by storm.

Although it is on the road to the fine beaches of the north, such as Cofresi, Costambar, and Playa Dorada, it has no coastline itself. It does however have one of the largest rivers, El Yaque del Norte. Santiago is the heartland of the country's fertile agricultural region, known as the Cibao. It's a town of crops and commerce, and lots of money. Tobacco and sugarcane are the key to Santiago's economy. Industries like rum and cigar and cigarette production are synonymous with Santiago. Its industrial free zone is one of the most successful, and its university, Universidad Catolica Madre y Maestra, is certainly one of the finest. The university, with its magnificent sloping campus, offers a hotel administration program in conjunction with Cornell University, and an exchange program with the University of South Carolina. It has its own domestic airport and an urban transportation system. Taxi service service is available at all major hotels.

Physically, Santiago is a pretty city of manicured lawns and a blend of architectural styles ranging from Neoclassical and anglo-antillean to modern. There are horsedrawn carriages, a fairly active nightlife, excellent shops, lovely hacienda-style houses, and a fair number of important landmarks. The monument of the heroes of the restoration, better known as "El Monumento" de Santiago, dominates the city's entrance and is visible from everywhere throughout the town. Santiago's Eiffel Tower is not only pretty to look at and the

129

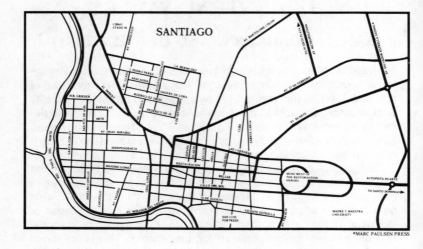

©MARC PAULSEN PRESS

most recognized symbol of the town itself, but is also a great point from which to take advantage of the view. The interiors are graced with murals by the Spaniard, Vela Zanetti, who was commissioned to do murals for the United Nations building in New York. 67 meters high, the top of the monument has a viewing gallery that is worth a visit. Like all the old towns, it has its central park square: Parque Duarte. This plaza faces the centennial cathedral of Santiago, built during the period of 1868 to 1895. The cathedral is a blend of Neoclassical and Gothic styles, and is particularly notable for its beautifully carved mahogany altar.

Another highlight is the Tomas Morel Museum of Folkloric Art, located in a lovely Victorian house. This museum contains a collection of carnival masks and folkloric objects. Many of the masks were recently on loan to the Parsons School of Design in New York for its 1986 display of carnivals masks of the Dominican Republic. There is also the Tobacco Museum, which explains the processing of tobacco from harvest to production. According to the March 1984 issue of *Connoisseur* magazine, some of the finest cigar manufacturing in the world takes place in the Dominican Republic today, involving a blend of tobacco leaves. The article's conclusion is that the old habanos of Cuba are, from the aroma of things, no longer invincible. For those with strong stomachs who are ready to sample a bout of cockfighting, only recommended for those the Gallera Municipal is the local cockfighting arena and might be another interesting point. Cockfighting is, after all, one of the most typical Dominican sporting events.

Like those of Santo Domingo and Puerto Plata, the marketplace of Santiago is brimming with handicrafts, woven baskets, flowers, fruit, potions, and incense. It is a fun place to visit and bargain. Shopping is generally enjoyable here, with many excellent small specialty shops and large department stores like El Gallo and Casa Hache for housewares. Santiago also boasts several excellent wicker and rattan furniture factories. These tropical furnishings are very well made for those who crave a Casablanca atmosphere. Santiago has its share of nightspots and piano bars, and it even boasts its own casino, which basically serves the Puerto Plata area as well. With all these factors to consider, it's small wonder the people from Santiago see themselves in constant rivalry with Santo Domingo, and it is left for you to decide if you prefer the leisurely pace of the *corazon* of the Cibao to the intensity of the capital city.

Roadside fishmonger displaying his wares

HIGHLANDS AND LOWLANDS

NATIONAL PARKS: THE LAST HAVENS

The Dominican Republic boasts a total of eight national parks, with Sierra de Bahoruco recently declared a national park and wildlife sanctuary. These preserves meet all the conditions of international requirements: undisturbed beauty, recreation, natural endemic life, refuge for endangered species, and unlimited opportunities for the student, scientists, and the just plain curious. The international community has made great strides in the design and management of national parks. From twelve parks located throughout five countries in the year 1900, there were twelve hundred parks located in over one hundred countries by 1975. The Soviet Union alone has 80 national parks. In South America, Brazil takes the lead with 20. The very first national park ever designated as such was the Yellowstone in the U.S.

In the Dominican Republic, the Direccion Nacional de Parques maintains a program to protect its natural sanctuaries under a specialized staff. They are more than happy to inform you of what each of the parks offers and set you on the right track for exploring these special parks. Among these preserves is the Parque Nacional del Este, located at the southeastern tip of the island. Many species of reptiles and amphibians are found here, including the native rhinocerus iguana and up to four species of sea turtles. This is also a refuge for the White Crown pigeon. Recent discoveries in this area have shown a number of caves used by the pre-Columbian Indian population for shelter and ceremonial purposes. Burial sites, fire pits, pottery, and petroglyphs have been uncovered. Part of this park of the eastern region is the Isla Saona. This island has beautiful beaches. Columbus once had to seek refuge there when he was caught in a storm in these waters during his second voyage. It is said he remained there for eight days.

Close by the coast of Samana Bay, Los Haitises was totally submerged in water hundreds of thousands of years ago. What emerged remains today as thousands of hills of approximately the same height. One third of the land is forest, and is currently undergoing a strict reforestation program. The moist conditions of the area provide breeding grounds and protection for many bird species including the parrot. Another shelter for both resident and migratory bird species is Isla Cabritos, inside Lake Enriquillo. Hundreds of these species visit the isle in October and November. One magnificent sight is the American Flamingo. You will spot quite a few of them in this sanctuary. Several species of reptile are also found in this natural habitat, including both species of threatened native iguanas, *Cyclura cornuta* and *Cyclura ricordii*. The endangered American crocodile (*Crocodylus acutus*) is protected on the island and its surrounding lake. The baby crocodiles take about 90 days to hatch and are no more than 10 inches long as newborns. There are several hundred crocodiles on the island, and the best time to catch sight of them is early morning or late afternoon. The island is said to have derived its name *cabritos*, from the hundreds of goats that populated it at one time. It still has some unusual residents, including wild donkeys that seem to thrive on the arid sand and cactus terrain. Not the prettiest place, its thorny vegetation seems to be just right for the strange ecological composition of the island and its surroundings. Lake Enriquillo is believed to have been part of some ancient body of water and to have been cut off from this ocean as a result of geological changes. This would account for its salty composition. Surrounded by land and constantly warmed by the intense Caribbean sun, the waters of the lake have evaporated to below sea level. The high saline content doesn't seem to bother any of the local residents, particularly *Crocodylus acutus*.

THE CARIBBEAN ALPS

Set between Parque Nacional Armando Bermudez and Parque Nacional J. del Carmen Ramirez are the towering cliffs of Pico Duarte, La Pelona, and La Rusilla of the Cordillera Central. These are the highest peaks of the Antilles, and one of the wonders of the Caribbean. A visit to this region of the Cordillera Central is not something to be planned casually. The department of parks can coordinate and schedule a guide for you. In addition to camping and first aid equipment, you will need rations and warm clothing. At dusk you're often enveloped by frost and fog. This is not for everyone; it is for the fit and the adventurous, and those who enjoy the stillness of mountains and forests at night.

Wilfredo Garcia, a distinguished photographer who has dedicated a great deal of time and effort to recording his impressions of the peaks, valleys, and woods of this remarkable area, has collected his work in a breathtaking volume entitled *The Cathedral of the Forest*. The book is available at most of the bookstores in the country, and it will give you some insight into the extraordinary vegetation of the parks which comprise the Cordillera Central. Here you'll see exotic ferns, wild flowers, and a pink moss that looks like heather, as well as endless stretches of forests as at La Comparticion. You'll find green valleys, the source of mountain rivers, and the rugged terrain that reaches up through mist to the highest peaks.

Traditionally, Pico Duarte was said to be 10,417 feet above sea level. However, recent studies seem to indicate that the peak reaches 10,128 feet, whereas La Pelona's height is estimated at 10,394 feet. There is considerable controversy over which of the two is the highest. To the climber, they are both awesome, and provide precious moments of communing with nature. Wilfredo Garcia suggests allowing three to five days for the trip, which can be started through Jarabacoa and Los Tablones, or from the opposite end, San Jose de las Matas. This latter is said to be a longer but more scenic route.

Under two hours from Santo Domingo, with a turn off the Duarte highway beyond La Vega, Jarabacoa is a world apart. Swiss chalet-type homes, mountain streams and waterfalls, pine trees, rich vegetation, bright flowers, and clean air make this a wonderful mountain retreat. A new highway has just been finished which should lead to improvements in facilities. Beyond Jarabacoa is Constanza, a town of beautiful mountain scenery, flowers, berries, and Nordic vegetation. Even though Jarabacoa and Constanza have not been developed to their full potential, they are rich in natural resources. To sit by a fireplace on a December night and listen to the rustle of pine trees may not be your idea of a "Caribbean" vacation and this may well be the reason why the mountain destinations of the Dominican Republic have not received the full attention they deserve and have limited hotel facilities.

Another tiny mountain village is San Jose de Ocoa, about a two-hour drive from Santo Domingo. There is lush mountain scenery here. The facilities are rustic, but there is plenty of opportunity for bathing in streams and river, horseback riding, and opportunity to practice your Spanish! It's a getaway.

The National Parks of the Dominican Republic are certainly some of its greatest treasures. In a recent map of the eight park sites, *The Santo Domingo News* pointed out that the combined area of the parks is larger than the state of Rhode Island. This is one Caribbean island where nature lovers will have no complaints about feeling crowded.

SUGGESTED TRAVEL ITINERARIES

Itinerary A. If you have one week or less, don't make the mistake of trying to do and see too much. After all, the object of travel is relaxation. We would advise you to concentrate on one destination within the country, either north or south. If you select Puerto Plata, a week will give you ample time to see this quaint gingerbread town, enjoy the resort at Playa Dorada, and visit Sosúa and Cabarete.

Should you visit Santo Domingo for a week, you will basically stay in the city. Between shops, museums, art galleries, restaurants, the colonial sector, and the night spots, there is more than enough to fill a week. You might want to include a few day trips to the beaches of Boca Chica and Costa Caribe, which are under an hour's drive from the city.

Itinerary B. Should you be in the Dominican Republic for two weeks, you have more time to plan side trips. Definitely include Rio San Juan and Samana in your northern coast explorations. From Santo Domingo, the obvious side trip should include La Romana and a visit to Casa de Campo and the artist village of Altos de Chavon.

An alternative to this plan is to spend one week in Puerto Plata and one week in Santo Domingo. American, Air Canada, and Pan Am are among the airlines flying into both Santo Domingo and Puerto Plata, so you could arrange your return in advance from either point. Bus travel between Santo Domingo, Santiago, and Puerto Plata is so frequent (each of several companies has at least three departures daily), that it is an easy matter to include both north and south in your itinerary. If you've decided to drive around yourself, this will allow you more flexibility with the scheduling of your travel plans.

Yet another possibility for a two-week stay, is a combination city and beach package. From Santo Domingo, for example, it is easy to arrange for a week at one of nearby Juan Dolio's many new resort properties. All of Costa Caribe is just under one hour from the capital, which affords a leisurely drive and a great way to see what the city has to offer while allowing yourself time on the beach.

Itinerary C. A three-week stay in the Dominican Republic should ideally include the above, as well as a visit to a lesser known area of the country. You could visit the beautiful east coast regions of Punta Cana and Macao, Barahona to the south, or Luperón and Monte Cristi to the northwest.

Another possibility would be the mountain towns of Jarabacoa and Constanza, or a visit to the national parks of the country, secluded wildernesses or wildlife havens like Lago Enriquillo.

Itinerary D. If you have a month of vacation time or more, try and spend a week on each coast and one in the towns of the interior, including the beautiful Cibao valley and the mountain towns in the central regions. An alternative to this is to spend the entire vacation period lounging on the nearest pool deck or beach, be it at Costa Caribe or the farthest reaches of the Samana Peninsula, doing absolutely nothing in plenty of style!

Fishermen along the road to Las Americas Airport

Chapter 6

HOTELS AND LODGINGS

The Dominican Republic offers a wide variety of hotels: Some are large, modern hotels while others are small, family-style guest houses. Basically, the cost of a hotel room will range between the equivalent in *pesos* of US$20 to $180. As regards the service, what may be lacking in efficiency is made up for in good will. The Tourism Ministry has a star rating system that goes as high as five stars. There are really only a few hotels that come close to an international rating of five stars, although many would like to think they qualify. What follows is a partial listing of adequate to excellent hotel properties in Santo Domingo, Santiago, Puerto Plata, Playa Dorada, Sosúa, the coastal towns, and the mountain destinations. All hotel rooms in the facilities listed have private bathrooms. Costs are designated as inexpensive (approximately 50 to 100 *pesos*), moderate (100 to 260 *pesos*), and expensive (260 *pesos* and up).

Both in and out of season, a number of packages are offered by wholesalers in the United States and Canada that include air fare, several nights of hotel accommodations, and tours. For current information, check with your travel agent and the airlines that serve Santo Domingo and Puerto Plata (see also *Tour Operators to the Dominican Republic*, chapter 2).

Modern apartments in Santo Domingo

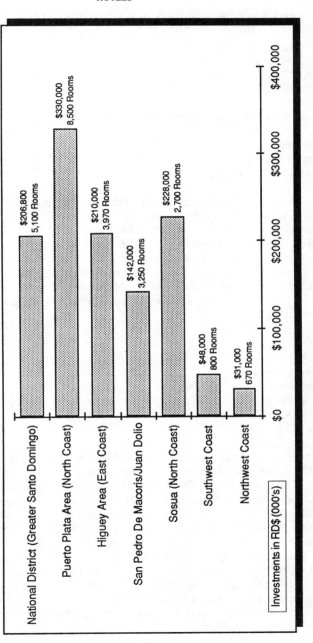

Hotel Rooms and Villas Currently Operating, Planned and Under Construction by Area, 1980 – 1989/90

National District (Greater Santo Domingo) — $206,800 / 5,100 Rooms

Puerto Plata Area (North Coast) — $330,000 / 8,500 Rooms

Higuey Area (East Coast) — $210,000 / 3,970 Rooms

San Pedro De Macoris/Juan Dolio — $142,000 / 3,250 Rooms

Sosua (North Coast) — $228,000 / 2,700 Rooms

Southwest Coast — $48,000 / 800 Rooms

Northwest Coast — $31,000 / 670 Rooms

Investments in RD$ (000's)

$0 $100,000 $200,000 $300,000 $400,000

©Marc Paulsen Press

HOTELS IN SANTO DOMINGO

Dominican Concorde
Tel. (809) 562–8222
Telex: ITT 3460179
  Affiliated with:

Loews Representation International
P.O. Box 1974
Anacaona Avenue
Santo Domingo
Republica Dominicana

316 rooms. Air-conditioned. Radio, cable television. Minibar.
Facilities: Spacious, modern hotel. Luxury restaurant "La Casa."
Informal restaurant "El Mercado." Elegant rooftop nightclub "La
Azotea." The art deco casino, although small, is easily the prettiest
casino in all of Santo Domingo. Lobby bar which dominates the
lobby. Pool bar. Olympic pool. Eight tennis courts with night lights.
Excellent convention facilities for 1,350 persons. For the business
traveler: secretarial and telex facilities. Car rental on premises.
Babysitter service.
Classification: moderate.

El Embajador
Sarasota Avenue
Santo Domingo
Tel. (809) 533–2131
    (800) 327–9226
Telex: ITT 3460528

310 rooms. Air-conditioned. Radio, cable television. Minibar.
Facilities: Elegant restaurant "The Jade Garden." Renowned nightclub "The Embassy Club"(the recently reopened Embassy is a nostalgic recreation of original dating back to 1956). Informal, poolside
garden coffee shop. One of the oldest casinos in Santo Domingo.
Inviting lobby bar. Certainly the most elegant traditional lobby of
Santo Domingo. Rooms are extremely spacious with traditional decor. Excellent shopping arcade. Beauty parlor. Swimming pool.
Country club atmosphere with beautiful gardens and grounds. Tennis
courts. Massage and sauna facilities. Business floor with complete
secretarial services and seminar facilities. Car rental. Babysitter
services. 24-hour taxi service. Convention capacity to 350 persons.
Classification: moderate.

The Dominican Concorde Hotel, Santo Domingo

Hotel Santo Domingo
Independencia Avenue
Santo Domingo
Tel. (809) 532–1511
(800) 223–6620
Telex: ITT 3460033

220 rooms. Air-conditioned. Radio, cable television.
Facilities: Luxury accommodations in this gracious, tropical, and
elegantly decorated hotel (interiors by Oscar de la Renta). "El Alcazar Restaurant" is one of the most beautiful you are likely to find.
Romantic courtyards. Poolside *bohio* style bar and lunch service.
Patio coffee shop for breakfast and lunch. "Las Palmas" nightclub,
intimate and dark. Lovely pool area. Tennis courts with night lights.
Volleyball. Sauna and massage. For the business traveler: American
Chamber of Commerce offices on premises. Complete secretarial
and telex service. "Premier Club" 66-room executive floor with rate
that includes secretarial services, breakfast and tea. Easily the most
elegant hotel in Santo Domingo. Convention facilities for up to 250.
Hairdressers, boutique, tour operator. Quiet and elegant facility.
Waiting lounge and offices at Las Americas International Airport.
Classification: expensive.

Hotel Hispaniola
Independencia Avenue, corner of Abraham Lincoln Avenue
Santo Domingo
Tel. (809) 533–7111
(800) 223–6620
Telex: ITT 3460033

160 rooms. Air-conditioned. Radio, cable television.
Facilities: The Santo Domingo's sister hotel, across the way from its
more luxurious counterpart. Convenient midtown location. Modern
rooms. Restaurant "El Vivero" known for local specialties. "Las
Canas" bar. Neon Disco. Pleasant pool area and deck. Three tennis
courts. Massage. Convention facilities for up to 400. Business ser-
vices: secretarial and telex. Hairdressers. Tour operator on premises.
Car rental. Gift shop. Waiting lounge and offices at Las Americas
International Airport.
Classification: moderate.

Gran Hotel Lina

P.O. Box 1915
Maximo Gomez Avenue, corner of Abraham Lincoln Avenue
Santo Domingo
Tel. (809) 689-5185
    (800) 223-6764
Telex: ITT 3460278

220 rooms. 15 junior suites and one presidential suite. Central air-condition. Radio, cable television. Minibar.
Facilities: The entire hotel was recently completely renovated and enlarged. One of the finest restaurants in the Caribbean, "Lina." Inviting piano bar. Spacious casino. Nightclub. Cafeteria and pool bar. Swimming pool. "Lina" nightclub offers live entertainment. Tennis courts with night light. Solarium, fully equipped gym, sauna. Full convention facilities with capacity for 1,000. Secretarial and telex facilities. Car rental on premises. Travel agency. 24-hour taxi service. 24-hour room service.
Classification: moderate.

Hostal Palacio Nicolas de Ovando

Las Damas Street
Santo Domingo
Tel. (809) 687-3101
Telex: ITT 3460446

60 rooms. Air-conditioned, telephone, and television. Minibar. Colonial decor. Beautifully restored 16th-century home of colonial governor and home of early colonial family all joined into one spectacularly romantic hotel property. Facilities: Adequate restaurant. Poolside for informal meals. Room Service. Several very appealing bars. Gracious interior courtyards and romantic Spanish patios with fountains. Small swimming pool. Accessible to museums and landmarks of colonial Santo Domingo. Recently refurbished.
Classification: moderate.

Santo Domingo Sheraton

365 George Washington Avenue
P.O. Box 1493
Santo Domingo
Tel. (809) 685-5151
    (800) 325-3535
Telex: ITT 3460529

Hotel Santo Domingo

260 rooms. Air-conditioned. Radio, cable television. Panoramic views of the sea. Presidential suite with spectacular view. Facilities: Elegant restaurant "Antoine's." Cafeteria. Poolside grill. "Petit Café" and "Yarey" lounge and nightclub. "Omni Discothèque." Large casino. Excellent convention facilities. Swimming pool and large deck area. Tennis courts with night lights. Gym and sauna. Secretarial services. Babysitter services. Tour operator on premises. Car rental. 24-hour taxi services. Excellent gift shops. One of Santo Domingo's busiest hotels with a great many activities and nightspots. Its location and facilities make it a great commercial hotel with a lot more class than most business-oriented hotels. Convention and banquet facilities for up to 550. One 50-person seminar room. Classification: expensive.

The V Centenario
218 George Washington Avenue
Santo Domingo
Tel. (809) 686–0000 to 686–0040

Scheduled to open mid–1988. 230 rooms, 30 of which are suites. Central air-conditioning. Cable television and radio. Facilities: This major property is under construction on Santo Domingo's seafront avenue, and all rooms will have sea views. The design calls for the most luxurious accommodations available. Two floors consist of executive penthouse suites with private executive club, restaurant, bar and lounge, library, and complete office services. 24-hour room service and taxi service. Convention facilities for 1,200. French gourmet dining at restaurant named in honor of Christopher Columbus: "El Gran Almirante." Tascamar fisherman's tavern for Spanish cuisine. Tennis, squash, swimming pool, gym and sauna, shopping arcade, disco named the "Galeon," and piano bar. Elegant casino. The hotel will have subterranean levels for entertainment facilities as well as parking. The name of the hotel honors the forthcoming 500-year anniversary celebration.

Hotel Cervantes
Calle Cervantes 202
Santo Domingo
Tel. (809) 688–2261
Telex: RCA 3264340

171 rooms. Air-conditioned. Radio, cable television.
Facilities: 24-hour "Bronco" steakhouse. Nightclub. Pool with ter-

The Santo Domingo Sheraton Hotel on the Malecon

race. Functional hotel facility. Convenient location. Taxi service. Massage and sauna. Babysitter service.
Classification: moderate.

Hotel Continental
16 Maximo Gomez Avenue
Santo Domingo
Tel. (809) 688–1840, 689–1151/58
    (800) 223–1900
Telex: ITT 3460425

100 rooms. Air-conditioned, radio, cable television. Panoramic view of city and seaside. Facilities: "Le Jardin" restaurant. Disco. Pleasant bar. A commercial hotel with a warm atmosphere. Tasteful and unpretentious. Small pool. Babysitter service. Convenient midtown location. The hotel is equipped with an information system software program designed to improve services for business travelers. Certainly one of the best in this category.
Classification: moderate.

Hotel Caribe I
Maximo Gomez Avenue
Santo Domingo
Tel. (809) 688–8141

39 rooms. Air-conditioned. Radio, cable television.
Facilities: Indoor/outdoor café-style Italian restaurant.
Piano bar. Secretarial services. Pool and deck area. Small and very appealing hotel. Family-style. Convenient location.
Classification: moderate.

Hotel Comodoro
193 Bolivár Avenue
Santo Domingo
Tel. (809) 687–7141
Telex: RCA 3264202

87 rooms. Air-conditioned. Cable television. Background music. Minibar. Facilities: "Le Gourmet" restaurant. Cafeteria. Nightclub. Conference facility for up to 200 persons. Swimming pool. Ice machine on every floor. Car rental. Taxi service. Babysitter service. Hairdresser. A popular commercial hotel. Convention facilities for up to 300 persons.
Classification: moderate.

Hotel Napolitano, Santo Domingo

Hotel Merengue
at Plaza Merengue
Santo Domingo
Tel. (809) 566–3151

New in 1987. 220 rooms (106 rooms first phase). Air-conditioned.
Cable television. Facilities: This property, at the corner of 27th of
February and Tiradentes Avenues, has an ideal location for business
people and shoppers. Nightclub. Casino. Hotel Merengue will be
part of a large commercial complex and shopping center like the
OMNI center in Miami.

Hotel Naco
22 Tiradentes Avenue
Santo Domingo
Tel. (809) 562–3100
Telex: ITT 3460382

105 rooms. Air-conditioned. Cable television, radio. Complete
kitchenette. Facilities: restaurant, cafeteria, popular casino. Small
convention facilities. Secretarial services. Tour operator on premises. Swimming pool and deck. Babysitter service. Convenient location, very near Plaza Naco. Pleasant commercial hotel. Excellent
midtown location.
Classification: moderate.

Hotel San Geronimo
1076 Independencia Avenue
Santo Domingo
Tel. (809) 533–8181
Telex: RCA 3264319

72 rooms. Air-conditioned. Radio and cable television. Restaurant
"San Geronimo." Cafeteria. Very popular casino. Swimming pool.
Small convention room. Secretarial services. Car rental. 24-hour
taxi service. Convenient midtown location (right behind "Vesu-
vio's"). Commercial hotel. Functional.
Classification: moderate.

Hotel Commercial
Conde Street, corner of Hostos Avenue
Santo Domingo
Tel. (809) 682–8161

75 rooms. Air-conditioned. Television. No frills. Downtown Conde Street location. Commercial hotel. Cafeteria and room service. Classification: inexpensive.

Hotel Napolitano
George Washington Avenue
Santo Domingo
Tel. (809) 687-1131
Telex: RCA 3464101

72 rooms. Air-conditioned. Television. Facilities: popular terrace restaurant and café. Seafront. 24-hour room service. Hairdresser. Banquet and convention facilities for up to 250 persons. Functional commercial hotel. Panoramic seafront views.
Classification: moderate.

The Jaragua Hotel & Casino
367 George Washington Avenue
Santo Domingo
Tel. (809) 686-2222
      (212) 921-0613
      (800) 223-9815
Telex: ITT 3460758

355 rooms, including 18 suites. Recently reopened, the Jaragua was the first major hotel property in the Dominican Republic and for two generations, locals and visitors alike enjoyed the spectacular nightlife of this hotel. The hotel was in later years allowed to deteriorate, but has now been reconstructed into a spectacular 231-room Jaragua tower, including 24 suites, six of which offer a jacuzzi. 100 additional garden rooms. The property itself has always enjoyed an exceptional waterfront location and is situated on 14 acres of choice land. All rooms have marble bathrooms, hair dryer, color TV, and computerized door locks. It has the largest casino in the country, the "Fiesta" nightclub for 760, a ballroom, five restaurants (including a New York-style deli), and a European spa for a complete fitness program. Add to this an Olympic-sized pool with 12 poolside cabañas, four clay tennis courts with grandstand facilities, and the spectacular seaside location on the Malecon and you can see that this is a major new addition to Santo Domingo's hotel industry. The Jaragua will also be a major convention center for up to 1,000. Represented by International Travel and Resorts.
Classification: expensive.

SMALL HOTELS AND APART-HOTELS

Residence Hotel
Danae Street
Gascue
Santo Domingo
Tel. (809) 682–4178
Telex (La Residence): ITT 3460001

24 rooms. Air-conditioned. A jewel of a small hotel. Located in Gascue on Danae Street, an easy walk from Santo Domingo's malecon and the downtown commercial district. European atmosphere. Spotless and tastefully decorated. Wall-to-wall carpeting. Everything looks brand new. Choice of standard double beds, king-and queen-sized beds. Room service and breakfast on the balcony.
Classification: inexpensive.

Hostal Nicolas Nader
Luperón and Duarte Streets
Sector Colonial
Santo Domingo
Tel. (809) 687–6674

10 rooms. Air-conditioned, spacious, and tastefully furnished.
This small and very romantic facility is certainly the most elegant of the small hotels of Santo Domingo. The location is a restored limestone building on Luperón Street in the old colonial sector. The rooms surround an inner courtyard which recreates the atmosphere of a 16th-century home.
Classification: moderate.

Hotel Senorial
Presidente Vicini Burgos Street
Gascue
Santo Domingo
Tel. (809) 687–4359

13 rooms. Air-conditioned. Television for extra charge.
Facilities: As far as small hotel facilities go, this is one of the most convenient, located on Presidente Vicini Burgos Street, just half a block from the Malecon's obelisk. Family-style dining. Dominican atmosphere. No points for decoration.
Classification: inexpensive.

Apart-Hotel Drake
29 Augustin Lara
Santo Domingo
Tel. (809) 567–4427

28 suites. Air-conditioned with color television.
Facilities: Fully equipped with kitchenettes. Convenient location
near Plaza Naco.
Classification: moderate.

Apart-Hotel Plaza del Sol
25 Jose Contreras Street
Santo Domingo
Tel. (809) 687–1317

Studio apartments. Fully furnished and equipped studios. Cafeteria
service. Convenient location.
Classification: moderate.

Apart-Hotel Arak
27th of February Avenue
Santo Domingo
Tel. (809) 567–4267

Air-conditioned and fully equipped apartments. All the amenities
including concierge and 24-hour security. Power plant. Intercom and
electrically-controlled entrance. Elevators. Located across from Nacional shopping center. Ideal midtown area.
Classification: expensive.

Plaza Colonial
Luisa Pellerano Street, corner of Julio Verne Avenue
Santo Domingo
Tel. (809) 687–9111

Air-conditioned and fully equipped one- and two-bedroom apartments located in residential Gascue district of Santo Domingo near
national palace.
Classification: moderate.

Plaza Florida
203 Bolivár Avenue
Santo Domingo
Tel. (809) 689–0151

32 apartments. Air-conditioned and fully equipped. Comfortably furnished, spacious one-bedroom apartments. Convenient Bolívar Avenue location.
Classification: expensive.

Plaza Naco Apart-Hotel
Tel. (809) 567-5281
or inquire at Dorado Naco Hotel

54 suites. 165 efficiency apartments, all with kitchenettes. Will be the tallest hotel in Santo Domingo, with spectacular views of city and sea. Apartments for sale. Hotel operation scheduled for winter 1988/89.

Apart-Hotel Turey
Gustavo Mejia Ricart Street, 8-A sd.
Santo Domingo
Tel. (809) 562-5271

Studios and one-bedroom apartments. Tastefully furnished. Air-conditioned and completely equipped with kitchenettes. Easily the best in this category. Good location on Gustavo Mejia Ricart, right near the Olympic Center. Swimming pool and snack bar.
Classification: expensive.

Plaza Central
Tel. (809) 565-6905

25 "Club Plaza" executive suites. The project includes an apart-hotel and hotel suites designed for executive travelers who will appreciate convenient location of the Plaza Central "Golden Apple" shopping mall and tower on intersection of 27th of February and Winston Churchill Avenues. The Club Plaza suites will offer an executive VIP facility including telex, secretarial services and seminar facilities. Scheduled for winter 1987/88.

HOTELS IN THE EAST

BOCA CHICA

Don Juan
P.O. Box 1348
Boca Chica
Tel. (809) 523–4511

140 rooms. Air-conditioned. This recently opened facility offers 70 junior suites (apartments) complete with bedroom, living/dining area, and fully equipped kitchenette. "La Caleta" restaurant. Casual eateries. Bar. Pool and deck area. Boca Chica beach. All water sports. Catamarans, jet skis, and sunfish. Accessibility to Santo Domingo Yacht Club.
Classification: moderate.

There are a number of small guesthouses on the beach ranging from very cheap to moderately expensive for that area.

Paraiso
Tel. (809) 523–4330

6 rooms. Newly redecorated. Ceiling fans. On the beach. Family style. Multilingual ambiance. Bed and breakfast.
Classification: inexpensive.

L'Horizon Hotel and Restaurant
Tel. (809) 523–4375

3 rooms. This is about as small as you're ever going to find! Swiss management. Excellent restaurant. Long on atmosphere.
Classification: inexpensive.

Neptune's Club
Tel. (809) 523–6703

3 rooms. Beach bar and patio restaurant. At east end of lagoon. Secluded.
Classification: inexpensive.

COSTA CARIBE RESORTS

Located at Guayacanes, Juan Dolio, or just outside San Pedro de
Macoris. These share proximity to International Airport, as does
Boca Chica, reasonable prices, and excellent beach. For the most
part these are low-profile resorts.

Talanquera Hotel and Villas
Country and Beach Club
Tel. (809) 688–6604/5
    (809) 685–6466

140 rooms. Air-conditioned. Facilities: Swimming pool. Sauna. Tennis. Open air restaurants. Disco. Cabaret entertainment. Game
room. Horseback riding. All water sports. Olympic-size pool. Also
available: condos for sale and homesites.
Classification: moderate.

Costa Linda Hotel and Beach Resort
Tel. (809) 541–2414

22 rooms. 132 apartments. Air-conditioned. Facilities: 11 cabañas.
Attractive stone and wood, rustic design. Piano bar. Restaurant.
Beach. All water sports. Tennis. Horseback riding. Members of
Resorts Condominiums International. Cabañas and apartments are
for sale or rental.
Classification: moderate.

Decamerion Beach Resort
Tumbacoco
Tel. (800) 223–9815

240 rooms. Air-conditioned. All inclusive package for room, three
meals and late-night snack, wine with lunch and dinner, and unlimited drinks. All gratuities and room tax included. Facilities: 96 apartments. Pool. Disco. Breakwater. Ideal for fishing and diving. Beach.
All water sports. Tennis. Children's playground with activities program.
Classification: moderate.

Los Coquitos Beach Resort
Juan Dolio
Tel. (718) 457–3211

80 one- and two-bedroom apartments. Air-conditioned bedrooms. Cable TV. Refrigerator and bar. Restaurant and grill. Pool. All aquatic sports. Children's activities and pool. Represented by Prieto Tours.

Punta Garza
Tel. (809) 533–2131

46 rooms. Air-conditioned, ceiling fans.
Facilities: Cabañas or two-story white stucco houses. Fully equipped kitchenettes. Nothing fancy but comfortable. Very relaxed atmosphere.
Classification: inexpensive.

Playa Real
Tel. (809) 529–3935
   (809) 533–1441/533–9549

56 rooms. Air-conditioned. Sea views. Seaside swimming pool. Coconut palm landscape. "El Coral" Restaurant. Outdoor bar and coffee shop. All water sports.
Classification: moderate.

Hotel Macorix
San Pedro de Macoris
Tel. (809) 529–3950

28 rooms. Air-conditioned. Sea views. Swimming pool. Tennis. Disco. Special student packages. Near the university and medical school.

Metrohotel
Juan Dolio (Costa Caribe)
Tel. (809) 565–3161
Telex: ITT (Atlantica) 3640086
Metro Tours: (809) 567–3138

Apartments currently for sale. Nine weeks guaranteed for owners' use. 174 rooms. 72 apartments distributed in three towers. 200 meters of beachfront. Marina. Aquatic sports. Two swimming pools. Clay tennis courts. One- and two-bedroom apartments and penthouse model. Central air-conditioning. Fully equipped with kitchenettes.

Tropically furnished. Spectacular panoramas. Proximity to international airport and to San Pedro de Macoris.
1987/88 winter season.

LA ROMANA

Casa de Campo
Tel. (800) 223–6620
    (305) 856–5404 (Premier Hotel Corp., in Florida)
    (809) 682–2111

Total 900 rooms (including villas). Casa de Campo was designed by the renowned Miami architect, William Cox. The interiors were designed by Oscar de la Renta, who maintains his beautifully rustic home "Casa de Madera" at Punta Aguila in Casa de Campo. This spectacular resort was created by Gulf & Western Corporation in the early 1970s. In recent years it was sold to the Fanjul Brothers from Palm Beach, Florida, and is managed by their company, Premier Hotel Corporation. Under the Premier banner, visitors have nearly doubled from 27,305 in 1983 to over 51,000 this year.

350 *casita* rooms (superior doubles), deluxe golf villas, deluxe tennis villas. A self-contained paradise. Facilities: The perfect playground for any price tag! Elegant "Tropicana" restaurant. Several casual eateries. Fourteen swimming pools, one with a bar inside the pool, swim-up style. 17 tennis courts (13 of which are clay courts and 6 of which have night lights). "La Terraza" tennis club. "Los Cajuiles" golf club. Two Peter Dye 18-hole championship golf courses. Las Minitas beach. Bayahibe beach. Altos de Chavon artist village complete with amphitheater, inns, several fine restaurants, and many worthwhile exhibits and boutiques. All part of the same complex which spreads along over 7,000 acres. Shuttle transportation provided by minibuses, horse- drawn carriages, and golf carts. Elegant main pool/bar/lounge complex. Two meeting rooms with a capacity of 75 each. Yachting. Horseback riding. Polo grounds. Stables. Marina. International airport for those arriving by private plane. Prices: US$180 for standard double and US$375 for two-bedroom villa, taxes not included. Casa de Campo has an office at Las Americas International Airport where you can arrange for transportation and reservations.
Classification: very expensive (but worth every penny).

La Posada Inn at Altos de Chavon
Tel. (809) 682–2111 for reservations (same as Casa de Campo)
ext. 2315 for direct calls

10 rooms. Air-conditioned. No TV (you won't miss it).
Part of the "lost in centuries" world of Altos de Chavon. Sheer
magic and romance. Lovely swimming pool. Perfect place to discover the artist village while still enjoying all the sports activities of
Casa de Campo. Accessible to the five restaurants that the village
offers, "Genesis" disco, magnificent 5,000-seat amphitheater, and
Museum of Taino artifacts. Also surrounded by interesting galleries,
boutiques, and artist workshops. Stop into St. Stanislas Church
(named after patron saint of Poland in honor of the papal visit) and
thank the good Lord that places like Altos de Chavon exist!

This friendly inn, like all of Altos de Chavon, was designed by set
designer Roberto Coppa, who was art director for many of Luchino
Visconti's films. Also look into the Altos de Chavon two- and three-
bedroom apartments (fully equipped). The two-bedroom apartments
here are less than the rate for the one- bedroom golf villa and Altos de
Chavon enjoys the same privileges for golf, tennis, and beach as Casa
de Campo since it is all part of the same complex. Reservations all
handled through Casa de Campo.
Prices: Posada US$110. Apartments US$275 and up.
Classification: expensive.

Dominicus Beach Village
Tel. (809) 533-4897
Telex: RCA 3464515 MAGNA DR

58 rooms. Lots of style with "primitive" decor. Beautifully rustic
stone and wood *bohios*. Hammocks. Raised platform beds. Cascading showers. Solitary beach. Very Creole flavor.
Classification: inexpensive.

Puerto Laguna
Tel. (809) 566-7464
     (809) 567-2812
106 rooms. Apart-hotel. Swimming pool. Bar. Creole restaurant.
Under half an hour from Casa de Campo.
Classification: inexpensive.

PUNTA CANA

Club Mediterranée
Tel. (809) 567-5228
     (800) 528-3100
Telex: ITT 3460550

600 beds. 320 rooms. 70-acre property located 145 miles east of Santo Domingo on beautiful eastern coast of the Dominican Republic. Strong emphasis on activity. Gracious GO's get you into the spirit of things. Tennis. Swimming pool and deck. Incredibly beautiful white sandy beach. Crystalline waters. All aquatic sports. Nightly entertainment. All meals with wine included in package rates. All-inclusive weekly packages. Charter departures from U.S. and Canada.
Classification: moderate

Punta Cana Yacht Club
Tel. (809) 565–0011
    (809) 565–3077
Telex: ITT 3460415 TREISA

520 hotel rooms. Air-conditioned. Facilities: The final project will consist of 140 two-bedroom villas and 120 one-bedroom apartments. Initial stage comprises 70 villas and 48 apartments. Swimming pool. Beach club. Four tennis courts. Discothèque. Boutiques. Ready for 1987/88 winter season. Punta Cana Golf Course under construction. All native materials: stone, wood, and marble. More than 100 acres of property. 2,200 ft. of beachfront shaded by coconut groves. Operated as condo-hotel.

Bavaro Beach Hotel
Higuey
Tel. (809) 682–2161/66
Barcelo Tour Office (owners/operators): (809) 685–8101
Telex: ITT 3460159

600 rooms. Air-conditioned. Nicely furnished apartments. Almost two kilometers of beach. Self-service buffets. Bar/lounge. Open, breezy design. Swimming pool. All water sports. All-inclusive budget packages. Medical services on the premises. Mini supermarket and gift shop. Closed-circuit color television.
Classification: inexpensive.

SAMANA

Hostal Cotubanama
Tel. (809) 538–2558

14 rooms. Ceiling fans. Family style. Looks out on Samana Bay. Breakfast included. Arrange day trips to beach at Cayo Levantado. Classification: inexpensive.

Bahia Beach Resort
Tel. (809) 685–6060
Telex: ITT 3460554

85 rooms. Air-conditioned. Ceiling fans. It has a beach. Lovely pool. The view is unsurpassable. Beautiful surroundings with vegetation and nature at its very best! Accommodations: simply decorated (you probably won't spend much time in your room). Clean and functional. Restaurant overlooking bay. Yacht takes you across to keys (one of these, Cayo Levantado, has magnificent beach). Casual, relaxed setting. Palm-laced coast and hillside. Many excellent beaches in area. Last of the best-kept secrets.
Classification: inexpensive.

Club Carousel
Telex: ITT 3460554
book through Bahia Beach or Carousel Tours of Toronto, Canada.

11 rooms. 9 cabins. Adequate furnishings, but nothing fancy. Extraordinary beach and natural setting. On small island key off the Samana coast. Operated in winter season by Toronto's Carousel Tours. All-inclusive week package.
Classification: inexpensive.

El Portillo Beach Club
Tel. (809) 585–0102

Air taxi service to Portillo available through Prieto Tours.
75 cabanas. Ceiling fans. Fully equipped with kitchenettes. Attractive tropical design. Wonderful restaurant. Minutes from excellent seafood restaurants of Las Terrenas (*Chez Paco*). All water sports. Excellent beach. Facilities are rustic but attractive. Private airstrip set between coconut groves.
Classification: moderate.

RIO SAN JUAN

Hotel Rio San Juan
Tel. (809) 589–2379
    (809) 589–2211
    (809) 567–3325 in Santo Domingo

38 rooms. Air-conditioned. Simply furnished. Extremely clean and well-maintained. A perfect country inn with plenty of small village life. Family-run operation. Bar and lounge. Pool. Tennis court. Nightclub and disco. One block to Gri Gri lagoon and spectacular boat ride through mangroves and out along northern coast to cave of swallows. Azure waters. Close proximity to some of the northern coast's finest beaches.
Classification: inexpensive.

SOSÚA

Koch's Ocean Front Guest House
Tel. (809) 571–2234

Nine cabañas and four rooms. Functional. Nos. 8 and 9, however, have a spectacular view overlooking ocean. The decor is not memorable, but it is one of Sosúa's traditional guest houses.
Classification: inexpensive.

Hotel Sosúa
Tel. (809) 571–2683

24 rooms. Air-conditioned. Facilities: This is one of Sosúa's most popular and better-run hotels. Recently refurbished and expanded. Some with kitchenettes. Pool. Short walk to beach and Sosúa's bars and restaurants.
Classification: inexpensive.

Los Charamicos Resort Hotel
Tel. (718) 457–3211/9628

Studios, two- and three-bedroom apartments and villas. Air-conditioned bedrooms in all units. Private balcony. Fully-equipped kitchenette. Recently refurbished. Represented by Prieto Tours.

One of Sosúa's many new small hotels

Villas Coralillos
Tel. (809) 571–2645
Telex: ITT 3462024

42 rooms. Standard rooms and villa accommodations. Functional decor within but the location is right on the beach and the view is breathtaking. Lovely terrace restaurant overlooking Sosúa Bay. Nightclub. Swimming pool. Villa 3 has a great view.
Classification: moderate.

Apart-Hotel Alcazar
Tel. (809) 571–2321

12 rooms. Graceful building with colonial arches. Kitchenettes. Pool. Ceiling fans. A few minutes walk to beach and to Sosúa's "restaurant row." Near the main road.

Auberge du Village Inn
Tel. (809) 571–2569

7 rooms. Ceiling fans. Small in size but big in style. Family-run guest house. Spotless. Tasteful decor. Lovely swimming pool set in tropical garden. Family table for breakfast. If you like sailing, classical music, or ballet, you'll have plenty to talk about with the Magnusson clan. Short walk to beach. Inquire about their Catalina Ranch for day trips and horseback riding.
Classification: inexpensive.

Woody's Hotel
Dr. Rosen Street (next door to Auberge).
Tel. (809) 571–2032
Telex: 202–346–2005

80 rooms. Double and triple rooms (three double beds). Air-conditioned. Brand new property, modern facility. Swimming pool complete with swim-up bar. Tasteful interiors.
Classification: moderate.

North Shore Hotel
Tel. (809) 571–2388

28 rooms. Air-conditioned. Swimming pool. Comfortable and well maintained. Short walk to beach and to Sosúa's shops and restaurants.
Classification: inexpensive.

Hotel Yaroa
Tel. (809) 571–2651

24 rooms. Air-conditioned. Ceiling fans. Tropical architecture, nice vegetation. Very clean. Facilities: Yaroa has a lovely rooftop deck. Family style restaurant. Swimming pool. Short walk to beach. Don't be surprised at finding a Star of David skylight. Hotel is owned and operated by the Benjamin family, one of Sosúa's oldest and most respected.
Two poolside rooms have king-sized beds.
Classification: inexpensive.

Sun Island Inn
Tel. (809) 571–2558

Five rooms with ceiling fans. Tropical garden restaurant.
Classification: inexpensive.

Condos Dominicanos Apart-Hotel
Tel. (809) 571–2504

12 studios; four one-bedroom and four two-bedroom apartments. Ceiling fans. Kitchenettes. Swimming pool. Near Playa Chiquita ("little beach").
Classification: moderate.

Hotel Mirador
Tel. (809) 571–2202

80 rooms total. 40 fully-equipped one- or two-bedroom villas. Air-conditioned. Ceiling fans. Hilltop hotel overlooking Sosúa and the beach beyond. Swimming pool. Pool/bar, restaurant. Tropical fabrics and furnishings. Tennis. All water sports. Transportation to the beach. Lovely countryside setting.
Classification: moderate.

Hotel Costa Sol Sosúa
Tel. (809) 571–3553
Telex: ITT 3462005

Studios, one- and two-bedroom villas. Air-conditioned, ceiling fans.
Swimming pool. Kiosk bar. Restaurant.
Classification: inexpensive.

Sosúa Sol
Tel. (809) 571–2334

16 units. One- and two-bedroom bungalows. Small kitchens. Three-
bedroom houses. Rancho bar. Barbeque. Creole restaurant. Short
walk to Playa Chiquita.
Classification: inexpensive.

Las Palmas Apart-Hotel
Tel. (809) 571–2545

Two-bedroom apartments. Comfortable and modern. Located near
restaurants and bars. A short walk to Sosúa beach. Its own boutique
and supply shop.
Classification: inexpensive.

Sosúa Caribbean Fantasy
Tel. (809) 571–2534
Telex: ITT 3462005

67 rooms. Apart-hotel suites. Air-conditioned. Cable television. Dir-
ect-dial phone. Presidential suite. Facilities: Cascading pool. Jacuzzi. Terrace restaurant. Disco. Short walk to beach. Modern and
comfortable.
Classification: moderate.

Tourist Studio
Tel. (809) 571–2212
    (809) 685–7851
Telex: ITT 3460313

12 apartments. One- or two-bedrooms. Air-conditioned. Nicely furnished. Two double beds each. Very comfortable. Short walk to the
beach and to Sosúa's restaurants and boutiques. Owner Mario Bonci
is an opinionated charmer.
Classification: inexpensive.

Seahorse Ranch
Tel. (809) 571-2374

This undertaking is in the early stages of development. There will be 176 residential lots for vacation homes in this exclusive 250-acre community. Also includes hotel and condo options. Secluded beaches, private beach club, equestrian center, nine competition tennis courts, and sports center. It will be some time yet before there are rooms available for travelers, but when it is finished, it will be worth looking into.

One Ocean Place
Tel. (809) 571-2360

Apart-hotel. Air-conditioned. Tastefully decorated apartments. Kitchenettes. Balconies. 24-hour security.

Playa Chiquita Beach Resort
Tel. (809) 689-9191

90 junior suites. Apart-hotel. Air-conditioned. Cable TV. Wet bar and refrigerator. Two double beds or one kingsized bed in each room. Pool with sunken bar. Jacuzzi. Situated right on Sosúa's smaller beach in an isolated little cove. Walking distance to shops, restaurants, and the main beach area.

Hostal de Lora
Tel. (809) 571-3939
    (809) 867-9690

32 rooms. Apart-hotel. 12 fully-equipped apartments. Executive and junior suites. Central air-conditioning. Swimming pool. Three minute walk to Sosúa's "little beach" (Playa Chiquita).
Classification: moderate to expensive.

Los Almendros Beach Resort
bookings through Dimargo:
Tel. (809) 562-7461
    (809) 562-3921
    (809) 562-4171

78 rooms. Apart-hotel. Fully equipped. Air-conditioned. Linked to beach through tunnel.

Villas Baleareas
Bookings through Dimargo:
Tel. (809) 562–7461
    (809) 562–3921
    (809) 562–4171

Six villas on a hillside overlooking Sosúa. Fully furnished and fully equipped.

****

Info about new hotel and apart/hotel properties in Sosúa available through Servicios Turisticos at (809) 571–2665; telex ITT 3462005.

****

CABARETE

Punta Goleta Beach Resort
Tel. (809) 562–2774

78 rooms. Air-conditioned and ceiling fans. Facilities: spacious rooms. Walk-in closets. Victorian theme in decor. Near beach, known for windsurfing. Lagoon with exotic birds. Swimming pool. Classification: moderate.

Hosteria del Rey
Guest house

10 rooms. Ceiling fans. Restaurant. Bar. On the beach. Classification: inexpensive.

Pelican Beach Resort

388 Mediterranean style condo units in this new time-sharing resort, funded in part by a private investment of US$50 million. Dr. Martin Vlietman, the builder, has developed major resort properties in St. Maarten, Curaçao, and Aruba. In St. Maarten, they own the prestigious Pelican Beach Resort and Casino. This operation will have 136 units in the first phase to be completed by November 1988. It will include a health spa, tennis club, stables, pools, jacuzzis, and a gourmet restaurant.

PLAYA DORADA

Jack Tar Village
Tel. (809) 586–3800
Telex: ITT 3462025

250 rooms. Apartments are air-conditioned. Cable television.
Tropical restaurant specializing in spectacular Caribbean buffets.
Bar. Swimming pool and deck. Tennis. Golf. All water sports. Convention facilities. Sauna. Horseback riding. Playa Dorada beach.
Jack Tar specializes in all-inclusive packages that cover your accommodations, food, drink, and activities. For further information, call
(800) 527–9299.
Classification: moderate to expensive.

Dorado Naco
Tel. (809) 586–2019
      (809) 566–9206
Telex: ITT 3460554

252 rooms distributed in 150 apartments. Fully furnished and
equipped one- and two-bedroom apartments and penthouses. Air-conditioned. Cable television. Very comfortable. Wall-to-wall carpeting. More of an urban concept than a beach design. You'll have
the best of both worlds: the comfort of a sophisticated apartment with
all the facilities of a beach resort. Living and dining area. Private
balcony. Complete kitchenette. Bar. "Flamingo" restaurant. Supermarket on premises. Swimming pool and deck. Golf. Horseback
riding. All water sports. Short walk to Playa Dorada beach.
Classification: moderate.

Heavens
Tel. (800) 828–8895
      (800) 223–9815
      (212) 840–6636

Due to open in 1988. 150 rooms and suites. Air-conditioned. Cable
TV. Olympic-sized pool. All of Playa Dorada's golf and beach facilities. All-inclusive rate for meals, liquor, and rooms.

Villas Dorados
Tel. (809) 586–3000
Telex: ITT 3462031/3460528

207 rooms, including 170 standard, 32 suites, and five villa-style. Air-conditioned. Cable television. Rustic decor. Pine furnishings. Tasteful but simple. Swimming pool. Casual eateries. All water sports. Romantic little bridge over lagoon leads right out to Playa Dorada Beach. "Las Garzas" restaurant. Golf. Tennis. Exchange bank on premises. Local entertainment.
Classification: moderate.

Eurotel
Tel. (809) 567–5159
Telex: ITT 3460757

402 rooms. Total of 290 apartments. Air-conditioned, cable television. The design calls for 8 different models of apartments ranging from studios to one- and two-bedroom suites. Complete with kitchenettes. Tropically furnished with an entire palette of Caribbean colors! Dazzling lobby area. Open design. Handpainted chairs by Dominican artist Ada Balcacer pick up motifs from murals she has done for the hotel. Footpaths lead out to Japanese rock garden with cascade and beyond to swimming pool, deck, bar, and beach. Right on Playa Dorada beach. You are not likely to see another property quite like this. Expect the flamboyant in the architect's fantasy world. Try not to collide with modular hangings in informal poolside eatery. Barbeque Room for seminars. Restaurant "America." All water sports. Horseback riding. Tennis. Golf. Also offers time-sharing vacation plans through Euroclub. "Own a vacation" program can be traded in over 1,000 comparable resorts.
Classification: moderate to expensive.

Playa Dorada Hotel
Tel. (809) 586–3988
    (809) 562–5616
Telex: ITT 3462030

254 rooms and suites. Air-conditioned. Cable television. Modern facility with plenty of Victorian details. Located right on Playa Dorada beach. Lovely seaside pool area and swim-up bar. "Las Brisas" for casual meals. International cuisine in "La Palma" restaurant. Banquet and convention facilities. "La Copa" room for international revues. Secretarial services. All water sports. Golf. Horseback riding. Tennis. Disco. A complete resort hotel facility. Attractive lobby area leading out to tropical verandas, pool, and beach. Elevators.
Classification: moderate to expensive.

The Playa Dorada Hotel on the northern coast

Villas Caraibe
Tel. (809) 562–8494

200 rooms. Air-conditioned. Television. Short walk to beach. Nicely furnished apartments. Landscaped surroundings. Tennis. Golf. Horseback riding. All water sports.
Classification: moderate.

Radisson Puerto Plata
Golf and Beach Resort
Tel. (800) 228–9822

336 rooms. Two-bedroom villas and fully-equipped apartments. Air-conditioned. Television. Kitchenettes. Facilities: Tennis. Tennis Club, including seven world class courts and exhibition center court. Gym and spa. The first property at Playa Dorada to offer a complete fitness facility. Horseback riding. Golf. All water sports at Playa Dorada beach. Swimming pool. Poolside bar. Lobby bar. Restaurant. Supervised playground and activities for children. The most complete convention facilities on the north coast. Facility is operated by York Hannover, the same as the St. George Club of Bermuda. Sales office for purchase of apartments: (809) 562–7666. Affiliated with Resorts Condominium International.
Classification: moderate.

Costa Dorada

Opened in 1987. 118 apartments. One-bedroom apartments with two double beds. Kitchenettes. Air-conditioned. Television. Private balcony. Fully-equipped. Lagoon Club situated on a shaded natural lagoon. Swimming pool. Playa Dorada Beach for all aquatic sports. Golf. Horseback riding. Tennis.

Puerto Plata Village

Scheduled for 1988/89 season. 488 rooms. 112 two-room apartments and 88 three-room villas. Two restaurants. Swimming pool. Playa Dorada beach. Will be done as a Victorian town. Village setting complete with central park and gazebo, clock tower, and "town hall" building for administrative offices, boutiques, tour offices, and car rental. Concert and convention hall. Golf and all aquatic sports.

PUERTO PLATA

Hotel Montemar
Tel. (809) 586-2800
Telex: ITT 3462019

104 rooms. Air-conditioned. Includes three suites. Three bungalows. Spacious pool area, deck, and lounge. Elegant "La Isabela" restaurant. "Los Cocos" disco. Conference facility for 250. Across from Long Beach (the beach that services the town of Puerto Plata). Hotel School—this explains why you see so much staff in each area. Short walk to all of Puerto Plata's shops, restaurants, and Malecon. Tennis. Full program of aquatic sports at nearby Mara Pica Beach (shuttle bus from hotel to beach). Beachcomber Bar at Mara Pica.
Classification: inexpensive to moderate.

Puerto Plata Beach Resort
Tel. (809) 586-4243
Telex: ITT 3462027

216 rooms. All-suite hotel. One- and two-bedroom apartments. Air-conditioned. Fully equipped. Kitchenettes. Private balcony. "Atlantica" restaurant. "La Chichigua" (the kite) informal dining. Disco. Elegant lobby with old-fashioned black and white tile floors. Hints of Victorian past throughout this modern facility. Swimming pool, deck, and bar. Landscaped gardens. Casino. Gazebo on beach across the boulevard. Beach grill with seafood by the pound. Tennis. Golf. 24-hour room service. Combines resort facilities with advantages of being in town of Puerto Plata itself.
Classification: moderate.

Hotel Caracol
Tel. (809) 586-2588

34 rooms, 23 of which are currently in service. Air-conditioned. Cable TV. Oceanfront terrace. "El Caracol" restaurant. New piano bar/nightclub with seaside view. Swimming pool. Convenient location in town. Modest but comfortable hotel facility.
Classification: inexpensive.

Hostal Jimesson
41 John F. Kennedy Street
Santo Domingo
Tel. (809) 586-5131

Puerto Plata Beach and Casino Resort

22 rooms. Air-conditioned. Lobby is decorated with antiques and period furniture. Even though it offers all modern conveniences, the atmosphere is one of "Old Puerto Plata." You feel like you are staying in someone's home rather than a hotel. Situated in the center of Puerto Plata, just a block off the main square, this hotel is a charmer.
Classification: inexpensive.

JUST OUTSIDE PUERTO PLATA

Costambar
Tel. (809) 586–3828
Telex: ITT 3460171

100 rooms in condo apartments. Vacation homes. Residential sites. This is a beach resort with a residential feeling. Seven minutes outside Puerto Plata town. Located near the cable car station for Mt. Isabel de Torres. Facilities: Costambar beach. Los Mangos golf course. Horseback riding. Club house with swimming pool and tennis facilities. Three miles of beach. Daily, weekly, and monthly rentals. Resort community.
Classification: moderate.

Las Caobas
Costambar
bookings through Dimargo in Santo Domingo
Tel. (809) 562–4171
    (809) 562–7461

40 rooms. Apart-hotel. Air-conditioned. Mahogany used for interiors. Fully furnished and equipped. 60 meters from the beach. Tennis. All aquatic sports.
Classification: moderate.

Cofresi Beach Club
Tel. (809) 586–2898
    (800) 223–9815
    (800) 828–8895
    (212) 840–6636

100 rooms, including 11 junior suites. Simply designed cottages facing the sea. Air-conditioned. Cable television. Recently remodeled and refurbished. Beach. Tennis. Both salt water and fresh water

pools bordering the sea. Archery, spa, and miniature golf newly added. Spectacular view. "Corsario" restaurant. Well-known "Sombrero" restaurant for casual meals seaside.
Classification: inexpensive to moderate.

SANTIAGO

Hotel Camino Real
Tel. (809) 583–4361
Telex: ITT 3460529

72 rooms, nine of which are suites. Air-conditioned. Restaurant "Hidalgo" with panoramic views of the city of Santiago. Piano bar "las Nubes." Commercial hotel with excellent midtown location.
Classification: inexpensive to moderate.

Hotel Don Diego
Tel. (809) 582–7186

36 rooms. Air-conditioned. Color television. Swimming pool. Tennis. Restaurant for Chinese and Creole specialties. Disco. Dingy and colorless. They are currently upgrading and adding quite a few new rooms. It may improve.
Classification: inexpensive.

Hotel Matum
Tel. (809) 582–3107
Telex: ITT 3461037

52 rooms. Air-conditioned. Cable television. Swimming pool. "La Nuit" discothèque. Spanish patio. Casino. Old Dominican-style hotel. Functional.
Classification: inexpensive.

MOUNTAIN RESORTS

JARABACOA

Alpes Dominicanos (Dominican Alps)

132 hotel rooms. Currently distributed in 11 villas and 66 apartments with more under construction. Fully furnished and equipped. You do

not need air-conditioning here! 1,500 ft. above sea level. Hundreds of pine trees.
Classification: inexpensive.

Pinar Dorado
Jarabacoa 2244
Tel. (809) 689–5105

Functional rooms. Cafeteria-style restaurant. No points for decor. Pretty countryside setting and nice swimming pool.
Classification: inexpensive.

CONSTANZA

Hotel Nueva Suizza
Tel. (809) 539–2233

59 rooms. Functional. State-operated hotel. Beautiful panorama and mountain countryside.
Classification: inexpensive.

BARAHONA

Guarocuya
Tel. (809) 685–6161

22 rooms. Air-conditioned. Functional. Small pleasant beach. Situated in the town of Barahona.
Classification: inexpensive.

Bahoruco Beach Club and Resort
Tel. (809) 685–5184
Telex: 3264248

90 rooms hotel and 84 rooms in apart/hotel. All hotel rooms in suites. In addition, 5 apartment blocks with a total of 34 apartments. Apart-hotel has one- and two-bedroom apartments. Air-conditioned. Deluxe property located 17 km. from town of Barahona on the Barahona-Enriquillo road, between the villages of Bahoruco and Cienega. Less than a three-hour drive from Santo Domingo. Minutes from Barahona International Airport now under construction. Facilities: Jacuzzi. Swimming pool. Restaurants, bars. Satellite television programming. Fully equipped apart-hotel. Time-sharing facility affiliated with Resorts

Condominiums International. Tennis. Horseback riding. All water sports. Mountain excursions and day trips to national parks. Breathtaking panorama and vegetation. Completion scheduled for fall/winter 1987/88 season.

UNUSUAL DESTINATIONS

SAN JOSE DE OCOA

Rancho Francisco
Tel. (809) 558-2291
or in Santo Domingo:
    (809) 565-7637
    (809) 562-1930

This is a small 10-bungalow project that consists of one- and two-bedroom units with private bathrooms. There is an Olympic-size pool and restaurant/club house. The nicer pool is a smaller one exclusively for the resident guests. If you come here on weekdays, it is nice and quiet. The Ocoa River is pleasant to bathe in. Nothing fancy, just the great outdoors. Family-style operation. Just outside the village of San Jose de Ocoa.
Classification: very inexpensive.

ON THE EAST COAST

MACAO

Hacienda Barbara
at Playa Macao
Tel. (809) 685-2594
    (809) 565-7176
in the U.S.: (516) 944-8060

A country home by the sea, Hacienda Barbara is perched on a ridge overlooking the wide expanse of beach. In addition to its tennis courts, swimming pool and deck area, and tropical gazebo, Hacienda Barbara borders a thousand-acre coconut plantation. Exclusive family-style inn. Each room offers two double beds. Private baths. Beautifully decorated. Swimming pool. Beach. Tennis. Home-style cuisine. A study in how to be in the middle of nowhere in plenty of style! Small, secluded, and exclusive.
Classification: expensive.

THE NORTHWEST COAST

PUNTA RUCIA

La Orquidia del Sol
Tel. (809) 583–2825 for reservations

28 rooms. Private bathrooms. Air-conditioning or ceiling fans. Restaurant for Creole specialties. Right on the beach. Aquatic sports. Boatrides. Picnics and hammocks! If you can get it, ask for the old family house right on the beach. This one is better if you are traveling with family group, as it involves a shared bathroom. You will see the wild orchids for which Punta Rucia is noted throughout the property.

Luperón Beach Resort
Tel. (718) 457–3211/9628

310 rooms, including 188 suites. Air-conditioned. Cable TV. Suites have separate living rooms with bar, sofabed, and balcony. Facilities include four restaurants, disco, bar, video room, conference facilities. Swimming pool and children's pool. Golf course. Horseback riding. Jogging trails. Car and motorcycle rentals. Heliport. Situated one hour's drive east of Puerto Plata in Luperón. Represented by Prieto Tours.

Chapter 7

DINING OUT IN THE DOMINICAN REPUBLIC

DINING OUT IN SANTO DOMINGO

Santo Domingo has become very diversified in cuisine. So much so that locals sometimes forget that the dishes they regard as part of their "national" heritage are sometimes of oriental or Middle Eastern origin. This city is certainly one of the most cosmopolitan places in the Caribbean and those with gourmet inclinations should be pleased to discover the range of cuisine served up in the capital city: Italian, Chinese, Bavarian, Creole (very much like Cajun), Spanish, North American, Mexican, Peruvian, French, and sort of a vague category termed "International" which, of course, covers a multitude of culinary experiments!

The restaurants in the capital encompass the large, lost-in-the-crowds variety, intimate restaurants housed in the various rooms of what were formerly private homes, outdoor café-style eateries, and fast food establishments. Even though the Dominican Republic can no longer be considered the "cheapest" offer of the Caribbean, unbeatable prices are offered in its restaurants. "Outrageously expensive" is in the neighborhood of US$40 per person, including wine. More typical is the 25–60 *pesos* (US$8–17) per person category. You can dine on lobster here for the equivalent of US$10-$15, depending on the going market price. There are buffet lunches where you can literally feast on about the equivalent of US$6.

Menu prices are always in *pesos*. The restaurants listed below—not a complete listing, but a selection—are among the best. Their price category per person start at 10–25 *pesos* (inexpensive) for a meal including beverage, and go up to 25–60 *pesos* (moderate) for a meal including wine, and 60 *pesos* and up (expensive) for a meal including wine. Many of the deluxe hotel restaurants which basically cater to the tourist crowd are in the latter category. But if your hotel plan is European Plan, by all means get out and sample some of Santo Domingo's finest! (Your waistline will hate you for it.)

SANTO DOMINGO

ALCAZAR RESTAURANT
Santo Domingo Hotel
Tel. (809) 532–1511 ext. 650
This one looks like a Moroccan palace and is worth a visit just to view the decor (interior design by Oscar de la Renta). 20-ft. tented ceiling, mirrors, trellises, and a total feeling of splendor. If you don't want to blow your bankroll on dinner, they offer weekday lunch buffets (each day brings you the cuisine of a different country) and a very reasonable Sunday champagne brunch. Although pretty during the day, it is simply magical at night. Try the Tournedos Alcazar (medallions of beef) and their heart of palm salad. *Travel and Leisure* magazine has called this one of the finest restaurants in this part of the world.
Classification: expensive (although the lunch buffets are moderate).

ANTOINE'S
Sheraton Hotel
Tel. (809) 685–5151
Another hotel restaurant that is well worth the trouble. This one is a study in understated elegance, all gray tones, fresh flowers, and flickering lights. The menu is "international" and endless, but seafood dishes are excellent.
Classification: expensive.

ASADERO LOS ARGENTINOS
809 Independencia Avenue (near Maximo Gomez Avenue)
Tel. (809) 687–6792
This is a very casual ranch-style restaurant where the roasting pit is the big attraction. You can smell it a block away! The choice is yours: rabbit, beef, lamb, pork, or try the *parillada*, which means mixed grill.
Classification: moderate.

AUBERGINE
Plaza Mexico
Tel. (809) 566–6622
Proprietor/chef Harald boasts this is the smallest restaurant in Santo Domingo. It has no more than eight tables, cluttered together with

plenty of charm. Everything German from smoked sausages to *wienerschnitzel*.
Classification: moderate.

DON PEPE
Santiago Street, corner of Pasteur Street
Tel. (809) 689-7612
Santo Domingo's newest in what was formerly the home of the
Azteca restaurant. Well decorated. Spanish atmosphere and cuisine.

BOGA BOGA
Plaza Florida
Tel. (809) 687-1539
Informal bar and restaurant which services the apart-hotel Plaza
Florida. The emphasis is on Spanish cuisine. Particularly good is the
seafood *cazuela*.
Classification: moderate.

BRONCO STEAK HOUSE
Hotel Cervantes
Tel. (809) 688-2261
All-night place for steaks and chops. American-style charcoal. Excellent beef. Surprisingly excellent wine list. Very informal. Drawback is the shabby decor; needs a new rug desperately. Not a place to
dress up for but you can count on a reliable meal at reasonable prices.
Classification: moderate.

LA BELLE MAISON
308 Independencia Avenue (near Pasteur Street)
Tel. (809) 685-6758
High-priced and high-style French cuisine prepared by owner/chef
Jean Pierre Decrequy. Pleasant setting of old Gascue residence.
Classification: expensive.

BOSTONIA
103 Calle Camini, corner of Coba
near Concorde Hotel
Tel. (809) 562-8879
Very casual. Informal trellis decor. New England-style seafood. Creole dishes. Steaks. Formerly Manny Mota's Dugout.
Classification: inexpensive to moderate.

CAFE ATLANTICO
152 Mexico Avenue
Tel. (809) 565-2841
Welcoming bar and casual eatery. Informal and youth-oriented. Indoor and outdoor sections. Excellent pastas and light meals.
Also has a very popular happy hour with young executive crowd.
Classification: inexpensive to moderate.

EL CASERIO
459 George Washington Avenue
Tel. (809) 685-3392
You have a choice of dining indoors or outdoors at this spacious restaurant. Seafood specialty. Popular bar.
Classification: Moderate.

CAFE GALERIA
27th of February Avenue
Galerias Comerciales (second level)
Tel. (809) 567-4059
Overlooking the Olympic center and stadium. Lots of atmosphere in this casual favorite. Combination eatery and gallery. Paintings exhibited throughout the restaurant are for sale. Excellent and imaginative crepes. Dessert crêpes, too. Free hotel transfer at time of this writing.
Classification: inexpensive to moderate.

CAFE ST. MICHEL
24 Lope de Vega Avenue
Tel. (809) 562-4141
Beautiful restaurant for French specialties. Wood and mirror decor, a cross between a chalet and a greenhouse. One of Santo Domingo's finest and most established. Excellent service. Friendly, helpful personnel.
Classification: expensive.

CANTABRICO
45 Independencia Avenue
Tel. (809) 687-5101
Popular restaurant with executive lunch crowd. Quiet spot for dinner.

Simple but tasteful decor in dining room. Excellent seafood and paella. But don't hesitate to select the roast lamb or the Segovia pork.
Classification: moderate.

CASA VIEJA
457 Independencia Avenue (opposite the Jaragua)
Tel. (809) 685-6334
The restaurant is pleasant, clean, and informal. Casual terrace decor. You feel you're dining in someone's greenhouse. Seafood specialties with a touch of old Spain. Dining indoors with an outdoor feeling. Their problem is parking facilities.
Classification: moderate.

CHINO DE MARISCOS
38A Sarasota Avenue
Tel. (809) 533-5249
Spacious restaurant. Very clean. Very typical in decor. You may need a sweater as they want you to remember them for their air-conditioning. Excellent wonton soup. All Chinese specialties. Conveniently near the Embajador hotel. Takeout section as well. Bakery adjacent to restaurant. Completely informal neighborhood restaurant.
Classification: moderate.

DA CIRO
Independencia Avenue near Pasteur Street
Tel. (809) 689-6046
Another landmark. Gracious manor house converted into high- spirited restaurant. Music and entertainment nightly thanks to Ciro and Ana. Italian specialties.
Classification: moderate.

DA CIRITO
George Washington Avenue, corner of Pasteur Street
Located behind Da Ciro's, this is pizza heaven! Great eatery for kids. Seafront views. Casual, no frills.
Classification: inexpensive.

D'AGOSTINI
9 Maximo Gomez Avenue (near Caribe I and Continental hotels)
Tel. (809) 685-4822
Excellent wine list and international cuisine at this restaurant geared
to an exclusive local clientele.
Classification: expensive.

DULCES CRIOLLOS DOÑA MARIA
Plaza Criolla
Open until 9 p.m., seven days a week. Specialties include *dulce de
leche*, guava paste, orange paste, coconut pastry, and other native
candies. Also offers special homemade cider.

EL BODEGON
Arz. Merino, corner of Padre Billini Street
Tel. (809) 682-6864
Vintage Spanish. Colonial setting in the old city of Santo Domingo.
Around the corner from the Cathedral. Very romantic spot. The best
of Castilian cuisine.
Classification: moderate.

EL BUREN
Padre Billini Street (next door to Bodegon)
Small restaurant. Creole theme. Includes a small museum of native
craft and utensils. All wood and thatch but crisp linen and flowers.
Excellent seafood, chicken, and stews. Rice dishes.
Classification: moderate.

EL PICNIC
Centro Europa, behind Palacio del Cine on 27th of February Avenue
Tel. (809) 542-6406
Tiny place for seafood specialties. Casual eatery. Excellent deli in
front for meat, cheese, and pastry shop.
Classification: inexpensive.

D LUIS
205 Santiago Street
Tel. (809) 689-3534
A beautiful house in Gascue sector of Santo Domingo. Stone detail,

lovely wood, and stained glass. Appealing bar completely separate from restaurant. The restaurant has an international menu, with delicious beef and seafood dishes but leave room for dessert!
Classification: moderate.

EL TOLEDO
Pasteur Street, corner of Casimiro de Moya
Tel. (809) 687–6343
Spanish to the core in this attractive multi-level restaurant.
Seafood, rabbit, lamb, and pork dishes specialties.
Classification: expensive.

FONDA DE LA ATARAZANA
5 La Atarazana
Tel. (809) 689–2900
Located on one of the new world's oldest streets which was the center of commerce in time of Columbus. La Fonda boasts a lovely interior courtyard for casual dining and a more formal upstairs with a spectacular view of the Alcazar. Occasional folklore shows presented in their patio. A touch of Andalucia in Santo Domingo!
Classification: moderate.

GERD'S HOFBRAUHAUS
Padre Billini Street, near Palo Hincado
Gerd himself does the shopping and cooking, and is ever-present in this tiny restaurant for Bavarian specialties. Next door is Lily Marlene, where dancing girls go through to the wee hours. The restaurant specializes in pork dishes and his soups are excellent. Simple decor. Completely casual. Downtown location.
Classification: inexpensive.

IL BUCO
152-A Arz. Merino
Tel. (809) 685–0884
Don't miss it. One of the most charming in the colonial city. A tunnel of a place, long and narrow. Smartly decorated and long on atmosphere. Excellent Italian cuisine. Try the veal. Pasta dishes are popular, particularly a house specialty, green lasagna.
Classification: moderate to expensive.

IL CAPO (two locations)
George Washington Avenue (next to Bella Blue)
the Embajador Gardens
Both these eateries are great for fast family meals. Very casual and
relaxed atmosphere. Pizza is the thing, but not exclusively. Good
selection of pasta favorites.
Classification: inexpensive.

JAI ALAI
411 Independencia Avenue (behind the Jaragua and Sheraton hotels)
Tel. (809) 685-2409
Residence turned restaurant with the emphasis on consistency. You
can always count on a good meal and good service. The atmosphere is
informal and friendly, with an ample bar leading into three separate
dining areas. Seafood is the specialty, with a Peruvian flavor. The
owners are always on hand to insure everything is in top form. One of
Santo Domingo's most frequented and most frequently praised!
Classification: moderate.

JAPONES (Japanese Restaurant)
George Washington Avenue
Tel. (809) 686-6566
This is the only show in town for Japanese cuisine. Strategically
located on seafront Malecon.

JARDIN DE JADE (Jade Garden)
The Embajador Hotel
Tel. (809) 533-2131
One of the most attractive restaurants in town. Beautiful encased
costumes, ceremonial crowns, and weapons imported from China.
Ample menu of Sichuan, Cantonese, and Mandarin specialties. Pe-
king Duck is a ritual. For something different, try the Beggar's
Chicken, a Hangchow tradition.
Classification: expensive.

JUAN CARLOS
7 Gustavo Mejia Ricart Street
Tel. (809) 562-6444
Originally a neighborhood restaurant, it has turned into one of snob

appeal. The decor is pretty but informal; however, the prices are formal. Spanish specialties and excellent service.
Classification: expensive.

LA FROMAGERIE
Plaza Criolla
Tel. (809) 567-8606
Winner of the Europa '85 gastronomic trophy. Pretty decor with mezzanine level. Natural woods. Ideal place for lunch break after shopping at the Plaza Criolla. Try their *bouillabaisse*, crêpes, and fondues.
Classification: expensive.

LA GRAN MURALLA
218 27th of February Avenue
Tel. (809) 567-2166
Walk over a lotus pond into a huge multi-level restaurant. Local Chinese residents consider it one of the best. Try the corn soup. Midday buffet on Sundays very popular. All you can eat for a modest fee.
Classification: inexpensive.

LA MEZQUITA
407 Independencia Avenue, behind the Jaragua and Sheraton hotels
Tel. (809) 687-7090
Excellent and recently refurbished place for Spanish cuisine. Pleasant and comfortable. Informal.
Classification: moderate.

LA PARILLA
George Washington Avenue
Tel. (809) 688-1511
Casual outdoor place for BBQ specialties. Steaks and chicken served on butcher block. Sit on benches at picnic tables and watch the action on the Malecon. Wear jeans.
Classification: inexpensive.

LA REINA DE ESPAÑA
103 Cervantes Street
Tel. (809) 685-2588
        687-5029

Opened for the 1987 season. Gorgeous stone house in Gascue section of Santo Domingo. Short walk from Sheraton and Jaragua hotels. Chef Ramiro is the name to contend with. He dazzles you with Spanish cuisine served up in style. Try the Sea Bass Isabel la Catolica (cooked in apple cider). Excellent lamb and beef dishes. Attentive service. Castilian tradition.
Classification: moderate.

LAGO ENRIQUILLO RESTAURANT
Mirador Park
Anacaona Avenue (across from the Dominican Concorde)
Tel. (809) 562-7924
International and Oriental cuisine at this family-style restaurant. Located right inside the park. Particularly popular on Sunday afternoons for family outings. Rowboats available for rental right on the lake.
Classification: inexpensive to moderate.

LE BISTRO
1353 Independencia Avenue, just beyond Hispaniola Hotel
Tel. (809) 533-7221
Owner/chef Jacques Naudine has put together a casually charming place. Unpretentious decor with plants, watercolors. Limited menu but try their seafood paté. The onion soup is excellent.
Classification: moderate.

LE CAFE
George Washington Avenue
Attractive casual eatery for crêpes, light meals, and desserts. Outdoor terrace overlooking Santo Domingo's Malecon.
Classification: inexpensive to moderate.

LAS PIRAMIDES
352 Romulo Betancourt Avenue (prolongation Bolívar Avenue)
Tel. (809) 533-0040
A terrace restaurant done in natural woods and a profusion of plants. Steaks. Mixed grill. Popular casual atmosphere.

LEE'S KITCHEN

27 Tiradentes Avenue (prolongation Bolívar Avenue)

Tel. (809) 562-4581

Chinese specialties in a plain setting. Totally informal neighborhood-style restaurant. Try excellent sizzling beef and sizzling fish specialties. Variety of appealing soups.

Classification: inexpensive.

LINA

Gran Hotel Lina

Tel. (809) 689-5185

Certainly one of the most famous in Santo Domingo. A tradition that goes back decades! Large modern dining room adjacent to the attractive Lina bar. The restaurant has about 17 seafood choices, all of them superb. Noted for beef dishes. Spanish cuisine. Their paella is one of the best. But leave room for dessert—the Lina specializes in a memorable ice cream cake *tarta helada*. You will hate yourself afterwards, but go ahead. They also have a takeout service and a pastry shop on the hotel premises.

Classification: expensive.

MARBELLA

Pasteur Street, corner of Casimiro de Moya (adjacent to Lucky Seven)

Tel. (809) 689-8936
     682-7588

Remodeled restaurant section of Lucky Seven. Now classier with seafood specialties. Lucky Seven is the sports enthusiasts' hangout with satellite broadcasting of games.

Classification: moderate.

MARIO

453 Las Mercedes Street (by Independence Park)

Tel. (809) 682-3944

Another landmark. The perennial neighborhood Chinese restaurant. Always dependable. Takeout orders handled as well. Sweet and sour everything. Best rice dishes in town. Casual. Very affordable.

Classification: inexpensive.

MESON DE CASTILLA
8 Dr. Baez Street
Tel. (809) 688–4319
Terrace and small rooms of former residence converted into one of
the city's most popular restaurants. Always crowded. Service is not
the best but the food is excellent. Try the rabbit. Their soups and
stews are noteworthy. Seafood dishes heavy on creams. Unless you are
a regular, don't count on attentive service.
Classification: moderate.

MESON DE LA CAVA
Mirador
Tel. (809) 533–2818
Natural cave setting is the star of this show. Careful with the spiral
staircase. Clients should receive hazard pay for attempting the descent. Specializes in beef dishes. Very tourist-oriented but the site
itself is worth a visit. Small dance floor for those ready to try the
merengue after their second rum punch!
Classification: expensive.

NAIBOA
703 Bolivár Avenue, near Maximo Gomez Avenue
Tel. (809) 685–0902
Pretty restaurant with a country feeling. All gingham tablecloths and
timber beams. Specializes in Creole dishes, seafood, and beef. Informal, quiet restaurant.
Classification: inexpensive to moderate.

PIANTINI
Lope de Vega, corner of Roberto Pastoriza Avenue
Tel. (809) 566–4230
        567–7385
Tasteful restaurant with attractive side rooms for small parties. Sea-
food specialties and pasta.
Classification: moderate to expensive.

PICCOLO GOURMET
605 Abraham Lincoln Avenue
Tel. (809) 566–6340

Attractive restaurant: brick, wood, stained glass. A warm feeling in casual atmosphere. Tradeoff is you have to listen to Giuseppi sing. Good food with pasta, beef, and seafood specialties. Spaghetti with lobster sauce.

Classification: moderate.

TAQUERIA ANTOJITOS
49 Lope de Vega Avenue
Tel. (809) 567–1118
Tacos, tamales, tacos, pizza. Very casual and appealing place. Family-oriented.

Classification: inexpensive.

VEGETARIAN ANANDA
7 Casimiro de Moya
Tel. (809) 682–4465
Very informal cafeteria-style place for vegetarian meals. Side counter also offers honey, granola, vitamins, natural cookies, and other health products for sale. Self-service. Clean and comfortable setting.

Classification: very inexpensive.

VESUVIO I
George Washington Avenue
Tel. (809) 689–2141
The classic. A landmark in Santo Domingo through the best of times and the worst of times. Over three decades of service. Something for everyone. Outdoor terrace overlooking malecon has to be the most popular place in Santo Domingo. Indoor restaurant is spacious comfort. Recently refurbished, it now offers a cavalcade of light tropical colors: mauve, peach, lime, white, and the occasional pink. Extensive menu for pastas, seafood, veal, beef, pizzas, and sinful desserts. The Bonarelli clan has gone all out to make it bright and cheerful in keeping with the Caribbean. Definitely a people-watching place. Always busy.

Classification: moderate to expensive.

VESUVIO II
17 Tiradentes Avenue
Tel. (809) 562–6060

The subsidiary. It's a smaller version of the seafront Vesuvio. Same offer but not as much atmosphere. Good food. Quieter setting. Location near Plaza Naco and midtown commercial area makes it a popular spot for lunch.

Classfication: moderate to expensive.

PIZZERIA
George Washington Avenue (next door to Vesuvio I)
It's part of the Vesuvio family but oriented to the kiddie crowd. Great for pizzas, hamburgers, and ice cream. Casual outdoor terrace and indoor eatery.

Classification: inexpensive.

NEAR SANTO DOMINGO

BOCA CHICA

L'HORIZON
overlooking Boca Chica Beach
Tel. (809) 523–4375
Lovely spot for lunch or dinner set in a thatched terrace restaurant. Swiss owner/chef Walter Kleinert specializes in fondues. Try the favorite Fondue Bourguignonne. There is even a Chinese fondue! International specialties ranging from Indonesian chicken to Zurich-style pork filet. The onion soup makes people drive out from the city regularly (except on Tuesdays).

Classification: moderate.

COSTA CARIBE

ALLEN'S
Juan Dolio (near Playa Real Hotel)
Follow the signs until you find it practically hidden in the overgrown brush. Worth the trip. The Levitts' touch in seafood specialties is memorable. By their own admission, a perfect place to escape from the noise of the city. Try it (except on Mondays).

Classification: moderate.

LA ROMANA

DE AMERICA RESTAURANT
52 Catillo Marquez Street
Tel. (809) 556-3137
Hot new place in town if you can get a table! Creole and middle eastern food personally prepared by Dona America. Moderate prices. Great cuisine. Cozy atmosphere. *Everyone* goes there including the Vice President.

ALTOS DE CHAVON

CAFE DEL SOL
at Altos de Chavon
Tel. (809) 682-9656 ext. 2346
Light meals are the specialty all day and all night, particularly pizza in every shape and flavor. Try the vegetarian. Also serves crêpes, sandwiches, ice cream, and tropical fruit drinks. The open terrace overlooks Chavon's magical piazza and is a great place for drinks at sunset!
Classification: moderate to expensive.

EL SOMBRERO RESTAURANT
at Altos de Chavon
Tel. (809) 682-9656 ext. 2353
Fiesta atmosphere for south of the border favorites! Moderate.

CAFE EL PATIO
at Altos de Chavon
Tel. (809) 682-9656 ext. 2265
Informal. Lush greenery and rustic decor. Dominican Creole specialties. Inexpensive.

CASA DEL RIO
at Altos de Chavon
Tel. (809) 682-9656 ext. 2345
Spectacular view of Chavon River and hillside at this favorite restaurant perched high on cliff overlooking the Chavon River. The seafood is sensational. Offers a number of continental specialties. Try to

reserve a table by the window for one of the most memorable sights. Rustic design in stone and wood. Formal attire required.
Classification: moderate to expensive.

LA FONDA
at Altos de Chavon
Tel. (809) 682–9656 ext. 2350
Along one of the side streets, almost hidden away, is this casual spot for Creole cooking. The best of native Dominican dishes, including a wonderful goat stew, *sancocho*, and seabass in coconut.
Classification: moderate.

LA PIAZZETTA
at Altos de Chavon
Tel. (809) 682–9656 ext. 2339
Italian restaurant beautifully done in country style with decorative tiles, wood, and crafts. Excellent veal dishes and pastas (try Risotto Primavera) along with extensive wine list. A strolling violinist completes the atmosphere.
Classification: expensive.

SANTIAGO

RESTAURANT PEZ DORADO
43 Calle El Sol
Tel. (809) 582–2518
A Santiago landmark for Chinese specialties and seafood. Comfortable setting. Ideal for business lunches.
Classification: moderate.

RESTAURANT OSTERIA
27th of February Avenue
Tel. (809) 582–4165
Regarded by many as Santiago's most exclusive restaurant. Italian specialties. Excellent choice for pasta lovers.
Classification: moderate to expensive.

RESTAURANT EL HIDALGO
Calle El Sol
Tel. (809) 583–4361

Elegant setting for international cuisine.
Classification: moderate.

PUERTO PLATA AND ENVIRONS

THE BOAR HOUSE
Avenue Colon (at the end of the Malecon, across from the electric plant)
American-style "hangout" specializing in BBQ spareribs, chicken, steaks, and chops. Open from noon "until the last person leaves." Complete with draft beer and country & western sounds.
Classification: inexpensive.

CAFE TERMINUS
Corner of Hermanas Mirabal Street and Malecon (right opposite Long Beach)
Tel. (809) 586-2882
French specialties in a simple seafront setting. Seafood in wine sauce, escargots, and beef flamande are favorites.
Classification: moderate.

CASYROS
near the stadium
Tel. (809) 586-3716
Stylish restaurant put together by former maître and chef from Santo Domingo's Alcazar Restaurant. Flambée dishes. Deviled oysters, rice, and seafood specialty. Many dishes are prepared in front of you with a great deal of flair. A variation of Crêpes Suzette prepared with banana and Grand Marnier.
Classification: moderate to expensive.

DE ARMANDO
Separacion Street
Tel. (809) 586-3418
Seafood specialties. Creole cuisine. Open daily noon to midnight. Recent addition to Puerto Plata's restaurants.
Classification: moderate.

INTERNATIONAL RESTAURANT AND PIZZERIA
Stadium traffic circle
Favorite with locals. Rustic casual atmosphere. Looks like a big ranch house. Italian specialties. Every conceivable pizza!
Classification: moderate.

JIMMY'S
72 Beller Street
Tel. (809) 586–4325
Residence converted into informal restaurant for seafood and beef specialties. Flambée dishes.
Classification: moderate.

LA ISABELA
Montemar Hotel
Tel. (809) 586–2800
Worth a mention. Easily one of Puerto Plata's most elegant, including Playa Dorada. As part of the Hotel School, the service is impeccable, if somewhat exaggerated. Tasteful decor, soft music, fresh flowers, and very crisp linen. Seafood and beef specialties. Try their seafood casserole. Excellent dessert selection.
Classification: expensive.

LA NUEVA CASONA
Separacion Street, corner of the Malecon
Tel. (809) 586–3891
Terrace restaurant located on Puerto Plata's seafront avenue. Nothing fancy. Zero decor. The food is the important thing. Seafood specialties.
Classification: inexpensive.

LOS PINOS
Hermanas Mirabal Street
Tel. (809) 586–3222
Recently remodeled and with new ownership. Creole specialties as well as international. Tasca tavern-style bar with a Mexican flavor.
Classification: moderate to expensive.

MAMIS KNEIPE'S (CAFE MARGARITA)

11 Calle Diagonal

Tel. (809) 586-4030

Austrian cuisine in a family setting. A real treat but let her
know you're coming. Between 3 and 5 p.m., Mamis prepares tea with
marble cake and other favorite pastries.

Classification: moderate.

NEPTUNO BAR & GRILL

Puerto Plata Beach Resort's seaside grill.

Right on the beach, this has become popular with locals as well as
guests for seafood specialties. You can weigh your own choice!

Classification: moderate to expensive.

OCEANICO

On the Malecon, near Separacion Street

Luigi Cataldi was a ship's chef. Now he prepares conch, octopus,
shrimp, and other seafood with a touch of Italian virtuosity! Terrace
overlooking seaside Malecon. Casual.

Classification: moderate.

ORIENT EXPRESS

Hermanas Mirabal Street

Tel. (809) 586-3962

An oriental garden atmosphere for French and oriental-style seafood
dishes. From breakfast straight through the day and night. Light
snack menu available in late hours.

Classification: moderate.

PIZZERIA ROMA II

Beller Street

Tel. (809) 586-3904

Everything from paella to pizza at bargain prices. Casual eatery
overlooking central park. A place to mix with locals.

Classification: inexpensive.

VALTER'S

Hermanas Mirabal Street

Tel. (809) 586-2329

''Gingerbread'' setting for one of Puerto Plata's prettiest terrace

restaurants. Valter Tapparo offers seafood and Italian specialties. Pasta in summer sauce. "Finger-licking" shrimp (*camarones chupa dedos*).
Classification: moderate to expensive.

RESTAURANT LA CARRETA
Separacion Street
Tel. (809) 586–3418
Creole cuisine in an old Puerto Plata house. Dominican atmosphere.
Classification: inexpensive.

VICTORIAN PUB
9 Separacion Street
Tel. (809) 586–4240
Authentic gingerbread turned restaurant. Lovely outdoor garden setting. International specialties. Good seafood at reasonable prices. Romantic choice.
Classification: moderate.

PLAYA DORADA

Each of the resort hotels at Playa Dorada boasts a distinguished restaurant facility. Many of them specializing in seafood buffets. The hotel section includes a discussion of the various facilities.

JADE GARDEN RESTAURANT
Tel. (809) 586–3000
A tropical jade garden that manages to be elegant and casual at the same time. The local branch of the original at Santo Domingo's El Embajador. Try the dim sum, shredded pork, and delicious Peking Duck. Seafood specialties as well.

SOSÚA (EL BATEY)

MORUA MAI
This is easily Sosúa's most beautiful restaurant, an open tent tastefully done in cream colors and exceptional for its seafood and friendly service.
Classification: moderate to expensive.

UNITED FRUIT COMPANY/LA ROCA
This was recently refurbished. The terrace is nicely done with white wicker peacock chairs. There is an attractive dark wood bar and a large area for disco dancing.
Classification: moderate.

CAFE MAMA JUANA
Tiny place. Open from breakfast straight through the day. Start your morning with a Mama Juana "MacMuffin." Rustic decor. Small outdoor yard with picnic tables as well.
Classification: inexpensive.

CAFE SOSÚA
at the entrance to El Batey
A small and very pretty little café for casual meals and light snacks.
Classification: moderate.

EL CARACOL
The restaurant at Villas Coralillos.
Lovely terrace restaurant overlooking Sosúa Beach. Spectacular during the day and just as lovely for dining *al fresco*! Excellent seafood specialties.
Classification: moderate to expensive.

PJ'S INTERNATIONAL BAR
Light meals, hamburgers, and generous drinks.
Classification: inexpensive.

EL OASIS
One of Sosúa's oldest. Covered terrace. Rocking chairs. Dominican-style eatery for native cuisine.
Classification: inexpensive.

LORENZO'S
Pizzeria with popular rooftop terrace and bar. Formerly Roma III. Popular prices and atmosphere.
Classification: inexpensive.

MARCO POLO RESTAURANT
Opposite Villas Coralillos in El Batey.
This spectacular terrace restaurant offers the finest view of Sosúa Beach, tasteful rustic decor, and certainly some of the best food available in the region. Try their Honey Chicken. Tables and bar stools overlook the bay. Tastefully done down to every detail. Classification: moderate to expensive.

SOSÚA (*LOS CHARAMICOS*)

ATLANTICO BAR RESTAURANT
Another favorite for the view. Spectacular terrace overlooking beach. Excellent seafood specialties. Classification: inexpensive.

MAURICIO'S
French Canadians love Mauricio's at Los Charamicos. Noted for seafood specialties and friendly ambiance.

CABARETE

CHEZ MARCEL
On the beach, next door to Cosme Tours
Madoni and St. Laurent have put together a winner on the beach at Cabarete. The menu varies daily with the emphasis on seafood. French flair with sauces. Soft jazz at night. All very casual. The day's catch and prices posted on blackboard.

LAS TERRENAS

CHEZ PACO
François Jarlier of Chez François fame in Santo Domingo, closed shop and moved out to Las Terrenas equipped with his pots and pans and his flair for making something spectacular out of just about anything. Seafood is the specialty here. The day's catch determines the menu.

Chapter 8

SHOPPING IN THE DOMINICAN REPUBLIC

Shopping in the Dominican Republic shows off the best in its native produce, mineral resources, and the artistic craftwork of its people, while bringing you into the heart of Dominican life. Although most fruits and vegetables cannot be brought back into the United States, it is worthwhile to take advantage of them during your visit. As for the rest, temptation awaits at every corner!

FLAVORS AND AROMAS OF THE DOMINICAN REPUBLIC

From pumpkin to avocado, from mango to papaya, the Dominican Republic is rich in tropical fruits and vegetables. Anyone who is health conscious will find a wealth of fruits in season to chose from. Root vegetables are also very popular and found in abundance. Manioc or *yuca*, as it is called here, has been an island staple since the times of the Taino Indians. It is not to be eaten raw as it can be toxic. It is most commonly boiled or fried and also prepared as *casabe* bread, a crunchy flat bread resembling pita in shape and size but not in texture. *Casabe* also goes back to the early days of the colony, when it was adopted by the Spanish conquerors as a substitute for wheat bread.

Rice and beans are sometimes referred to as "the Dominican flag" because it is a daily ritual for most Dominicans and many don't feel they've eaten well if they haven't had their *arroz con habichuelas*. A serving of plantain completes the menu, either boiled or mashed with a little oil to make the popular *mangu*.

Sancocho is a popular dish comprised of every imaginable root vegetable, beef, chicken, and pork. It should have at least seven varieties of meat to be a "respectable" sample. Fish with coconut sauce, crabmeat Creole style, skewered beef, pork in every imaginable style, goat meat, and meat pies called *pastelitos* are also typical dishes.

FRUITS AND VEGETABLES OF THE DOMINICAN REPUBLIC

PINEAPPLE

Cultivated varieties of pineapple belong to the species *Ananas Comosus*. With just one exception (Spanish Moss) which is native to the west coast of Africa, pineapples are native to this island and the other islands of the West Indies.

Called yayama by the Indians, pineapple was first tasted by Columbus and his men when they arrived in the Caribbean on their second voyage.

The earliest records of this indigenous fruit are references made to the fruit by Columbus, Oviedo (the historian of the early colony), and Sir Walter Raleigh. The pineapple was taken on one of Columbus' voyages back to Europe, from which it was introduced to many other parts of the world. By 1550, it had reached as far as India. Before the end of the 16th century, cultivation had spread over most of the tropical zones of the world. This included the islands of the South Pacific. Pineapple spread quickly throughout the far reaches of the globe because of its resilience. Crowns of the fruit carried on board ships survived the crossings with no spoilage and were used to propagate the fruit once the ships reached port. The crown part does not spoil even when detached from the mass of the fruit for long periods.

In 1986, fruit imports from the Dominican Republic into U.S. ports totaled US$42,624,000. The latest development on the pineapple story is the arrival of Dole Pineapple in the Dominican Republic (see section on Agribusiness, chapter 11).

ORANGE

Visitors from northern climes will be quite surprised when first viewing this orange. It really isn't orange at all, but light to medium green in color. The inside is very light. In fact, there will be found few, if any, orange-colored navel varieties in the country. The Dominican orange is one of the staples of the country. When in season, it is very popular, and you will see it being hawked from many three-wheeled bicycle carts. The orange is very sweet, almost non-acidic, and has many seeds. As many as 140 seeds have been counted in one orange. The juice has a color that is somewhere between that of a navel orange and a North American lemon. It is the custom to sell the oranges peeled, and it is fascinating to watch the vendors peel one for you. In some cases, a vendor will peel it with a knife, making a continuous peel surprisingly long. Others will use a small hand-cranked machine much like an old-fashioned apple peeler. When he is finished peeling, the orange will remain exceptionally clean until he sells it. The vendor will pile the fruit neatly on his sales cart, arranging it like a stack of cannon balls, or bag a few oranges together in clear plastic bags. Street vendors will be found selling the small plastic bags at intersections. You must certainly partake of this unusual fruit!

100-year old mango trees

LEMON

Columbus took citrus fruit seeds to the country on his second voyage, and it is generally agreed that this was among them. What is known as a lime in North American countries is known here as a lemon. The fruit is exactly the same as a lime, green in color, and somewhat smaller as a rule. These are a big item for the street vendors. You might as well forget trying to find a typical yellow lemon, for they are seldom seen.

MANGO

Some of the finest and largest mango trees in the world are found in the Dominican Republic. The fruit thrives here and are in full season during May and June. Mango trees can bear fruit numbering in the thousands each. These are exceptional, but do exist and are a wonderful sight to see, as they sometimes reaching a height of 75 feet and more. According to the best authority, the mango was introduced into the West Indies about 1740. It is considered indigenous to Asia, Burma, and the Assam state of India. It thrives in the Caribbean climate, and has become an important source of food for native Dominicans. If you haven't eaten a mango, this is your chance to enjoy an interesting fruit that is so important throughout the tropical world.

PAPAYA

The origin of the papaya is somewhat obscure. It is thought to be native to Mexico and Central America, although there is a distinct possibility that it is indigenous to the Caribbean as well. Be that as it may, it is another important item in the food chain of inhabitants of the West Indies. As you travel about the country, you will see groves of the fruit in the areas that support typical jungle greenery, as the fruit requires high humidity and a great deal of water to flourish. This is an item you will find on most hotel menus to add taste and color to you repast.

PLANTAINS AND BANANAS

You may be surprised to see what appears to be a green banana being sold everywhere in the country. These are not, as many northerners assume, ordinary bananas in the ripening process. These are plantains. They are an extremely important staple in most of the tropical world. The plantain is a cooking variety of the banana. There is no time in its growing process when it is edible without cooking. There are over 100 varieties of banana throughout the world, but the common characteristic of all varieties is their exceptional nutritional value. It is a staple food which is extremely rich in vitamins A, B, and C.

The plantain belongs to the genus *Musa*. One of the ancient legends is that sage men ate this fruit, which is why the botanical name is *Musa Sapientum*. This is probably the origin of the idea of the Muse who inspires wise men. Historians trace the fruit to Asia and India. It is said the Greeks saw it in India during an expedition of Alexander the Great. The origins are definitely believed to be Asiatic.

The banana was brought from the Canary Islands to the New World shortly after the discovery of this island by Columbus. It was first established in Hispaniola from which it later spread to other islands.

There is an enormous demand for bananas and plantains in U.S. markets. The United States imports more bananas than any other country. In 1986, the Dominican Republic shipped US$783,000 worth of banana and plantain exports to the United States. Undoubtedly, a great part of the demand comes from the Hispanic communities there. This market should not be underestimated, since it represents a US$60 to $70 billion market annually for goods serving 15 to 17 million Hispanics. This is why many large U.S. corporations with Caribbean area sourcing are targeting the Hispanic market with special products and selective advertising (US$333.5 million in 1985).

RICE

A surprising amount of rice is grown in the Dominican Republic. There are many small producers, and it is considered another one of the country's staples. As much as twenty-seven percent of the calories of the poor are provided by this crop, so its importance is clear. Many northern travelers are surprised to see rice growing here, thinking that it is probably too hot for this crop. On the contrary, because there are several separate climates in the country, and some have the right soil, humidity, and moisture, rice grows very well. When you visit a market, check the shelves and you will find a substantial quantity of rice on them. In restaurants, many of the dishes will include rice. This is a tropical country, and typical tropical weather with its frequent sudden warm rainshowers make possible the cultivation of rice as well as many exotic fruits.

Bags of rice awaiting a truck

CORN

Corn is produced by thousands of small farmers in relatively small quantities for their own consumption and as feed for poultry. It is used as livestock feed and as a result, will continue to grow in production in the future. Since the plantain (see above) remains the key staple in the typical Dominican's diet, corn will probably continue to be used chiefly for livestock.

COCONUT

There are many areas of large coconut groves. You will find them almost everywhere you look. Coconut oil is a big export item, and coconut nectar is hawked on the street from small three-wheeled carts. If you haven't tried this, we recommend it. Keep in mind that when you buy the drink, the vendor cuts the top off the coconut on the spot, thereby insuring a safe, clean drink.

CASHEW NUTS

You may be surprised to learn that cashew nuts come from a tree on which one nut grows on a fruit about two and a half inches long. When in season, you will see many roadside vendors selling the nuts and the fruit. You will form a new appreciation of the value of the nuts when you realize how many fruit must be harvested to gain just a handful of nuts.

THAT LEGENDARY DOMINICAN COFFEE

In the earliest known advertisement for coffee (circa 1652) on display at the British Museum, you can read: "Coffee quickens the spirits and makes the heart lightsome…" Although it is usually claimed that coffee originated in Africa, there is evidence of early cultivation in Arabia. The name has also been linked with Kaffa, a region of Ethiopia reputed to be the birthplace of coffee. There are many legends about its origins. One tale involves the discovery of coffee around the year 850 by an Arabian goatherd named Kaldi. The story goes that he noticed his goats acting strangely after eating the bright, colored berries from a bush. He is supposed to have followed their example and tasted the berries, thereby discovering coffee.

It is also said that the effectiveness of coffee in fighting drowsiness was a major factor in its popularity with Muslims, who used it to help them get through their prolonged religious services, although orthodox leaders considered it an intoxicating beverage prohibited by the Koran! This didn't deter much of the Middle Eastern population, as its use flourished throughout the Arabic countries.

Introduced to Europe in the 16th and 17th centuries, it was said to have medicinal properties and "soul-stirring" qualities. The popularity of coffee in Europe was such that Johann Sebastian Bach even composed a "Coffee Cantata" in 1732!

Coffee gained its first real popularity in the coffeehouses of London. In the mid–1600's, these were the meeting places of the literary people, the artists, and the local intelligencia, who gathered to discuss everything from philosophy to politics.

The 17th century also saw coffeehouses become popular in the major cities of North America. Boston, Philadelphia, and New York all had these establishments. In fact, the Merchants Coffee House in New York (1737) is claimed by historians to have given birth to the plan of American Independence. How coffee found its way to the American colonies is uncertain. There is no evidence that it came aboard the *Mayflower*. Some writers of the period credit John Smith, founder of Virginia, for having been the first to bring coffee to America, as early as 1607.

It is known that coffee was being produced in the Caribbean islands in the early 1700's. There are references to this in letters and early histories of Santo Domingo which place local production at around 1715.

The most charming theory of how coffee found its way to the islands is the story of Gabriel Mathieude de Clieu, a young French naval officer assigned to Martinique in the early 18th century. He believed the climate and fertile soil of the islands would be perfect for the cultivation of coffee. The few coffee plants in existence in Paris were in the Royal Hothouse of King Louis XV. Somehow, de Clieu managed to steal one and carry it across the Atlantic. The ship's supply of water was so low during the crossing, that he had to share his meager ration with his fledgling coffee plant. Somehow, the plant and de Clieu survived and he nursed his coffee plant to harvest. Legend has it that many of the coffee plants throughout the West Indies are descendant of that first one that thrived in Martinique. It is said that by 1777, Martinique had over 19,000,000 coffee trees!

Coffee grown in the different Central and South American countries vary by types and grades. Coffee looks different from one plantation to another. In the parlance of the coffee industry, Brazils and Milds are terms used to denote coffees grown in the region. All those grown in the Caribbean fall into the mild classification.

The method of processing coffee is true and tried. It involves the natural drying properties of sun and air. It generally takes two to three weeks in the sun for coffee to become thoroughly dry and, during this time, the beans must be turned over regularly to ensure that every bean receives the benefit of tropical warmth no machine process can rival. After hulling, there is a careful hand inspection to remove imperfect beans. This ensures that the highest quality coffee is packed for shipment to the coffee ports of North America. If you ever saw Juan Valdez (''the demanding one'') in commercials on U.S. television, you know this is true.

Dominican coffee is packed in conveniently compact, moisture-proof bags to carry home the taste of the island. It most certainly rates among the finest coffees in the world.

An indication of just how important coffee is to the Dominican economy is that the Dominican Republic exported US$115.9 million worth in coffee to the United States in 1986.

TOBACCO

Christopher Columbus and other early explorers who came to Hispaniola and the other islands of the Caribbean, found the natives smoking tobacco. Many of the early encounters were celebrated with the smoking of a peace pipe as a shared moment of trust. In those days, it was believed that tobacco had positive medicinal properties.

The name tobacco is said to have been derived from the tube used by the aborigine population for inhaling smoke and to refer as well to the leaf itself. Tobacco cultivation by settlers started in Santo Domingo in 1531. It soon became the principal trade commodity in exchange for articles needed by the early colonists. The demand in Europe was overwhelming from the start, largely because of the novelty of this new sensation and the addictive nature of tobacco. It is still a strong force in the Dominican Republic's economy today. This country exported close to US$10 million in unmanufactured tobacco to the U.S. market in 1986; while US$18.5 million worth of cigars were exported to the United States from the Dominican Republic in the same period. in its March 1984 issue, *Connoisseur* magazine featured Dominican-made cigars in an article praising the quality of the Dominican product in comparison with the Havana cigar. The Dominican Republic is a strong contender for some of the best tobacco production in the world today. Its blends are considered among the finest.

Santiago is the urban center of the Cibao, a fertile agricultural region known for its excellent tobacco cultivation. The national tobacco industry is very strong in its quality production of blonde and

Overseer directing the planting of tobacco shoots in this depiction of a 17th-century Caribbean plantation.

dark tobacco. The manufacturing of fine cigars by Industrial Free Zone companies like Consolidated Cigar and General Cigar has raised the country's reputation in the estimation of international markets. *Connoisseur* magazine lists the Dominican Republic as a strong candidate for some of the best cigar production in the world using national leaves together with other fine blends.

A visit to the Tobacco Museum of Santiago on 30 de Marzo Street in the historical downtown area of Duarte Park, is well worthwhile. It takes you through a botanical study of the leaf itself, the historical development of the industry and what it has meant to the Dominican economy.

DOMINICAN RUM

A visit to a Dominican supermarket will reveal an amazing array of attractively-bottled and more attractively-priced Dominican rums. The "three Bs," Brugal, Bermudez, and Barcelo are the most prominently displayed labels found in an assortment of sizes and shapes. From the sophisticated packaging to the high-powered advertising Dominican rums utilize, it is clear that the product has come a long way from its image as the drink of pirates, sailors, and banana republic machos. Actually, rum's "yo-ho-ho" past started with the arrival of sugarcane in the early days of the colony. Some historians claim this took place as early as the second voyage of Columbus. Sugarcane is believed to have originated in the South Pacific or Monsoon Asia. It arrived in the Mediterranean area relatively late, most likely with the Arabs after A.D. 636. As late as the 16th century, its production was a scarce luxury in the western world.

Rich moist soil, abundant sunshine, and a tropical climate are the recipe for successful cane cultivation, which is why the Caribbean has always been an ideal place for it. Rum spirits result from the distillation process of fermented sugarcane. All rums begin with molasses (cooked sugarcane juice) that has been fermented with special strains of yeast.

Production started in the West Indies where the Spanish conquistadors knew all about distillation. Over the years, it spread throughout the American colonies, where it took on considerable popularity in the preparation of somewhat colorful libations such as Kill-Devil, Rattle-Skull, Whistle-Belly Vengeance, and other concoctions that must have done wonders for the liver!

By the early days of American Independence, rum began to give way to the more popular whiskey derived from distilled American grain. It was not until World War II that rum made a comeback in the

U.S. market, mostly because the reduction of grain supplies resulted in a severe whiskey shortage during the war years. In those days, however, rum was produced in small quantities and it was impossible to meet market demands.

As the century progressed, so did the systems for producing, aging, and blending, and it wasn't long before modern plants and sophisticated equipment made rum the spirit of the islands.

Each of the Caribbean islands has its own distinctive rums, ranging from the fruity to the dry. There are basically three types of rum: white, amber, and *anejo*. White rums are the lightest and driest. They are used in mixed drinks, generally with tonic or fruit juice. White rums are distilled to a very high proof which results in a clean, muted flavor. The amber rums are fuller in flavor and more aromatic. They seem thicker to the taste. Amber rums are distilled with a slightly lower proof, which results in a more robust flavor in the final product. As a rule, it was these golden-colored rums that were the preferred substitute for whiskey. In the Dominican Republic, they are frequently mixed with Coca Cola or enjoyed on the rocks. Proofs are determined by the addition of distilled water and the rums are aged a minimum of one year in oak barrels before they are blended and bottled. *Anejos* are specially selected golden rums, aged several years in wood casks. These are by far the richest and most flavorful. They are sometimes compared to brandy. The aging of *anejos* results in a smoothness best enjoyed straight.

In the U.S. market today, white rums are big sellers because they are lighter and easy mixers. Some of the most famous contemporary rum drinks include the Cuba Libre, Frozen Daiquiri, any fruit flavor Daiquiri cocktail, Rum Collins, Rum Toddy, and Zombie. But the list of rum-based selections also includes some picturesque items like the Quaker's Cocktail, Mary Pickford, Fair and Warmer, and the Fireman's Sour. Even Christmas Eggnog contains rum, but we don't recommend too much experimenting on a hot Caribbean day!

A trip to Santiago or Puerto Plata isn't really complete without a tour of their famous rum plants, where visitors can view all aspects of the process to the final product which for centuries has been synonymous with the Caribbean.

BEER

Dominican Beer is regarded by many to be one of the best on the market. The industry here has its roots as far back as the late 1920's, and names like Charles Wanzer and James Stuart had a great deal to do with the origin of "Cerveceria Nacional Dominicana."

Presidente beer has become as much identified with the Dominican Republic as baseball, and this very first beer has also become the most recognized outside the country. It is regarded as one of the very finest beers to come out of the Caribbean. Other popular Dominican beers are *Quisqueya*, *Bohemia*, and the low-calorie beer called *Coral*. *Carlsberg Lager* and *Heineken* are also available in the Dominican Republic.

HEALTH FOOD

For the best in health foods, Santo Domingo has the Ananda Institute, corner of Casimiro de Moya and Pasteur Street (where Lucky Seven Restaurant is located), turn right and walk half a block to Ananda's driveway. The institute has a health food cafeteria and sells excellent honey, vitamins, coconut cookies, bee pollen, and other health food items over the counter. Also, look for the health food shop at Plaza Naco along the side street garage entrance.

All pharmacies in Santo Domingo and the interior towns sell vitamins and other nutrition products.

SEMI-PRECIOUS STONES

Larimar and amber are the semi-precious stones that come to mind when there is any discussion of what to buy in the Dominican Republic. Larimar is a stone that resembles the American turquoise in color. "Dominican turquoise," as it is often called, tends to have lighter, pale blue shades, and has the strength of agate. The stone is found along the southern coast and in the Bahoruco mountain range and is largely mined in the area east of the river of Pedernales, which forms a natural frontier with Haiti. According to Aldo Costa, founder of the Amber Museum of Puerto Plata, Larimar is a variety of pectolite not known elsewhere in the world. Its distinctive light blue color is caused by the presence of cobalt oxide during its geologic formation. The Dominican Republic is the only country in the world to date, where this variety of turquoise is mined, and it has only been mined in the last decade. Its promoter, Miguel Mendez, named the stone "Lari" for his daughter Larissa and "Mar" because it is the color of the sea. The recognition of larimar by professional artisans did not occur until 1974. That was the year a member of the Peace Corps brought a sample of the stone to Mendez, who was the first to recognize its potential in the jewelry trade. Larimar can be found in all the major gift shops in Santo Domingo, Santiago, Puerto Plata,

Sosua, and the towns of the interior. Its popularity has made it easily available and it is usually set in Dominican silver, although we've occasionally seen it set in gold. Recently, necklaces combining larimar and black coral have been a popular and very striking item. If you don't see the stone set in a way that appeals to you, it is likely that the shop will have it set for you according to your specifications.

Amber has traditionally been identified with the Dominican Republic, although many shoppers fail to realize that when they buy Dominican amber, they are investing in a stone that holds the key to millions of years of history. Throughout the ages, amber represented different things for different civilizations. Early concepts linked it to the sun because of its glowing quality and many men came to call it the ''burning stone.'' The early Greeks called it *elektron*, meaning substance of energy, associated with the sun. From that early civilization, there is also a magical legend of Phaeton, son of the sun god Helios whose death caused his sisters such grief that the pitying gods turned them into poplar trees and transformed their tears to drops of amber. In the Christian era, amber was regarded by many as a talisman to ward off evil spirits. The Romans believed in its supernatural powers, and many a gladiator entered the arena with amber adorning his garments. Medicinal qualities were also ascribed to amber and in later centuries it came to be used in the treatment of asthma and fever. Aristotle was the first to determine the scientific origins of amber as that of vegetable. He defined it as the fossilized resin of trees. As the sap ran down the trees, it trapped tiny insects and leaves, bits of flowers and ferns in its flow. Today, these crystallized fossils tell a tale in the Dominican Republic of ancient land formations dating back over 30 million years!

Artisans have always used amber for decorative purposes, in both jewelry and religious art. In the Dominican Republic, it has traditionally been used to craft jewelry. Today it is being used to shape everything from delicate figurines to chess sets. Many shoppers even prefer amber in its rough form, to use as paper weights or unusual conversation pieces! Amber deposits have been found in Japan, Mexico, and the Baltic region. Dominican amber, however, is considered by artisans to be particularly resilient. It is also noted for its wide variety of color. A true chameleon, amber can be found in clear white, lemon, ruby red, cobalt blue, near black, and the more popular caramel.

Amber can be authenticated by the use of ultraviolet light which shows the blue transparency of the stone. However, because of its organic origin, amber will burn, so a more practical experiment is to rub the stone and test its magnetic properties. The most productive region for the mining of amber is in the mountains between Santiago and Puerto Plata. Areas like Palo Alto, Palo Quemado, El Valle, and Los Higos are some of the regions rich in amber deposits. The deeper the excavation, the harder the amber. Usually the presence of fossils makes the stone more valuable since only one stone in about every hundred has some evidence of early life frozen in amber for eternity.

Again, most of the gift shops along La Atarazana, El Conde, and Plaza Criolla, as well as the old marketplace, will offer an abundant selection of amber in Santo Domingo. The gift shops of Puerto Plata, Santiago, the international airport gift shops, and all the resort hotels are stocked with this appealing semi- precious stone, particularly in its more available caramel shades. The rarer shades are also available in the finer shops. The milky white shade is the rarest of all, and is really a collector's item. If you are in Santo Domingo, stop at Joyas Criollas at Plaza Criolla. Adjacent to the gift shop, you'll find a tiny exhibition area that displays a not so tiny sample of amber. The largest piece mined to date in the world, it was found in Sabana la Mar in 1979, weighs 8,000 grams, and measures 18 inches by 8 inches. The highlight for those interested in the history and variety of amber, is a visit to the Amber Museum of Puerto Plata. Here, the collection of Aldo and Didi Costa has been made in the permanent museum under the Costa Foundation. The selection, beautifully displayed with special lighting, is staggering, and the history of amber is explained in both English and Spanish. According to the Costas, the geological age of certain Dominican ambers date back to about 120 million years ago. The Amber Museum is a must on any Puerto Plata itinerary! You will find it at 61 Duarte Street, on the second floor of the Tourist Bazaar.

SHOPPING FOR ALL BUDGETS

THE MODELO MARKET

If ever there was a study in contrasts, this is it! The old marketplaces in our urban centers have become increasingly popular attractions for tourists who want to sample a bit of local atmosphere. On Santo Domingo's Mella Street, you'll discover the Mercado Modelo. Over the years, it has evolved from the central, fly-infested market of the town to what it is today: a much cleaner and more congenial market-place, full of handicrafts, woven baskets, straw hats, hand-carved wood items, and side shops for jewelry and accessories. In its central stands, it is still a cornucopia of fruit, vegetables, medicinal herbs and potions, flowers, and confusion. Like any living thing, the market seems to have evolved. Today it is a much more tourist-oriented potpourri of wares, sights, sounds, and smells. Despite its newfound sense of hygiene and its eye-catching displays of merchandise, in one respect, the marketplace has not changed. The contagious frenzy of the place is still as it was many decades ago. Its vendors, like in all the great bazaars of the world, still assault you with their offers and still have an endless capacity for bargaining. This is the one place in town where you can best put your bargaining prowess to the test! The Mercado is located on Mella Street, which runs at an angle to Conde Street. If you stand at the Conde Gate by Independence Park, walk toward the left for two corners (down by the fire department), you will see the flow of chaotic traffic into Mella Street, a more economical shopping street than Conde.

THE PLAZA CRIOLLA

In contrast to the old Mercado is the Plaza Criolla, a "village market" design shopping center located on 27th of February Avenue, facing the Olympic Center. If you are staying at the Lina Hotel, just cross Maximo Gomez Avenue and walk along the intersecting avenue just over one block. You could also conceivably walk over from the Caribe I or the Continental. Its midtown location is a short taxi ride from the other hotels. What Plaza Criolla sacrifices in Creole flavor, it makes up in style and comfort. The split-level arcade is designed in a village format centered around the village clock tower. The central plaza offers a mini-market of fruit and vegetables across from the ice cream shop. The "village market" houses about a dozen gift shops with fine items ranging from crushed shell picture frames, tortoise-shell evening bags, horn, black coral, the perennial amber and lari-mar selection, summer clothes, T-shirts galore, swimsuits, hand-painted pareos, ceramics, weapons, Dominican coffee, jams, and preserves. A word of caution: the tortoise is an endangered species, and items made from this material will be confiscated by U.S. Customs. Plaza Criolla is not cheap. You're paying for midtown convenience and the comfort of air-conditioning. No matter, it's a delight, and worth a visit whether you are here for browsing or hassle-free shopping.

The Plaza Criolla also has a number of facilities for casual snacks. Some are very charming informal eateries, and then there is the more formal Fromagerie for lunch and dinner, which is one of the city's oldest and best-known restaurants. You can go through most of your shopping list here, but you won't have the fun of bargaining. Discounts are sometimes given at the shop-owner's discretion, but it is not on the same level as the old market downtown. All the boutiques accept major credit cards, with which you get the favorable exchange rate. Most shops close at midday to allow time for lunch but some do remain open straight through the day.

LA HORTALIZA

La Hortaliza on Winston Churchill Avenue—about three blocks north of the intersection with 27th of February Avenue—is a minia-ture version of the Modelo Market, but more sophisticated and lack-ing its chaotic fascination. Aside from fresh produce, this one offers an assortment of baskets, brass beds, ''antique'' sewing machine stands, ceramic dishes, pottery, glazed decorative tiles, and other handicraft items. It is also an outlet for Granix natural products. Because of the uptown location, prices tend to be higher than at the downtown market. It offers a nice selection of fruit for you to snack on back in your hotel room!

PLANARTE

In the section on colonial Santo Domingo, Planarte was mentioned as an essential stop on your shopping itinerary. Located inside the For-tress of Bastidas complex, it has a wonderful assortment of handmade handicrafts ranging from wood to ceramic items. Planarte is spon-sored by the Dominican Development Foundation (*Fundación de Desarollo Dominicano*) and is a high point on a tour of the old city. Look for the hand-tooled leather and the wonderful selection of rag dolls and birds!

DOWNTOWN SANTO DOMINGO

Conde Street. Downtown shopping in the Conde district will allow you a taste of local flavor. Here, you won't be isolated in the air-conditioned comfort of a self-contained shopping center. Conde Street means sensible shopping at sensible prices and a lot of elbowing to get from point A to point B. The stores themselves are comfortable, air-conditioned, and spacious, and offer a wide variety of apparel, handicrafts, housewares, fabrics, toys, shoes and items both imported and domestic. Conde Street is narrow and brimming with street vendors, and has been converted into a pedestrian walkway. This is the traditional shopping street of Santo Domingo, and you will find some excellent buys here. If you are buying several items, most stores will give you a break on the price. A number of the larger houseware specialty shops like "Mary," the department stores like Puerta del Sol and Gran Via, and the shoe stores that you will find along Conde also have uptown branches at one of the various shopping centers mentioned.

Duarte Street. This is as far downtown as you are going to get. Best buys at bargain prices but total mayhem! One place of note if you are going to taxi down there is the brand new Plaza Lama, an all-inclusive department store with shoes, clothes, toys, handicrafts (nice selection), pharmacy, and photography department.

DUTY-FREE

The largest selection of duty-free items is at the principal International Airports. In Santo Domingo, however, the shops immediately behind the Atarazana and the shops at Centro de los Heroes have the same facilities and price list as the airport shops. Keep in mind that purchases must be made in U.S. currency, and delivery is made to you at the airport before boarding your flight. There is a good selection of watches, cameras, fine silver, and jewelry, but the big sellers are liquor, cigarettes, and perfume.

MODERN SHOPPING PLAZAS

SANTO DOMINGO

There are several, and they are reminiscent of what you would see in any modern shopping center in North America. The difference is that there is more emphasis on handicrafts. The arcades are spacious, air-conditioned, and offer ample parking facilities. The shopping centers are comfortable, clean, and expensive. One point to keep in mind, whether you are shopping at one of these arcades or along the downtown shopping district, is that most shops close at midday and reopen at about 2:30 or 3 p.m.

Plaza Naco. Located on Tiradentes Avenue, it offers two levels of department stores, houseware specialty shops, small boutiques, hair-styling salons, sporting goods and apparel shops, shoe stores, jewelry stores, toy stores, a video shop, and several casual eateries. Watch for the pizza place at the entrance! Keep in mind that many of the boutiques at Plaza Naco also do custom orders. In many instances, custom clothing is only slightly more expensive than off the rack. You will see a lot of fine quality work in linen. The variety and excellent quality of children's clothing makes handmade baby clothing a top selling item at Plaza Naco.

Centro Comercial Nacional. At the intersection of Abraham Lincoln and 27th of February Avenues, it is one of Santo Domingo's most modern and spacious supermarket facilities. It has a small commercial center which offers a few specialty shops, shoe stores and small department stores for ladies', men's, and children's apparel. Make a stop at the bakery section of the supermarket, and don't miss the flower market located in the supermarket's parking lot.

Plaza Lincoln. Across from Centro Nacional, this new mall specializes in very fine boutiques and home accessory shops which are top of the line and high-priced.

Galerias Comerciales. On 27th of February Avenue, just a few doors down from Plaza Criolla, this center offers two levels of small shops ranging from furnishings for the home to sportswear, fabric, and bed and bath linen. It also houses the charming Café Galeria for a sampling of art together with some tasty light meals.

Plaza Central. There are a number of other commercial plazas on the principal avenues, but none as ambitious in scope as the Plaza Central at the intersection of 27th of February and Winston Churchill Avenues. Popularly known as the ''golden apple,'' the center is one of the largest in the Caribbean. Its consists of three levels of which the first two are used for shops and the third for fast food restaurants, a movie theater, and sport facilities. The second phase of the project calls for an apart-hotel and casino complex, with the 25th floor designed as a gymnasium with a sauna and swimming pool area. It was completed in November 1987.

Street scene in Old Santo Domingo

UNUSUAL ITEMS

SANTO DOMINGO

One shop you definitely do not want to miss while in Santo Domingo is **Tu Espacio**—which translates as "Your Space"—at 102 Cervantes Street. Go out behind the Sheraton, cross Independence Avenue, walk two blocks—you will pass the beautiful manor which houses the Ossaye workshop, also well worth a visit—and spot a little corner house with a carved bird perched above a small, brightly painted birdhouse advertising the shop. Tu Espacio offers antiques, art, handicrafts, and other odds and ends. What they have done is to furnish every room in the house with furniture and accessories, all of which are for sale. The selection is beautiful and the displays imaginative. You will find antiques mixed in with modern pieces, baskets, pottery, ceramics, whimsical handpainted trees carved and designed by Rafael Morla, handpainted plates and canvases by Albuquerque, a beautiful collection of music boxes and jewelry boxes, cushions, lithographs, sculpture, everything put together with considerable flair. Don't miss the bathroom menagerie and the doll closet. It is a fun place to visit and should definitely be included in your shopping itinerary.

No one will ever believe me when I tell them that one of the best places for a selection of interesting gift items is one of the local hardware stores! **La Ferreteria Americana** has plenty of pots and pans, garden hoses, and paint brushes to sell you, but they also have a gift section that rivals many in the city. It is both imaginative and surprising in its selection of local and imported items. Here you will find Italian pewter trays and brass accessories from Taiwan, fine crystal and silver, attractive dinner china from Sri Lanka and the Philippines, and an ample selection of imaginative handicrafts from local artisans. There are some lovely handpainted wood boxes and picture frames made in crushed shell and bull horn. In ceramics, you'll find the traditional Lime dolls that are by now very identifiable favorites. These dolls are "working dolls," usually portraying vendors, carrying baskets of fruit or flowers, or with Dominican women at their work. They have a universal quality and are faceless. It seems this is an attempt to give Dominican woman an "everywoman" quality since the ethnic mix in the country doesn't really allow one defined "type" to represent the whole. These faceless beauties are very popular gift items, and are found in many of the leading gift shops for an average of 30 to 40 *pesos*. Sabor, S.A. also creates some very sensual ceramic beauties and the Americana carries an ample selection. Omixam, M.M. is another producer of ceramic figures, each an original. Americana offers a line of their "follies" girls, and these ceramic originals can run between 100 and 200 *pesos*.

Another hardware and department store that offers a beautiful selection of housewares and crafts is **Casa Hache** on John F. Kennedy Avenue. Everything from candlesticks and baskets to teapots and fine glassware is artfully displayed in the front section of the store.

El Gallo on Romulo Betancourt Avenue (the prolongation of Bolívar Avenue between Abraham Lincoln and Winston Churchill Avenues) is another favorite for housewares, Italian and German china, crystal, and gift items. You can also try Casa Virginia at Centro Comercial Nacional and both Mary and Alfonso, located at Plaza Naco. These are mostly for imported items and are more highly-priced. El Gallo, however, still has enough range for all budgets, and you can pick up gift items from anywhere between 15 *pesos* and several hundred *pesos*. El Gallo and Casa Hache both have main branches in Santiago, as well as their branches in Santo Domingo. Take note of their baskets, a beautiful assortment in a variety of weaves and colors.

On the second floor of Plaza Naco, you'll find **Triana** for a lovely selection of handpainted ceramic plates, vases, coffee and tea services, candlesticks, and fruit bowls. Some of the crafts are local, but many are imported from Spain and Central America. If you are after handpainted pottery and ceramic items that are 100 percent Dominican and original in design, then you must visit **Marialejos** downtown at 53 Nouel Street, parallel to Conde Street. They carry wonderful lamps, ashtrays, vases, and other crafts. You can actually select your own design from their portfolio and have it done in distinctive original colors. Their selections range from 10 to 300 *pesos* and the work you see is exclusively theirs.

Cenadarte (Centro Nacional de Artesania) is a government-sponsored and operated handicraft institute which exhibits and sells the crafts of local students and artisans. To get there, follow Tiradentes Avenue past Plaza Naco, then cross John F. Kennedy Avenue, proceed to the Office of Public Works and make a left turn. Cenadarte is the second building, at the corner of Calle San Cristobal. It is not one of the more accessible craft centers in town, but it will be well worth the trouble. The workshops of the institute train artisans in the skills for leather crafts, macrame, weaving, ceramics, glazed clay pottery, wood furniture, jewelry, and handbags. The prices in the shop on the premises are quite reasonable. The giftshop and workshops are open from 8 a.m. to 2 p.m.

MAI (Mujeres Aplicadas a la Industria), on Las Mercedes Street at the corner of Duarte Street, is within walking distance of the heart of the colonial section. Las Mercedes Street is easily recognized by the anchor leaning against the Museo de las Casas Reales at the corner of Las Damas Street. This project, which translates as Women Applied to Industry, consists of a series of microindustries throughout the country, in both rural and urban centers. They are all under MAI's direction regarding design, quality control, marketing, and administration. The brainchild of one of the Dominican Republic's most outstanding artists, painter Ada Balcazar, MAI offers woven bedspreads, area rugs in bright colors, cushions, wall-hangings, dolls, sportswear, T-shirts, placemats, table linen, greeting cards, Christmas decorations, carnival masks, and other gift items at "giveaway" prices. Hand-painted *pareos* are 50 *pesos*, dolls 15 *pesos*, colorful rugs around 200 *pesos*, and gift items for as little as 2 *pesos*. One unforgettable section of the showroom is the cotton and linen sportswear in tropical designs with a "peasant" look. These were made by Italian designers commissioned to design a special line specially for MAI under a program sponsored by the Bank for Interamerican Development (BID). You'll discover everything from gold jewelry to woven hammocks here. The center also handles special orders for individuals and wholesalers.

For those interested in handicrafts from other Latin American countries as well as those of Dominican trademark, be sure to visit **Artessa** on Roberto Pastoriza Street. Here you'll find handicrafts from Mexico, Peru, Panama, Guatemala, Honduras, and Haiti. These include jewelry boxes, woven belts, inlaid mosaic tables, miniature dolls handpainted by Ruth Op Den Bosch from Santiago, and crystal figurines that are sure to keep you in the business of browsing for hours.

Nuebo is an exciting little shop located across the side street from Plaza Naco, at 36 Fantino Falco Street. It is stocked with lovely frames, pottery, handpainted bird modules, Haitian cushions, imaginative wall hangings and striking mahogany furniture, enameled in bright colors. Also look for the handpainted birds of Laura Pezzotti.

Habitat, at the elegant Plaza Lincoln shopping center (located on Abraham Lincoln Avenue near 27th of February Avenue intersection) offers a fine selection of exclusive handicrafts designed for this very select store. The designs are very modern, ranging from gold leaf apples to exotic birds. Plaza Lincoln has a number of high-priced boutiques.

Plaza Criolla boasts several shops specializing in items for the home, including everything from picture frames and decorative boxes to chess sets and the beautiful mother of pearl craft of Maria Teresa Ramos.

FURNITURE

SANTO DOMINGO, SANTIAGO, AND PUERTO PLATA

Craftsmanship in the Dominican Republic has reached very high standards, particularly in the production of wood, wicker, and rattan furniture, much of which is currently exported. There are a number of fine furniture stores and workshops in Santo Domingo, Santiago and Puerto Plata. **Alfonso's** at Plaza Naco has its own craftsmen producing the store's exclusive designs under their mobleart trademark. **Palacios** at 81 Jose de Jesus Ravelo Street has been a name in furniture production for generations.

Von features original designs in mahogany which are very modern and highly finished. The showroom is at 503 27th of February Avenue. They also have their factory in the Industrial Free Zone of Herrera, near Herrera Airport.

Ambiente Decoraciones, located at the corner of Independencia and Doctor Delgado Avenues, is a great place to shop for furniture at budget prices. They have a large selection of handpainted cushions, mirrors, birds, decorative boxes, and small easy-to-travel gift items. In addition to the pieces on display, they can make furniture to your specifications.

La Nueva Dimension is a high-priced but beautiful furniture shop at 79 Gustavo Mejia Ricart Street in Naco. In this same category is **Hipopotamo**, located at 31 Max Enrique Urena Street. Also stop at the **Bonsai** furniture boutique, just a few doors from Nuebo on Fantino Falco Street, which is the side street that runs along the left side, as you face the entrance, of Plaza Naco.

D'Arquin at Plaza Paraiso is a newcomer specializing in clean lines, simplicity, and style in furniture designed for compact spaces and uncomplicated lifestyles.

Wicker and rattan furniture are exceptionally well made in the Dominican Republic although prices are high. There seems to be a great deal of emphasis on the Victorian or on the Sidney Greenstreet variety of peacock chairs and chaises lounges.

Domus is the place to go for world-class furnishings. The stock carried in their present location is unquestionably the finest in the country. Here you will find the names Stendig, Artifort, Knoll, Sherle Wagner, Roche Bobois, and many other of the finest names in the business. The owners of this showroom clearly understand and appreciate the word "classical" when it comes to interior design and furnishings.

At first, one might be taken aback to see such wonderful items when most offered are not nearly so grand. After talking with the owner it soon becomes apparent that they travel the world searching for the finest. Much of the stock comes from Italy, but many countries are represented.

Soon, they will move to a new location of 20,000 square feet. That is very large for this type of operation. They state that *Architectural Digest* would be proud to illustrate a showroom of the quality they are planning.

Artesania Rattan located on the ground level of the San Carlos building at Romulo Betancourt Avenue (prolongation Bolivár Avenue), has a definite oriental flavor to its designs. The store offers many home accessories at reasonable prices in addition to furniture. Of particular interest are the lovely woven placemats, baskets, and chests. Their factory is located in Santiago on Carretera Duarte, kilometer 4–1/2.

Gonzalez Muebles on 27th of February Avenue at the corner of 30 de Marzo Avenue has a huge selection of wicker and rattan furniture and accessories for the home.

Delgados is another major producer and exporter of wicker and rattan furniture. Their showroom is conveniently located at 58 Maximo Gomez Avenue, around the corner from the U.S. Consulate.

Casa Bibely on Conde Street offers two levels full of beautifully designed wicker and rattan furniture and accessories. They can also show you their catalogue for special orders from their factory.

Hogar del Mimbre at 1424 prolongation Bolivar is a necessary stop if this style of furniture interests you. They have an ample selection and good prices.

Along this same avenue at number 2056, you will find **Sauce**. They happen to have a branch in Puerto Plata at the Plaza Comercial Luis Ginebra (near the stadium) which is convenient to the Playa Dorada Resort. Again, they handle exports.

Rattan Y Decoraciones has a very fine selection of beautiful designs in Avenue Luperón's industrial zone. They handle both individual and large export orders.

Rattan Industrial is yet another well-known exporter of wicker and rattan furniture, located in the Alma Rosa section of Santo Domingo at 136 Calle Costa Rica.

The list goes on, but those mentioned are among the principal furniture manufacturers in the country.

OTHER ITEMS

ACCESSORIES

Putting aside the fact that all the major hotel and resort facilities have some lovely gift shops and boutiques, there are a number of shops that can satisfy specific needs during your stay, or where you can pick up some good buys at good prices. One place you may want to visit while in Santo Domingo is the workshop of Maria del Carmen Ossaye at 52 Cervantes Street. Cervantes is the street that is directly opposite the rear exit to the Sheraton Hotel parking lot, on the Independencia Avenue side. It's a short walk from there to this lovely old manor house, where the workshop is located on the ground level. The Ossaye name is synonymous with beautifully designed and crafted accessories, for the home and for you. Her handpainted mahogany handbags are one of the most original gift items you can carry home with you. The designs range from floral pastels to striking geometrics. Many of the finer boutiques carry these purses, but you can visit her workshop directly. Her handbags are sometimes found in fine stores in the United States for three times the cost. An original Ossaye purse bought here can range anywhere from 85 to 150 *pesos*. They are exquisitely done and you will probably want a suitcase full of them! The workshop doesn't have a sign, but you can't miss the house once you pass the Dominicana Supermarket because it occupies the entire next block. The workshop also offers a selection of furniture and some lovely "valenciana" guitars crafted by Ossaye's husband, Dario Arias.

Bouganvilia, at Altos de Chavon, features fine Dominican handicrafts, particularly ceramics, silkscreen, and embroidery. **Macramé Chavon** has wonderful handbags, belts, and other fashion accessories. **Rancier Boutique** on Duarte Street in Puerto Plata is a "micro" department store featuring Dominican-made accessories for men, women, and children.

FABRIC

Although a good deal of the fabric found here is imported from the United States, you will find an ample selection of fabrics brought in from both Europe and the Far East, as well as the linens and cottons produced locally. Conde Street in Santo Domingo is a good place to browse for fabric. The prices are reasonable and there seems to be a fabric store on every corner! You will see names like Flomar, Palacio, Gran Via, Gonzalez Ramos, and La Opera. Novia de Villa on Lope de Vega also offers a large selection of fine fabrics, with many imported from Europe. Certainly one of the best wholesalers of fabric here, who also sell directly to the public, is Almacenes Doble A. They have a downtown store right off of Conde Street at 19 de Marzo Street, and a less hectic branch store located at 103 prolongation Mexico Street. They have a wonderful selection of fine fabrics at very fair prices. Manikin, at Galerias Comerciales on 27th of February Avenue, is a small fabric boutique, select and expensive, as is the Mundo Modas fabric store at Plaza Lincoln. Many of the boutiques in town also have a selection of fabrics for you to choose from if you want to order something custom-made.

MEN'S APPAREL AND CUSTOM-MADE CLOTHING FOR MEN

La Coruña at 804 Winston Churchill Avenue, just a few blocks from 27th of February Avenue, is a high-quality, high-priced establishment. They are some of the best tailors in town and the selection of fabrics includes fine English cashmere. Take into account that no matter what it costs, it will still be much more reasonable than custom-made clothing in the United States, Canada, or Europe.

Ciprian is a more accessible and equally fine establishment located on the second floor of Plaza Naco. Here you can order custom tailoring of shirts, and sport shirts known as *chacabanas* which are worn over trousers, blazers, and suits. They have an ample selection of linens, blends, and cashmere. A three-piece suit will run just over US$150 and that is made-to-order in your choice of fabric. Ladies might consider having a tailored suit made here in a variety of summer fabrics.

Cavalieri at 18 Lope de Vega Avenue is a smart new shop for menswear from dresswear to casual.

Solo Para Hombre is a menswear specialty shop recently opened at 1560 Betancourt Avenue at the prolongation of Bolivar Avenue.

Sunny is another shop to consider for menswear, mostly off the rack and very modern. It's one block from the Merengue Hotel. On your way to Plaza Naco, make a left turn on Roberto Pastoriza Street and it is right there at no. 152. Almost their entire stock is made in their own workshop.

LADIES' APPAREL AND CUSTOM-MADE CLOTHING FOR WOMEN

It was a known fact some time back that the ready-to-wear clothes available in the Dominican Republic were imported by the local boutiques, mostly from the U.S., and consequently were very high in price. Not so anymore. A great deal of clothing is being produced right here, and the prices are reasonable. Almost every important boutique has its own seamstresses producing most of the outfits in their own workshop.

Mercy Jaquez is an up-and-coming young Dominican designer who has her own boutique across from Nacional supermarket on Abraham Lincoln Avenue. In addition to buying off the rack, you can have something made to order.

Cachet Boutique on the second level of Plaza Naco is another that will handle custom orders in addition to their off-the-rack selections for both men and women.

Mi Boutique on Independencia Avenue—next door to the Salon Rosita at the corner of Pasteur Avenue—offers plenty of flair, a lovely selection of fabrics, and a workshop right on the premises. They also have some nice ready-to-wear items, and there is special emphasis on eveningwear in their own designs at very reasonable prices.

Vielka, who often has showings at the Embassy Club in the Hotel El Embajador, is a little out of the way but worth the trip. She has a boutique line off the rack, much of it designed and made in her own shop. Her boutique and workshop are at 101 Nicolas Urena Street, corner of Charles Sumner Street in Los Prados.

Mimosa. If linen is your thing, head for this shop around the corner from Plaza Naco at 59 Fantino Falco Street. The blouses are works of art. You can have something made to order in their fine selection of fabrics and designs.

Ready-made and designer clothing are easily available at many of the finer boutiques in the city. At Plaza Naco, for example, you'll find **Abraxas** and **Maria Cristina Boutique** (Cacharel, Charles Jourdan, Rafael, and Rizo's), and at Centro Comercial Nacional, there is the **Casa Virginia** boutique, a very youthful shop with some very attractive fashion accessories!

Patapoof at Plaza Criolla is a unique shop for swimwear, Danskins, beautiful handpainted *pareos*, shorts, T-shirts both long and short, and anything that spells tropics and beach. They also have a number of skin care sun products, rich in aloe and moisturizers.

Babette Butti boutique located at Galeria Comercial on 27th of February Avenue, is another stop for ladies' clothing, belts, jewelry, and other accessories.

La Pavilion Boutique at Plaza Lincoln is at the top of the list for imported designer clothes and fine Italian shoes and sandals.

Ocasion on Pasteur Street, corner of Bolívar Avenue, offers a nice selection of cotton, silk, and linen dresses.

Europa at 71 Gustavo Mejia Ricart Street offers a good selection from casual cottons to dressier eveningwear in silks and satins.

Natacha is a wonderful store for lingerie and hand embroidered nightgowns. It is located at 30 Carlos Sanchez y Sanchez Street, at the corner of Lope de Vega Avenue. Also look for their very fine infant clothing, all handmade in the Dominican Republic.

For larger sizes in ladies' clothes, **La Dama Elegante** is located at 47-A Manuel de Js. Troncoso Street, and specializes in large sizes and maternity clothes. While in the tropics, white linen and cotton have a special appeal. Stop into **D'Sport** on the corner of Alma Mater and 27th of February Avenue for an attractive selection of sportswear. Another good and convenient place for ready-to-wear and a nice selection of accessories and handicrafts is **Jaez Boutique** in the Sheraton Hotel shopping arcade leading up to the main door.

CASA DE CAMPO

The Oscar de la Renta boutique line is carried at Altos de Chavon by Freya, who also has the Freya Boutique of Santo Domingo across the avenue from Plaza Naco at 3 Tiradentes Avenue. Here they specialize in linen apparel.

CHILDREN'S AND INFANT APPAREL

Some of the best buys are in clothing for children. Generally speaking, they are meticulously made and prices are excellent.

Bebelandia on Conde Street in Santo Domingo, has a selection for infants and children in linen and cotton. **La Casa de los Niños** at 35 Gustavo Mejia Ricart Street is another store exclusively for children's wear and toys. Original designs for children can be found at **Gabriela** at 323 Romulo Betancourt Avenue (prolongation Bolivar Avenue). Plaza Naco has a number of children's and infantwear boutiques. Look into **Babex** and **El Rinconcito** on the second level.

JEWELRY, LEATHER, AND OTHER ITEMS

Jewelry. There are a number of fine jewelers on Conde Street. One excellent choice is DiCarlo, which has a tradition of responsible craftsmanship. Here you can have a favorite stone set in gold or silver, or select from their tasteful display of fine jewelry. Seiko at Centro Comercial Nacional carries watches in addition to a fine selection of gold chains and other jewelry, including the Mallorca pearls imported from Spain. For native jewelry, amber, larimar, and black coral, the gift shops of La Atarazana are an excellent choice. Mr. Ortiz from Amber Tres will take the time to explain how you can tell real amber from a phony. His shop offers fair prices and a good selection of local gems, expertly crafted.

Altos de Chavon in La Romana has a fine jeweler, Everett Designs, that offers the gold escudos and silver pieces salvaged from eight sunken galleons, set in Dominican gold or silver. They also work in the native stones and coral. Coins from the same wrecks can also be purchased directly from the Museum of the Royal Houses (Casas Reales) in Santo Domingo's downtown colonial district, and set by one of the local jewelers. This is not only an attractive piece but also a valuable collector's item as many of these wrecks date back to the 17th and 18th centuries.

If you are interested in something rustic and very special, the ceramic jewelry designed by Carlos Despradel and Eduardo Fiallo can be found at art galleries and gift shops. Check at Nouveau Gallery on Independencia Avenue next door to the Sheraton Hotel, and also inquire at the Plaza Shop on Plazoleta de los Curas (the square behind the cathedral).

PUERTO PLATA

The town of Puerto Plata has some of the finest jewelry and accessories shops in the country. Harrison's specializes in gold jewelry, but you will find a large selection of work in coral, native stones, and antique crystal. The designs are originals and the prices are realistic. The shop itself is located in a wonderful old building with an enormous staircase leading up to a small gallery, three showrooms, and a friendly bar where you can sample a local beer. Harrison's is located at 14 John F. Kennedy Street. Also inquire about their new "Jungle Jungle" location.

Puerto Plata is full of gift shops that carry a large assortment of the native amber and larimar. One that we recommend is Macaluso at 32

Duarte Street, where the native crafts and jewelry are plentiful and the prices are fair. A visit to the Tourist Bazaar is highly recommended, not only for its fine gift shop but also for the Amber Museum located on the second floor. Another place for stones is the Grand Factory Gift Shop at 23 Duarte Street and 27 John F. Kennedy Street. Enjoy a free tour of their workshop and watch amber and larimar being set in Dominican gold and silver by their craftsmen. Puerto Plata's Centro Artesanal, located at 3 John F. Kennedy Street in a remodeled warehouse is certainly worth a visit. They are designing attractive jewelry and setting native stones, such as amber, larimar, black coral, and jasper in gold and silver. You will see the students working on the premises, learning all aspects of faceting, modular design, and insetting. The students' work is on exhibit and is all for sale at very reasonable prices. Other items there on sale include a large variety of dolls and toys which are all handmade, chess sets, domino sets, a large selection of gift items, and toy train sets carved of native wood.

The resort hotels all have fine boutiques, many of which carry some of the same handicrafts and accessories already mentioned in addition to locally-made clothing, with a strong emphasis on beachwear and sportswear.

Handpainted dresses, blouses, and T-shirts can be found at Norma Monte Silverio's Puerto Plata workshop at no. 20 on the Malecon (seafront avenue). Many of the local boutiques also carry her creative work.

Rancier Boutique has a nice selection of ladies casual apparel made locally. Also carries some fine quality underwear.

La Plaza shopping mall has recently opened to house the Terrabus terminal, a casual eatery for hamburgers, ice cream and sandwiches, and a number of interesting small shops. One for Mexican clothes and handicrafts is of special note. Plaza Los Messones at the corner of Beller and Separacion Streets, houses an ice cream parlor and three small shops, one of which specializes in antiques.

If you are in Sosúa, Coconuts Boutique is of special interest for ladies' casual clothes.

Leather Accessories. In downtown Puerto Plata, your best place for leather is the Centro Artesanal where you can buy directly from the artisan. The selection is appealing although the craftsmanship is rustic. Offers mostly purses, schoolbags, belts, sandals, leather frames, and boxes.

Santo Domingo's Planarte is under the direction of the Dominican Development Foundation and offers much the same selection of leather handicrafts as the Centro Artesanal of Puerto Plata. You will find Planarte on Calle Las Damas, adjacent to the fortress compound.

Anyone interested in fine leather work should visit the Dpiel workshop at 405 Santiago Street in the capital, or look for the Dpiel name in fine boutiques throughout the city. Briefcases, ladies handbags, wallets, folders, credit card holders, and related accessories all crafted in genuine leather are available. These items are not inexpensive but are top quality and well worth the price.

Luggage. If you've gone shop silly and need an extra piece to carry home the goods, stop at La Maleta on February 27th Avenue (just a block in from the Abraham Lincoln intersection) in Santo Domingo. Here you will find a fine selection of luggage, garment bags, attaché cases, travel totes, and other fine leather accessories carrying the Dpiel trademark. Much of the luggage is imported, however, and this is reflected in the prices.

Rocking Chairs. It may seem a little peculiar to go from leather accessories and luggage to a discussion of rocking chairs, but many visitors consider this a priority item on the shopping list. Many gift shops in both Santo Domingo and Puerto Plata offer a fine selection and they come boxed for easy traveling. Rocking chairs are traditionally great for thinking, relaxing, and pampering a bad back! The Dominican rocker made a name for itself in the Kennedy years, when the famous Kennedy rocking chair became a familiar sight as it was known to be a presidential favorite.

Macaluso's in Puerto Plata will take phone orders and deliver the rocker to your hotel. Many of the resort shops carry them as well and they are always available at the old marketplace in downtown Puerto Plata. Dominicans have a preoccupation with things Victorian, and this is evidenced in the popularity of the Victorian-design rocking chairs known as the ''Maria Teresa'' style. This and the ''Kennedy'' rocking chair are the two big sellers, preferably in mahogany. The Modelo Market in Santo Domingo, and the gift shops located on Conde Street, La Atarazana in the colonial sector, and the uptown Plaza Criolla all carry a selection of rocking chairs.

Mink and Other Furs. Granted, this is not what usually comes to mind when shopping in the tropics, but it is interesting to point out that one of the largest fur coat manufacturers in the world is located in the Puerto Plata Industrial Free Zone. Mink America will see you by appointment (586–4396) and will show you quality mink and Norwegian fox coats at about half the U.S. market retail price. They handle custom orders and there's no duty to pay, since they deliver to you at your point of departure.

Saddles. English, Spanish, and Western riding saddles, holsters, belts, and handbags are available at Juan Francisco de los Santos workshop, a tiny hole of a place not far from the Gran Parada on the road to Sosúa (10 km.). Taking home a saddle may not be your idea of souvenir shopping, but the artisan sells a variety of leather items, all hand-tooled and at very reasonable prices. He will also do special orders for you. His workshop has no sign, but is located on the right by the fork of the road as you head towards Sosúa. We first learned of this out of the way workshop through *The Santo Domingo News* and found the trek out there worthwhile.

Stained Glass. Extremely creative stained glass gift items, mirrors with stained glass frames, wall modules, tiffany lamps, and glass engravings are found at Arte Vitral located at 151 Hatuey Street in Piantini sector of Santo Domingo.

ART GALLERIES AND RESTORATION

Both Haiti and the Dominican Republic are known for their richness and abundance of art. The Dominican Republic has a number of outstanding artists: Ada Balcacer, Guillo Perez, Leon Bosch, Dario Suro, Clara Ledesma, Candido Bido, Justo Susana (the naif painter of the Dominican Republic), Oviedo, Andujar, and Azar, among others.

Works by all the great Dominican painters can be viewed at any number of prestigious galleries throughout Santo Domingo. Many of the galleries are easily accessible to the major hotels in the city. Gallery Nader on La Atarazana is an essential stop for art lovers in the colonial city. The gallery is situated in a colonial landmark building, complete with Spanish patio. It holds a representative collection of the finest artists from both sides of the island. Don Roberto Nader is usually on hand for advice and consultation. George Nader has his own gallery on Gustavo Mejia Ricart Street, an easy walk from Plaza Naco. George's is located at number 49. The Centro de Arte Nouveau is a progressive gallery located on Independencia Avenue, just outside the Sheraton Hotel (rear parking lot exit and to the right). This one is a favorite for established masters as well as works by young artists new to the art scene. In addition to regular exhibits (weekly) they have an excellent framing business with a beautiful assortment of locally crafted frames. The Arawak Gallery is another accessible and well-known establishment on Pasteur Street. In addition to paintings, they usually have a selection of prints and lithographs. Galeria de Arte Sebelén, located at 209 Hostos Avenue, is another important gallery.

Sometimes it is possible to go straight to the artist in cases where his gallery or *taller* (workshop) are open to the public. For art lovers a stop on the agenda should be the Centro de Arte Cándido Bido at 5 Dr. Baez Street in a lovely old Dominican house in the heart of Gascue. The wonderful thing about the Bido center is that you always see a lot of activity: his school, special exhibits, and an impressive array of gift items to select from including his beautiful handpainted ceramic plates, birds, his brightly colored canvases, limited edition lithographs, as well as the reproduction of his work on greeting cards. Bido's work is an explosion of vibrant color. Look for the warm sun colors and the deep "Bido blue" that has become his signature. Bido is one of the most acclaimed Dominican painters of our day.

Guillo Perez at 302 Hatuey Street, just west of Winston Churchill Avenue, also has a gallery and workshop. He is usually there at his flamboyant best! Gallery Paiewonsky on 260 Espaillat Street features modern Dominican artists, and the proprietor is bilingual and helpful.

Arte Espanol has its original gallery at 466 Avenue Mella and has since opened at 339 27th of February Avenue, at Abraham Lincoln and 27th of February Avenues. It is one of the largest gallery and framing establishments in Latin America with framing services guaranteed in 24 hours for a fraction of stateside prices, and a huge selection of locally crafted frames. Galeria El Greco at 16 Tiradentes Avenue has an excellent selection of works by Dominican artists.

In **Sosúa**, a gallery to visit is the Viva Art Gallery in the Batey section of town, located at Calle Alejo Martinez. Here you will find works by a number of Dominican artists on exhibit, as well as works by foreign artists now residing in the Dominican Republic.

A Word on Restoration. A number of galleries also handle restoration work. One of the best restorers in the city is Eduardo Fiallo, who studied restoration of canvases in Italy. He can be contacted through Centro de Arte Nouveau. Another team of restorers who can work on anything from canvases to old photographs are Victorio & Pichardo at Calle 3, no. 2, Alfimar, km. 7–1/2, carretera Sanchez (532–6379).

SPORTING ITEMS

If you forgot your tennis racket or your jogging shoes, don't worry. Santo Domingo has a number of shops specializing in all the equipment and clothing you might need. Remember too that the resort facilities in Puerto Plata and La Romana's Casa de Campo have Pro

Shops for their Tennis and Golf facilities where you can buy or rent what you need. Among the better-known shops for athletic equipment and accessories are El Molino at Plaza Naco, Casa del los Cuadritos, conveniently located at Galerias Comerciales, Luis Lugo at Plaza Criolla, and Galvans Sport Shop at Plaza International on the prolongation of Independencia Avenue, km. 9–1/2, carretera Sanchez.

THE PERFECT PUP

Dog lovers rejoice! The Dominican Republic has some excellent breeding and training facilities. If you are interested in the purchase of a pedigree pup, it can run you upwards of 400 *pesos*. The breeds most easily found here are Doberman, German Shepherd, Cocker Spaniel, Poodle, and the irrepressible Irish Setters! There are a number of highly recommended veterinary facilities that can steer you in the right direction. The Dr. Peguero Clinic and Pet Shop on 27th of February Avenue and the Dr. Pineyro Clinic just off Winston Churchill Avenue opposite Centro Comercial El Paraiso are two of the most reputable. On your itinerary include a visit to Servican, a hotel and training center for dogs at Plaza Flor on Lope de Vega Avenue (just behind Carabela). Servican's Dr. Jose Raul Nova is a breeder of champion German Shepherds. He can put you in contact with other breeders and tell you what you need to know for the purchase and export of your dog. Servican offers short-term training program for pets in basic obedience, attack, and exhibition. These programs are reasonably priced and compliment their pet hotel and veterinary facilities.

Chapter 9

DAY AND NIGHT
IN THE DOMINICAN REPUBLIC:
RECREATION AND
ENTERTAINMENT

SPORTS

GOLF COURSES

There are four principal golf courses in the Dominican Republic. The Country Club in Santo Domingo has a traditional golf course which, although for members only, can be available through arrangement with your hotel. Inquire at the activities office or with the social director of the hotel.

Casa de Campo at La Romana has two outstanding courses. Both are 18-hole championship courses designed by Pete Dye. Golf pro Victor Elis is the man you want to talk to here. The "Dientes de Perro" (teeth of the dog) course is a 6,774-yard course with seven spectacular shoreside holes. As a coastal course, it is very windy and requires great control. It has been the site for the World Amateur Golf Team Championships (1974). The second course stretches inland and is known as the "Links." This course has narrow fairways, ferocious rough (take plenty of golf balls), and requires great accuracy. Green fees for Dientes de Perro are 120 *pesos* per person, including the use of a golf cart. The green fees for the Links run 90 *pesos* per person, also with the use of a golf cart. The use of a caddy is optional. Costs are 6 *pesos* per person for 18 holes. If your game is a bit rusty, lessons are offered at 30 *pesos* for half an hour. The pro shop rents everything you need except shoes. They have a good selection of clubs. Casa de Campo offers an all-inclusive golf package for a minimum three-night stay which includes accommodations, breakfast, all taxes, green fees, and cart. Inquire when making your reservations.

Another exceptional golf course is the 18-hole championship course at Playa Dorada designed by Robert Trent Jones. The pro here is Joe Rivera. The course is very windy. All greens are guarded by sandtraps and most fairways also have sandtraps. It is a remarkably subtle course. Lessons are available with Mr. Rivera for 25 *pesos* per half hour. In keeping with the reasonable rates charged by Playa Dorada facilities, green fees are only 25 *pesos* for nine holes and 40 *pesos* for 18 holes. The use of a caddy is compulsory and the charge is 6 *pesos* for nine holes and 10 *pesos* for 18 holes. The golf cart is an additional 20 *pesos* for nine holes and 30 *pesos* for 18 holes. Eurotel Playa Dorada plans to hold an annual International Golf Open in addition to local tournaments, both in coordination with the Dominican Golf Association. There are attractive club houses at both Playa Dorada and Casa de Campo, with all the feel of an exclusive country club!

TENNIS

All the major hotel properties in Santo Domingo, Playa Dorada, Casa de Campo, and all the coastal resorts have tennis courts, the majority of which are clay. They all have resident tennis pros and lessons will range between 50 and 80 *pesos* an hour. Most tennis shops have equipment for rent, but it is a good idea to bring tennis balls. There are sport supply shops in Santo Domingo where these can be purchased. You will have to reserve well in advance for late afternoon time slots. Avoid the midday sun, it's too hot to be healthy. Fees run from 8 to 10 *pesos* per hour. Most of the hotel facilities have night lights. The Marlboro Cup is the big international tournament to look for in November. Inquire at your hotel's activities desk or with your pro.

POLO AT CASA DE CAMPO

The most ancient game played with stick and ball, polo is the precursor of hockey, golf, and cricket. The game is played with four players on each team, on the same operating principle as hockey or soccer. A match lasts about an hour and is divided into periods of play known as *chukkars* (or *chukkers*) with ponies changed at intervals. Earliest records indicate that polo originated in Persia, from where it was taken to Constantinople and eastwards to Tibet, China, and Japan and then on to Manipur from China. It flourished in India during the Mogul dynasty. In ancient cultures, heads literally "rolled" in the polo games, as the heads of the enemy were sometimes substituted for the ball! By 1859, the first European Polo Club was founded, and the Calcutta Polo Club was formed by 1860. Who would have thought that less than a century later, the son of the Maharajah of Jodpur would be preparing the foundations for what is today a major center for polo in the hemisphere!

Casa de Campo spreads over 7,000 acres and encompasses all that would be expected of a playground for the privileged. This world-class Caribbean resort is ten times as large as Monte Carlo! Today, thanks to the driving force and creative efforts of the Maharajah Jabar Singh, Casa de Campo boasts what many regard as the world's most complete polo facilities. These include two 300-yard polo fields and two fields for stick and ball practice. The stables have over 400 horses of which, in addition to those that are privately-owned, there are 100 riding horses and over 100 polo horses for hire. The property's Equestrian Center, featuring the Dude Ranch and Polo facilities, serves itself from over 2,000 horses available at the nearby breeding farm.

Brigadier Arthur Douglas-Nugent, a former British Cavalry Officer, takes charge of all polo events and instruction at the resort. Maharajah Jabar Singh died in 1986. His son, whose name is also Jabar, is the present director of all sporting activities at Casa de Campo, not an easy task considering the amount of competitive sport that takes place at the resort. In addition to polo, there are frequent golf, tennis, sailing, and fishing tournaments, in addition to the day-to-day supervision of all sports facilities. Although each division has its pro, Jabar must oversee the entire operation. Jabar admits his sports are polo and golf. He explains that the polo facilities at Casa de Campo are unique in that they comprise the most complete club in the world. Most clubs only have about 20 or 25 polo ponies for hire. Since about 5 or 6 horses are used in an average game, this means players visiting from outside the country must bring their own horses at substantial cost and risk. Not so at Casa de Campo. This is the only club in the world where the player can come and find everything: "You can come with your helmet and mallot and nothing else!," says Jabar. Players are tested for handicap and then given a stable full of horses from which to select. Everything they need in order to play is there, ready and waiting. Polo lessons are available for those at beginner level for as little as US$30 an hour.

If everything needed for polo is so accessible at Casa de Campo, why then has it always been regarded as a game exclusively for the very rich? For one thing, the facilities available at Casa de Campo are not the usual fare. If a potential player were to keep his own horses, he would need a fair number as they are changed at frequent intervals during a match. Each polo horse costs from US$10,000 to $15,000, or more. Between veterinary care, stables, grooms, feed, and related expenses, the figure for upkeep would be around a quarter of a million dollars. Galloping over fresh green lawns and experiencing the exhiliration of the "most noble sport" is available to many, only because the facilities at Casa de Campo are so exceptional. Jabar points out that it takes about two years to prepare a polo horse: one year of specialized training and one year to thoroughly teach them the game. It is a sport where the horse and player become one, moving in perfect harmony.

In addition to running the school and polo clinics, Brigadier Douglas-Nugent organizes yearly tournaments. These are held as frequently as four times a year. The most important of these is dedicated to the memory of Jabar's father: the 1st Maharajah Jabar Singh tournament, which was amply covered in the May 1987 issue of *Polo International* magazine. Teams in attendance at this first tournament represented some of the best international clubs. Teams from Argentina, Colombia, Venezuela, the United States, and the Dominican Republic competed. Jabar played with the Dominican team. The tournament is a fitting tribute to a man who was the greatest promoter of polo in this country.

The story of Jabar's father is an interesting one. He left India at the end of the dynasty, to live and play polo in Europe. With a handicap of nine, he was one of a handful of élite players in the world. During the mid–1950s in Europe, he met the world-famous Dominican playboy, Porfirio Rubirosa who, according to the American press in those days, put the Dominican Republic on the map! Rubirosa convinced this extraordinary polo champion to return with him to the Dominican Republic to set up a polo club there. The Trujillo regime was in its heyday and the dictator was supportive of the project from the outset. Trujillo was an avid fan of quality horsemanship and had a passion for the breeding of horses.

Jabar Senior brought specialized trainers and horses, structured and organized a team that in time was to include some outstanding players. This included the dictator's son, Ramfis, who is said to have been an exceptional polo player of considerable natural ability.

Jabar, the younger, was born to a Dominican mother, Dona Mireya de Singh, who currently lives in Casa de Campo. After Trujillo's fall, the family decided to move back to Europe and took up residence in Spain, where Jabar was educated and where he grew up with his love of polo.

When Casa de Campo took off in the early 1970's, Charles Bluhdorn invited them back. The challenge of directing polo activities as well as the breeding and training of the horses was sufficient motivation to come "home" once more. For the last 14 years, the family has been an intrinsic part of the evolution of Casa de Campo.

Jabar and his wife, Gindy—whose father was a Gulf and Western executive—were married at Casa de Campo in the family villa. Believing that Casa de Campo is a community and a home to many residents, they miss it whenever they are away for any length of time. Their eldest child was "the first baby of Altos de Chavon" and their two children now have the opportunity to grow up in a place of remarkable natural beauty which combines healthy outdoor life with the activities of a thriving cultural community.

The contribution made by Jabar Senior goes beyond what has already been mentioned. He had his own ideas about the ideal polo horse for this country.

Before World War I, English- and Irish-bred ponies were considered highly desirable in Europe. In India, it was the Arabian horse. Argentina, Australia, and New Zealand also had great demand for their thoroughbred polo horses. In the United States, Texas and Wyoming were recognized for excellent breeding.

For the climate and conditions in the Dominican Republic, a sturdy horse was required. The Singh solution was to cross an English thoroughbred stud with an American quarterhorse or a Dominican mare. The result is a stronger horse of considerable endurance.

As Casa de Campo, Jabar Singh and the Brigadier prepare for the 2nd Maharajah Jabar Singh International Tournament scheduled for early 1988, there is optimism that teams from Spain, England, France, and possibly Germany or Italy will be participating in this major world event.

Whether as a spectator, enjoying the game of kings on the most spectacular fields of the Caribbean, or as a participant eager to test one's skill, Polo at Casa de Campo is always an event.

HORSEBACK RIDING

In Santo Domingo, there is an International Riding Club (tel. (809) 533–6321) and the National Horseback Riding School (tel. (809) 682–5482).

OTHER HORSE ACTIVITIES AND INFORMATION

The Dominican Republic is also known for the breeding of fine Paso Fino horses. In fact, Colombia, Venezuela, Puerto Rico, the United States, and the Dominican Republic are the forerunners in efforts to produce the finest in Paso Fino horses. Paso Fino horses are not new to the Dominican Republic. The first of these fine horses were warrior horses known as *ambladura* or amblar horses. They first galloped onto the Dominican stage in the days of colonial conquest, as early as 1493. They were originally brought from Spain to Santo Domingo on Columbus' second trip. According to the *Encyclopedia of Dominican Horses* written by Emilio Rodriguez Demorizi, Columbus opened the first horse trail for riding on American land and was among the first men to go horseback riding on Dominican soil. Eventually, after the need for conquest and fighting diminished and riding for pleasure or travel purposes took priority, the Paso Fino appeared.

The first Paso Fino competition in the Dominican Republic took place in 1944. These beauties, with their regular rhythmic gait and their light gracefulness, are actively bred in the country by a number of established ranches. Public enthusiasm seems to increase every year, and horse shows and competitions are held yearly, both at La

Romana and at the summer competition of Paso Finos on the lawns of the Santo Domingo Hotel. The Dominican Republic boasts two principal associations: Asociación Dominicana de Paso Fino (ADO-PASO) and the Federación de Dueños y Criadores de Caballos de Paso Fino.

DEEP SEA FISHING

For a detailed account of angling in Dominican waters, see Jaak Rannik's article on fishing in the Dominican Republic below. You can fish for dorados, dolphins (the fish, not the mammal), marlin, barracudas (you'll see plenty at Punta Rucia), sharks, and bonitos in Santo Domingo, Boca Chica, Bocca de Yma (20 miles east of La Romana), La Romana, and Samana. Ask the activities director at your hotel or resort. Boca de Yma is the sport fishing capital of the Dominican Republic, and has been the site of many important international fishing tournaments. River fishing for snook and tarpon (mouth of the river) is also available at Boca de Yma, La Romana, Samana, and the northern coast. Flatboats with guides can be rented at these locations for about 35 *pesos* for a half-day.

A SPECIAL REPORT:
FISHING IN THE DOMINICAN REPUBLIC
by Jaak E. Rannick

Many veteran anglers from all over the globe have begun to discover the world-class fishing in the waters around the Dominican Republic. Most of the attention is attracted by offshore species which are abundant at different times of the year, although respectable-sized snook and tarpon are taken in the river mouths and coastal estuaries, and an exciting new bass fishery is beginning to develop in the many man-made lakes and dam reservoirs.

Blue marlin, dolphin, wahoo, and bonito are caught year-round, but generally speaking, the peak fishing months are from January to June. Sport fishing in the Dominican Republic has evolved over the past twenty years to a highly developed stage, with numerous anglers from this country traveling abroad and competing successfully in world events such as the International Light Tackle Tournament Association's World Cup. Coincidentally, in 1987 the ILTTA was hosted by the Club Nautico of Santo Domingo in the waters off Cabeza de Toro on the Atlantic side of the island.

Numerous world records have been broken in the Dominican Republic, and records for dolphin in the 30-lb., 50-lb., and all-tackle line classes have been held at different times by anglers fishing the waters just south of Boca Chica. It is not unusual to hook bull dolphin in the 50- to 60-lb. size and a number of larger ones are boated every year. An annual dolphin tournament is hosted by the Club Nautico in Boca Chica every spring, using 16- and 20-lb. line, and you haven't lived until you land a 60-pounder on light tackle!

Blue marlin are found in Dominican waters year-round, although most years on the southern coast they seem more numerous in June and again in October, while on the northern coast the run is better from August to October. Blue marlin here are usually taken off the 100-fathom curve and deeper, unlike white marlin and sails, which seem to prefer shallower water. Most local anglers still troll large mullet on a wire leader for blue marlin, but artificials are starting to come into their own, with more and more fish falling for the occasional Kona Head, Soft Head, or "Yap." To my knowledge, nobody here has tried trolling a live bonito Hawaiian-style, but it should be successful as large blues can sometimes be seen feeding on schools of juvenile bonito in the late winter and early spring.

Most blues caught here are on the small side, 150–250 lbs. being the most common, but occasional "granders" have been reported. On February 16, 1980, the 50-lb. tackle world record for Atlantic Blue Marlin was set with an 830-pounder caught by Randall Lama fishing off San Pedro de Macoris in a 42-foot Hatteras. Lama's record still stands today.

White marlin also frequent Dominican waters in large numbers from March through June, although occasional catches have been reported as early as December. They are most numerous in the waters from Punta Espada to Punta Macao, where during the height of the season catches of seven or eight marlin a day for a single boat are not unheard of. White marlin in the Dominican Republic run from under 50 to about 120 pounds, with 50–60 being the normal. They are usually taken on 20-lb. tackle with fresh ballyhoo and a mono leader. Whites here are unusually finicky eaters and successful hookups don't necessarily follow a strike. On very light tackle, the locals use the Venezuelan technique of a long drop-back and then aggressively backing the boat down on the fish before it can go deep.

The best white marlin fishing is out of Cabeza de Toro, an idyllic barrier reef anchorage where the Club Náutico operates a fuel dock and minimal shore facilities. Both Club Med at Punta Cana and the Bavaro Beach Hotel are within a 15-minute drive, along with the international airport at Punta Cana.

Wahoo is found year-round in these waters, although surface trolling usually doesn't produce strikes, so most are taken with bally-hoo trolled with a 2-oz. sinker. Wahoo usually run between 50 and 70 pounds, and are often taken in schools together with dolphin wherever these congregate.

There really isn't a developed tuna fishery. The deep trenches just off the shelf on the northern coast should be good for bluefin as they pass by on their way to Cat Cay and Prince Edward Island each year, but this has yet to be explored sufficiently. Yellowfin tuna in 100–150 lbs. sizes are sometimes seen off the southern coast in the winter, while bonito, albacore, and skipjack make their appearance in large numbers every spring.

Some of our local anglers who experimented with drift fishing for swordfish at night were able to demonstrate that broadbill do exist in these waters, but apparently not in enough numbers to justify serious angling for them. Sailfish are caught, usually in 30 fathoms or less, all along the coastline, but are definitely less numerous than marlin. Local commercial fishermen have more success with live bait on handlines than do sport anglers using trolled baits, but live bait techniques as practiced in Florida have not yet come into widespread use. Kite fishing is still relatively unknown here.

Maybe it is because of the excellent trolling action offshore, but deep bottom fishing hasn't become overly popular here. There are excellent deep reefs with good-sized snapper and grouper, but these are normally taken by commercial fishermen using headlines. Reefs like these would undoubtedly be productive for deep jigging and chumming in the daytime as well, although traditionally what bottom fishing there is is done at night using a 12-volt light bulb lowered into the depths as a fish attraction device.

Since weather conditions offshore are often demanding, local boats are as good as any in the world, with many well-equipped Hatteras and Bertrams in the 40- to 55-foot range. Some of these, as well as smaller boats, are available for charter, mostly through the hotels. As a rule, captains and mates are normally excellent fishermen, equally good with the gaff as with the bait needle. A number of captains also mix a mean drink to cap off an exhausting day in the chair.

SCUBADIVING AND SNORKELING

Scubadiving. When a country is referred to as "a real dive," the implications are not always the most complimentary. In the case of the Dominican Republic, the expression is most often used in a positive sense by avid divers from all parts of the world. This is one island country that offers a special place in the sea as well as in the sun for all who visit. There are dives ideal for inexperienced divers, as well as more challenging ones geared to expert divers.

An easy way to find out about great diving opportunities in the Dominican Republic is to visit Mundo Submarino (Submarine World) at 99 Gustavo Mejia Ricart Street (tel. (809) 566–0340). There is always someone on hand who speaks English. In addition to selling and renting equipment for divers, they also organize classes and offer P.A.D.I. instruction for everyone from beginner level on. Mundo Submarino also organizes excursions to the best diving sites around the city.

For those who prefer to remain in the vicinity of the capital, and not sink too far below surface, there are excellent locations near the International Airport of Las Americas such as La Caleta. At La Caleta, one has the options of either shallow or deep diving with clear visibility and fertile underwater life. The aquatic scenery here is truly spectacular and La Caleta has long been a favorite with local divers. Those who have more time to travel around the coast might enjoy a dive on the northern coastal area of Las Terrenas, known for its remarkable reefs and underwater caves. Bayahibe, near La Romana on the southern coast, is within easy reach from Casa de Campo. It provides an outstanding beach as well as excellent dives in an underwater world filled with vibrant coral reef formations. Nearby Palenque is another choice location for dives. Watch for wrecks of warships.

Few realize that some of the Dominican Republic's most outstanding museums for historical artifacts are underwater! Dominican territorial waters hold some 400 shipwrecks, mostly along the coral reefs of coastal waters. Some of these ships wrecked in storms, while other wrecks are part of the island's military history throughout the centuries, owing their fate to famous battles fought during attempted invasions. See the section on Colonial Santo Domingo for information on galleon wrecks in coastal waters. Tight security is kept on these wrecks during salvage operations. You can see much of the treasure retrieved from Samana Bay and from the Silver Shoals at the Museum of the Royal Houses.

Many divers have been richly rewarded by exploring the ancient graves of our coastal seas. In another section of this book, we discuss the precious finds in Samana Bay and along the Silver Shoals of the north coast. The salvaging of the galleons *Conde de Tolosa* and *Guadeloupe* in Samana and the Silver Bank's *Concepción,* have yielded valuable artifacts, treasure, gold, silver, jewelry, pottery, hundreds of pearls and diamonds and tons of silver coins from these 17th- and 18th-century wrecks. The touring diver is not likely to surface with a find of equal note, but there are plenty of more recent sites where parts of skeletal ships and cannons and anchors can produce a tingling sensation and the thrill of discovery!

Karin Galliano, a fellow journalist, helped interview some noted divers who know about Dominican waters to provide tips on choice diving locations and trade underwater tales. These experts are in agreement about one thing, and that is that the Dominican Republic is a "jackpot" for those willing to take the plunge.

Tracy Bowden, captain of the salvage vessel *Hickory*, started diving and exploring here in 1957. He currently holds a salvage contract with the Dominican government and is responsible for the outstanding finds of the "quicksilver" galleons of Samana Bay. As an expert diver with decades of experience and a specialist in underwater archaeological recovery, he was asked to answer some questions:

Q: What are your two favorite diving locations in the Dominican Republic and why?

A: Number one is the breakwater at the mouth of the Haina River due to the mixture of fresh and salt water, along with the deep drop off. The area is very prolific with sea life. Samana Bay, which is like a time capsule, slowly releasing fascinating historical data to modern man, is my other choice.

Q: Of all your scuba diving adventures in this country, which do you consider to be the most memorable?

A: On Friday, March 23, 1979, at approximately 3:30 p.m., I was diving on the Spanish galleon *Tolosa* in Samana Bay. I happened to be alone on the wreck. The rest of the crew were topside cleaning artifacts or resting, while I was working with an airlift at the base of a submarine sandbank. Now and then, the airlift would trigger a small avalanche down the side of the bank, which is normal. What was not at all normal was that the bank suddenly began to vibrate and the avalanches grew bigger; before I knew what hit me, I was swimming in sand! There was an eerie sort of pulsing in the water that picked up speed and volume, until it sounded like a distant machine gun. It occurred to me briefly that a large ship must be passing overhead somewhere nearby. Then I realized that just was not possible. No ship of any size could make it through the maze of coral reefs, otherwise, I wouldn't be down there salvaging a shipwrecked galleon!

By that time, I had begun to vibrate all over, not just my eardrums, but my entire body. I glanced at my air pressure gauge, thinking my tank might have ruptured, but I had plenty of air. Just as I began to think of heading for the surface, the vibration stopped, as suddenly as it had started. I worked a while longer, and then called it a day. When later I headed for surface and came alongside the *Hickory*, I was told by a crew member that the radio had announced that we had experienced an earthquake! Not having had any previous experience to relate this to, it just would never have occurred to me this was the explanation. The earthquake had taken place in the Mona Passage, between the Dominican Republic and Puerto Rico. I had felt and heard the telegraphed vibrations of an underwater earthquake.

Pedro Borrell, Architect and Director of the Commission for Underwater Archaeological Salvage:

Q: Which are your two favorite diving locations?

A: Number one is the Silver Bank near Puerto Plata because it is one of the largest coral reefs in the entire Caribbean and, curiously, one of the least known. The coral formations are unique and the waters are incredibly transparent.

Number two would be Beata Island which is surrounded by unexplored reefs abundant with marine life. There are caves where thousands of marine organisms live. Interestingly, these do not flee from man, since this coast of the Dominican Republic has been little explored by fishermen and divers.

As to an unforgettable diving experience, there was one in 50 feet of water, while trying to photograph some Isabelita fish. I didn't notice the presence of a nine-foot long tiger shark resting on the sand. I almost tripped over it. After the first fright, my buddy and I began to take shots of the school of fish. It happened that both flashes went off simultaneously, this awoke the shark from its lethargy. Initially, it swam off slowly into the distance, but after apparently reconsidering, it turned and steered itself quickly towards us. We hid between some coral formations as best we could waiting to see what he had in store for us. Fortunately, after giving us a bad scare, he went back to sleep on the ocean floor. We had the opportunity to take some pictures and then, since we had hardly any air left in our tanks, we returned to the surface delighted that we had photographed such a fascinating experience.

Eddy Rodriguez, student of Veterinary Medicine at UNPHU, taught diving as a certified instructor in Florida and in the Dominican Republic:

Q: Is there any one experience you would single out for our readers?

A: There were six of us aboard two small skiffs sailing out for a night dive at La Caleta. As I looked ahead, it was difficult to distinguish sky from sea, it was so dark. The churning from the small outboards was beginning to produce a tense feeling in me similar to what an athlete feels just prior to a competition. I was anxious to arrive at the site, and yet a little wary as it was the first night dive for many in the group.

At the dive site, everyone geared up and rolled back into the night. As I descended through the blackness, all I could see were the five glowing dots emitted from the safety lights on each diver. The ocean floor was at 60 feet. After settling on the bottom, we grouped into pairs and began exploring the coral heads in the area. I was at the rear of the group with my dive buddy, Charlie.

We had been wandering over the reef for about five minutes, when I decided to make a routine head count. As I turned to count Charlie, the beam from my underwater light focused on a huge jet of bubbles streaming towards the surface. It took me completely by surprise but one second didn't pass before I realized they were coming from his regulator. That degree of free flow usually means the diver is not receiving air. I raced towards him, banging on my tank and flashing the ''something wrong'' signal with my light, attracting everyone's attention.

Between the frantic ascent on my buddy's part and the bubbles gushing from his regulator, his safety light was obscured from my vision and I lost sight of him. Well aware of his limited diving experience, the danger of air embolism raced through my mind. I made an all-out attempt to stop his crazed ascent, but he was so scared a barracuda couldn't have caught him.

I found Charlie on surface, coughing, gasping, and mumbling in a state of shock. We checked him over thoroughly and, gratefully, he was uninjured. After correcting his problem, we returned to the dive. After all, who's afraid of the dark?

Q: What would you choose as a favorite diving location?

A: Definitely La Caleta, because of its easy to reach location, greatly diversified diving and excellent boatmen. I'd also say Samana because it is the ultimate adventure.

SCUBADIVING

Patrick J. Greene has had over 15 years diving experience in places such as the Canal Zone, Mexico, Belize, Bay Islands, Honduras, Curaçao, and the Florida Keys:

Q: Name two favorite diving locations.

A: My first choice would also be La Caleta for excellent visibility and the great variety of fish, coral, and sponges. Las Terrenas has nice caves with a surprising variety of fish, coral, and species of sponge.

Q: What about your most memorable experience?

A: Three friends and I were cruising at 80 feet off Bayahibe. We'd been examining basket sponges and tubular sponges. Out of the corner of my eye, I saw movement in the water. As I watched, a very large spotted eagle ray glided up to within 15 feet of us and proceeded to circle around, curious about these strange denizens with large yellow tanks on their backs. These rays are magnificent with white underneath and black on top with large gray spots. Our beauty had about a six-foot wing span and a long thin tail about seven feet long. After swimming back and forth for about 15 minutes carefully examining us, he made a stately departure.

Billy Fothergill, professional diver for Sea Quest International which handled the salvage operation of the *Concepción* in the Silver Bank under Burt Webber:

Q: Favorite diving location?

A: The Silver Bank, which is located about 85 miles northeast of Puerto Plata. It offers coral reefs that are full of life and some remarkable night diving experiences.

Q: Your most unforgettable diving experience?

A: The day was November 30, 1978, and it would go down in history. It was the day that a member of our diving team, Jim Nace turned over a ballast stone lying on the ocean floor and found a 17th-century silver coin from the Spanish galleon *Concepción* that sank there in 1641. I joined the crew late in the operation, so I hadn't suffered through weeks of fruitless search. I felt privileged to share in the ecstasy of the find.

After the excitement of finding the first silver coin, the divers split into two groups to comb the site for the rest of the treasure. My group happened to come across a wall of coral in a trench. I looked up and there was a huge hill of embedded silver coins. We were about 100 yards from the wreck site and, apparently, the bow area of the ship drifted away from the wreck site carrying with it thousands of silver reales until it was encrusted in this stretch of coral. This is one possible theory. I will never forget what it felt like to look up that wall of silver. Everywhere you looked there was nothing but silver.

I remember thinking that here I was, just a hillbilly commercial diver from Kentucky, right smack in the middle of the romance and adventure of the *Concepción* galleon.

Donna Smith is a psychometrist and teacher:

Q: Select your two favorite diving locations and explain your reasons for the choice.

A: An area I found off the Malecon, about two or three kilometers out. This is a little explored location, and there you find lobster and the biggest barracudas! Giant fissures, caves, and caverns in the coral formations make for some very interesting exploring.

I'd also say a wreck site in Palenque, where there is a French warship that sank in the 1800's. It has many large cannons, and an anchor visible at only thirty feet. After all, if shipwrecks are your thing, this is sure the right place to come.

OTHER AQUATIC SPORTS

It goes without saying that boating, swimming, and all water sports are part and parcel of your vacation at all the major beach resort hotel facilities and at Boca Chica, where you can find everything for rent from catamarans to jet skis. Casa de Campo's 52-foot schooner, the *Merengue*, offers daytrips to Catalina Island for sailing, swimming, snorkelin, and relaxing. Inquire at activities office.

JOGGING

There are two ideal places for your jogging rituals in Santo Domingo. The Olympic Center and stadium on 27th of February Avenue, across from the Lina Hotel, is ideally suited to this type of activity. The Mirador/Paseo de Los Indios behind the Embajador Hotel is a lovely park and avenue popular among joggers, dog walkers, and children.

GYMS AND EXERCISE FACILITIES

Most of the major resort properties have some type of fitness program, including aerobics classes, yoga, fully equipped gyms and as in the case of the new Jaragua and York Caribe, spas. Both the Lina and the Sheraton Hotels have excellent gym facilities for men and women, as well as saunas and massage. There are also a number of excellent gym facilities throughout the city of Santo Domingo, so that if your hotel does not have one, you still have a few options.

Club Body Health (27th of February Avenue, Santo Domingo; tel. (809) 565–5156) is certainly the most modern and complete facility in the city, offers Nautilus equipment for men and women. Classes include aerobics, jazz, and freedance. Sauna facilities and massage services are available on the premises.

If gyms are not for you, but you would like to catch a dance class or dance/exercise instruction that doesn't break your bankroll, try the dance workshop offered by **Taller Dansa Moderna** (Centro Comercial Paraiso on Winston Churchill Avenue; tel. (809) 567–8261, ext. 46). These jazz/modern/aerobic classes are offered by director Eduardo Villanueva and his assistants. Classes are small in number and inexpensive. Very rewarding classes are scheduled at several times during the day.

Condominiums at Playa Dorada

SPECTATORS ONLY

BASEBALL FEVER

Tourism, sugar, coffee, and rum may be the backbone of the Dominican economy, but they are not the only priorities for a people who are anxious for a chance at a winning hit. The Dominican Republic has for some time been heavily into the "cultivation" of another remarkable export: the Dominican baseball player. Right now, there are more Dominicans playing in the U.S. minor and major leagues combined than are supplied by any other Latin American country or any single state in the U.S.

Why the wealth of talent? For one thing, Dominicans of all educational and economic levels eat, live, and sleep baseball and have been indulging for years in a passion for the game which they admit is obsessive. The national pastime took root here in the early part of the century, during the American occupation, and went international when the Dominican champions encountered Puerto Rico in 1922. In the 1950's, Dominicans found their way into the big leagues and Dominican winter season baseball (from October to January) became a sort of scout paradise for the U.S. major league recruiters in search of talent.

"The Heart of the Latin Baseball Cradle," as the July 20, 1986 *Miami Herald* called it, the Dominican Republic has surpassed Puerto Rico in pure numbers. Twenty-five years ago, there were five Dominicans in major league baseball, twelve Cubans, and seven Puerto Ricans. Currently, more than a third of major league starting shortstops are Dominicans and seven major league shortstops are even from the same town, San Pedro de Macoris!

There is no doubt but that San Pedro is a Mecca for those who follow contemporary baseball. There are at present roughly 300 Dominicans in the minor and the major leagues in the United States, and half of them are from San Pedro de Macoris. Two of the greatest shortstops ever in the majors, Tony "Cabeza" Fernandez of the Toronto Blue Jays and Alfredo "the Magician" Griffin of the Oakland Athletics are from San Pedro. Alfredo Griffin was the American League Rookie of the Year in 1979, when he was with the Blue Jays. Fernandez had a splendid season in 1986 when he made only 13 errors to lead American League shortstops in fielding percentage (.983) and earn a Golden Glove. He also batted .310 with 25 stolen bases. His 213 hits were the most ever recorded by a shortstop.

They are not alone. There are over 70 shortstops from the Dominican Republic in organized baseball under contract to major league teams. The list headed by Fernandez and Griffin includes names like Rafael Santana for the New York Mets; Julio Franco for the Cleveland Indians: Mariano Duncan for the Los Angeles Dodgers; Rafael Belliard for the Pittsburgh Pirates; Jose Uribe for the San Francisco Giants; and Andres Thomas and Rafael Ramirez for the Atlanta Braves.

What is the secret recipe that has made San Pedro such a baseball landmark? The answer has a great deal to do with its neighboring sugar mill, the Consuelo. Almost all the great Dominican ball players have come from towns where sugar production was for decades at the center of the economy. For the most part they lived in poor communities (called a *batey*) of field workers. In most cases, their fathers worked at the mill while the children played ball in the open fields or in the alleys between their shanty houses. Towns like La Romana, Boca Chica, and San Pedro all shared the same characteristic: sugar production was the core of their existence. Every sugar mill had a baseball field, and as the sport developed a stronger following, many sugar mills sponsored their own teams.

The young boys who came out of these towns had lean muscular bodies from working in the fields or helping out at the mills and the warm climate meant that they could play all year. More than these conditions, the determining factor for many was the chance to get out of the *batey* and achieve the American Dream.

Today, children in these communities are given baseball gloves and brand new balls along with the opportunity to enter the camps sponsored by major league teams. About twenty major league U.S. teams invite prospects to these camps or baseball farms, as they are often called, every year after the Dominican winter ball season that extends from October through January. Players like Rico Carty, formerly of the Braves and Blue Jays and winner of the U.S. National League batting record in 1970 with his .366 average, can recall when life in the sugar production communities was not so hopeful and baseball was the only long shot on the horizon. Rico Carty and the Alou brothers, Jesus, Felipe, and Matty, are of a generation that remembers using discarded cement bags to shape gloves and sugarcane stalks for bats. For these legends of the sport, the only lifeline was a career in baseball. Children in the small villages of the interior still fashion their equipment with imagination: empty milk cartons for gloves, palm fronds for bats, and anything from a stone to an unripe orange for a ball. The only difference is that now they have the example of those who went before, and the American Dream is a much more tangible goal for them.

Over the years, more than 60 of the professional players who played in the U.S. began at the Consuelo Sugar Mill in San Pedro.

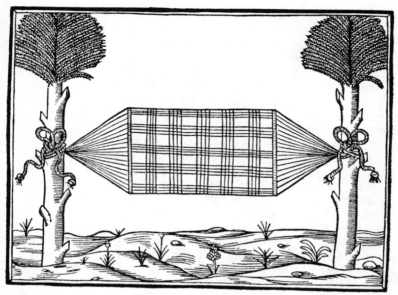

An Indian hammock, from a 16th-century print

Many of them, like Alfredo Griffin and Tony Fernandez, worked as ballboys at the local stadium or jumped the fence to see the games and learn what they could from the players. The fact that it has produced the greatest number of ballplayers of any town at any time in history has earned San Pedro de Macoris its place in the history of sports. When the stars come home after the major league season, they often coach at the baseball camps to guarantee that the Dominican Republic holds on to its deserved reputation as the "land of shortstops."

GREYHOUND RACING

This is a recent phenomenon in Santo Domingo. **El Coco Cano-drome** (tel. (809) 567–4461, 565–8333) is a modern facility equipped with a restaurant and bar. Watch those greyhounds run on Wednesday, Saturday and Sunday at 7:30 p.m. and Sunday at 4 p.m. Entrance fee is from 1 to 4 *pesos*.

COCKFIGHTING

Cockfighting pits gamecocks against each other who have been specially bred and trained to fight. Its origins can be found in the ancient civilizations of India, China, Persia, and other eastern cultures at least 1,000 years before Christ. By the fifth century B.C., the sport had been introduced to Greece. Themistocles, when leading his troops into combat with the Persians, is said to have spotted two cocks fighting by the side of the road and to have stopped his troops to view the courageous combat of the feathered gladiators.

After the victory of the Greeks against the Persians, cock-fighting caught on as a sport. On the chair of the high priest Dionysus in the Theater of Athens, there is a carved figure of Eros holding a gamecock about to fight. In Asia about 3,000 years ago, they used partridges and quail for lack of gamecocks. These gamebirds possess the attributes of natural fighters.

From Athens, the sport gradually spread throughout Europe and it was said that the best cocks were bred in Alexandria, Delos, and Rhodes. At first the Romans looked down on this ''Greek diversion,'' but by the first century A.D., they too were hooked by the gamble of it. From Rome, cockfighting spread north and, although greatly opposed by the Christian church, it became very popular in Britain, Germany, Spain, and the colonies.

During the time of Henry II, schoolboys in England took part in the sport with their schoolmasters directing the events. It was an immensely popular sport in Wales and in Scotland, where cockfights had been introduced in 1681. Occasionally the authorities would try to repress the sport, particularly during the Cromwell years, but the game survived despite these measures.

By the reign of Henry VIII, cockfighting had taken on the reputation of a game favored by the court. The King had a royal cockpit at Whitehall and this is where it started to be regarded as a royal diversion or ''pleasure of princes.'' James I and Charles II were also among its devotees and the position of ''King's Cockmaster'' became an official court appointment to preside over the pits at Whitehall.

In the early 17th century, the fighting cocks were matched to fight in pairs or in a variation called ''battle royal'' where a number of birds were simultaneously placed in the cockpit until all but one were killed or disabled. There was also a Welsh variation called the Welsh Main, in which eight pairs were matched and the survivors were then rematched until a final pair of victors remained and then these were brought together for a decisive match.

A cockfighting ring

There was a famous London cockpit at Westminster, as well as in Drury Lane and Birdcage Walk along St. James Park. Of all the English breeders, Joseph Gilliver was the most famous and the blood of his cocks is said to still run in the best breeds of America.

In Wales, however, the sport was practiced with surprising fervor. The games known as "the mains" were held in churchyards, and in many instances, they were held inside the church proper! Until the middle of the 19th century, the mains were frequently held in British schools. Parents were actually expected to contribute to the expenses of the annual main and this money came to be known as the cockpense. Cockfighting was ultimately banned by law in Britain in 1849, but not before it was introduced to the English colonies in North America.

In many of the North American colonies, the practice was frowned upon. Massachusetts was the first to forbid the sport by law in 1836. Today, laws for the prevention of cruelty to animals ban the sport in Canada and most of the United States, although it is still practiced privately, particularly where there are large Hispanic communities. Public pits are forbidden, but the games are still secretly held in many of the southern states.

Today, cockfights are still popular in Asian countries such as Thailand and the Philippines. They are widely prevalent in Hispanic cultures, where cockfighting can be traced to the time of the Spanish colonies. Although a substantial number of South American countries have banned cockfights, they are popular and legal throughout many of the Caribbean islands. In the Dominican Republic, it is a major league event. Here, the sport has many enthusiasts and dedicated breeders who stress pedigree and the blending or strains from the most courageous cocks.

Some of the most famous 20th-century strains are the Irish Gilders, Red Quills, Dominiques, Clairbornes, Baltimore Topnots, War Horses, Irish Grays, and in spite of the legal restriction on the sport, American-bred fighting cocks which are highly regarded and exported to centers where cockfighting is allowed.

Gamecocks are put in matches or bouts when they are between one and two years of age and between approximately three and nine pounds in weight. Before they are placed inside the pit, they are given extensive training. They do not need to be taught to fight, but they are trained in technique and the "art" of fighting, which is basically a form of martial arts for gamecocks! As part of this rigorous preparation, breeders exercise them greatly in order to develop muscles. They also have special diets of cornmeal, hard-boiled eggs, raw beef, and special feed. This diet of champions, is accompanied by a long list of methods to ensure that the prized cocks are groomed for the fight. They are massaged, for instance, with a mixture of alcohol and ammonia to toughen their skin, their wings are trimmed, and the comb cut to minimize the risk as a target for opposing fowl. The gamecocks are sometimes put in the pit at a measured distance from another cock because it results in stronger muscles when they strain to get at each other. After all this special training, the gamecocks receive actual fight training in the pit, with padded leather across their spurs. In ancient times, fighting spurs were usually made of silver, while today they are made of metal or horn. Sometimes, the natural spurs of another cock are slipped over the spurs of the fighter.

There are different rules applied to the tradition of the games. The ancient cultures allowed the gaming cocks to fight to the death, but modern rules allow the withdrawal of a badly injured cock. Other rules establish a time limit.

In contrast to the early history of the game, when the gamecock was revered and held a special place of honor even in death, in the Dominican Republic of today, many losers end up on the table for Sunday dinner! In the campos, cockfights are usually held in the open or in a rustic arena structure called the *gallera*. In the city, the facilities and the attitude towards the sport are far more sophisticated. The flurry of feathers and hysteria in the pit are matched by the excitement of the fans. The thrill is in the gamble; bets are placed even while the fight is in progress and odds are constantly changed.

There are occasions when the gamecock himself wants to call it quits. He lifts his hackle, the underside of which is trimmed with white feathers. This is the origin of the white feather as a symbol of cowardice. Throughout military history, ''showing the white feather'' was the ultimate disgrace.

The cockfighting community in the Dominican Republic is strong and growing stronger. Tourists are often surprised that it is not just a game for the rural communities. Fanatics and breeders in Santo Domingo include some very established members of the community, like the owner of the Naco Hotel, Mario Bonetti, whose trophies and mementos decorate the hotel coffee shop, Ramiro Espinola, an engineer, and Dr. Angel Contreras, one of the country's most highly regarded cardiologists. The princely game is a not-to-be-missed experience for those who want a taste of an unusual sport in the Dominican Republic.

NIGHTLIFE

CASINOS

At the time of this writing, Puerto Plata is in the process of giving birth to its first casino at the Puerto Plata Beach Resort in the town itself. (This casino opened in 1987.) This is an event which should stimulate Puerto Plata's nightlife considerably and which will be a welcome addition to the activities available for tourism in this area. As tiny a destination as Samana is, it offers a small casino facility at the Bahia Beach Resort (not operational at this time). Santiago also has a casino (until now the only one for the Cibao and the Puerto Plata region) at the Hotel Matum.

The major casino properties, however, are located in Santo Domingo. The capital is gradually developing a reputation for gaming in the Caribbean, made more attractive by the fact that you can play in either U.S. dollars or Dominican *pesos*, and be paid in the currency in which you play. Las Vegas-type games (craps, blackjack, roulette, baccarat) are offered by the capital's casinos. The exception is that there are no slot machines at the present time. In November 1988, a law to permit the operation of slot machines in casinos was under consideration by the National Congress and is expected to pass. Las Vegas rules and odds apply with small variation from casino to casino. Some are more liberal than others. Ask before you play. There is no trouble communicating, as the executive staff in most casinos is completely bilingual.

Bets vary from half a *peso* on roulette to 2,000 *pesos* on blackjack and 5 *pesos* to 1,000 *pesos* on craps. Limits depend on the individual casinos. The actual format of the casinos in Santo Domingo may vary from intimate eight table clubs to large international-style casinos of approximately 45 tables, as is the case with the new Jaragua. Casino hours are generally between 4 p.m. and 4 a.m., but there are variations.

CASINOS IN SANTO DOMINGO

THE MAUNALOA
Nightclub/Casino complex located at the ''Feria''
This one is very popular with local players and the style of the place is lively, with a noisy atmosphere.

THE NACO
at the Naco Hotel
The atmosphere is warm and friendly. Staff is attentive. Popular with regular local clientele.

EL EMBAJADOR CASINO
At the Embajador Hotel.
An old and established Santo Domingo Casino which is currently operated by Chinese.

THE OMNI CASINO
At the Sheraton Hotel (separate building)
A large and active casino popular with both tourists and locals.

THE LINA CASINO
At the Gran Hotel Lina.
Grandly decorated room with bright chandeliers and canvases by great island artists. The upstairs houses the Lina nightclub.

SAN GERONIMO
At the Hotel San Geronimo.
Very popular with Dominicans. Boisterous place; lots of fun if you want to get in with the locals. Usually the very last to close. Always busy.

JARAGUA
At the new Jaragua Hotel.
Very much in the tradition of Las Vegas: grand scale and flashy. Offers a large selection of games and activities. The biggest casino in the country at present. Brand new.

THE CONCORDE CASINO
At the Concorde Hotel.
Certainly the prettiest casino in Santo Domingo with its blue tones and its art deco glass panels. Located in the hotel lobby.

THE HISPANIOLA CASINO
At the Hispaniola Hotel.
The rebirth of a casino. The Hispaniola formerly had an attractive casino. They have now reactivated their license and the new facility is scheduled for a 1987 reopening. At this writing, its license has not yet been approved.

V CENTENARIO CASINO
At the new Centenario Hotel.
Scheduled for an early 1988 opening.

DISCOTHEQUES IN SANTO DOMINGO

Cover charges run between 5 and 15 *pesos*.

ALEXANDER'S
23 Pasteur Street
Attractive discothèque with a good blend of music from rock to reggae. Popular with very young crowd.

COLUMBUS/CLUB 60
60 Maximo Gomez Avenue
Lots of shimmer. Good atmosphere. Caters to young crowd.

BELLA BLUE
George Washington Avenue (next to Vesuvio's)
Sheer elegance by any standards. Dance under miniature blue lights or sit along mezzanine designed for comfort and conversation. Mid 30's and over feels right here.

OMNI DISCOTHEQUE
At the Sheraton Hotel
Located along the driveway leading up to the hotel lobby. Very well-designed with dancefloor that can be raised or lowered. Attractive mezzanine/bar, great sounds, and audiovisuals.

OPUS
Independencia Avenue
An attractive stone facade building houses this newcomer. Popular with a mixed crowd. Everything from rock to merengue and salsa rhythms.

NEON 2002
At the Hispaniola Hotel
It seems Neon is on its second generation of Dominican youth. It has always been a popular spot for disco, although the crowd gets younger. Attractive bar area.

In Puerto Plata

VIVALDI STUDIO
Hermanas Mirabal Street
Attractive discothèque with mezzanine dining overlooking the dance floor. Disco, merengue, salsa, and rock for a mixed crowd; everyone feels comfortable regardless of age.

LA LECHUZA (THE OWL)
Puerto Plata Beach Resort
A wise choice for disco and merengue rhythms or the perfect night-cap to a Puerto Plata evening.

NIGHTCLUBS

L'AZOTEA
Dominican Concorde Hotel
Santo Domingo
This is a rooftop nightclub decorated with a lot of style. Spacious and dimly-lit. A comfortable setting for drinks and dancing: merengue, boleros, salsa. Welcome to the Caribbean.

LAS PALMAS
Hotel Santo Domingo
Santo Domingo
A very elegant piano/bar/club. Live entertainment on weekends. The right place for a quiet drink, conversation and a spin around a small dance floor. Intimate and elegant.

PLAYA DORADA HOTEL
Puerto Plata
Their attractive disco is one of the most popular in the area.
But the news at this resort is their "La Copa" room which boasts a wide stage and seats 400 persons comfortably. Currently featuring "Latino '87," the only live revue at Playa Dorada.

PUBS

In Santo Domingo

DRAKE'S PUB
La Atarazana (colonial sector)
This has to head the list for a one-of-a-kind attraction. Housed in restored colonial building that could have well been the site of the first tavern in the New World...certainly there was one along this street which was the commercial hub of colonial days.

Lovingly restored by Gary Hampton and John Gillam. Remarkable establishment. Particularly nice on weekdays, when you beat the late crowd.

BLOODY MARY
La Atarazana (next door to Drake's)
Rustic and attractive. In addition to popular bar, they serve pizzas and light snacks. La Atarazana could well develop a "pub row" reputation.

RAFFLES
Hostos Avenue
Across from ruins of Hospital San Nicolas in the colonial sector.
Lovely graceful colonial home restored into attractive pub. Owner Gerd gives the place style and warmth. Good music and generous drinks.

BLUES BAR
George Washington Avenue
Attractive seafront establishment with outdoor terrace for enjoying the Caribbean setting and doing some people-watching. Neon lights welcome you to this modern and appealing bar and club. Popular happy hour between 5 and 8 p.m. with light jazz sounds.

CAFE ATLANTICO
Corner of Mexico and Abraham Lincoln Avenues
Very appealing and spacious bar/cafe establishment that caters to a young crowd. Excellent light meals and popular bar. Serves Mexican snacks during their happy hour.

DEMIAN'S CAFE CONCERT
Tiradentes Avenue, corner of Roberto Pastoriza Street
Live entertainment at this establishment with folklore shows starting at 10:30 p.m. on Wednesday, Thursday, and weekend.

MENTHE BAR
Independencia Avenue
Another popular bar/meeting place for locals as well as tourists. Located just a block east of the Sheraton's back entrance.

VILLAGE PUB
Hostos Avenue (next door to Raffles)
Lovely colonial house and garden overlooking the ruins of San Nicolas de Bari Hospital (the first hospital in the Americas).

IBIZA
Roberto Pastoriza Street, corner of Tiradentes Avenue
A favorite with Santo Domingo youth and the regular "drinking place" of the Prince of Spain when he and his mates are in port. Tropical, spacious, and attractive.

D'GOLDEN
Roberto Pastoriza Street (next door to Ibiza)
Another popular and very stylish bar.

In Puerto Plata

LOS PINOS
Hermanas Mirabal Street
This bar is attractive and spacious. Rustic decor and nautical maps. Very pretty mirror modular hangings over bar. Good drinks and friendly atmosphere. New ownership.

All the resort hotels at Playa Dorada have attractive piano bars.

In Sosúa

P.J.'S INTERNATIONAL
A pleasant establishment in the middle of Sosúa's popular restaurant row. Attractively rustic. Good drinks. Unpretentious and popular.

UNITED FRUIT COMPANY/LA ROCA

Very appealing dark wood paneled bar. Good place for mixing with Dominicans. Generous drinks and friendly conversation.

ADULT ENTERTAINMENT

The most widely known and advertised of the adult entertainment nightclubs in Santo Domingo is **Le Petit Chateau**. It has an attractive open seafront location on Autopista 30 de Mayo (there is not one cab driver breathing who does not know the exact location). The open tropical structure has a center dance floor surrounded by several tiers of small tables. The show is costumed and choreographed and there are elaborate buffets every night. Not all the ladies are performing on stage. Many are seated along the terrace, but they will not approach customers unless invited.

Number One is located in the elegant setting of the Embajador Gardens. It was formerly called Julissa but is under new management. This nightclub has very comfortable seating in a lounge atmosphere with the emphasis on discretion. There are live shows nightly.

MUSIC

Santo Domingo has one of the finest symphony orchestras currently performing in Latin America. The National Symphony Orchestra (OSN), under the direction of Maestro Carlos Piantini offers regular concert programs at the modern Teatro Nacional on Maximo Gomez Avenue. The Teatro is part of Santo Domingo's Plaza de la Cultura complex and has proven to be a grand and versatile theater. 1,600 spectators can sit in its principal hall and be assured perfect visibility from any vantage point. The stage has a height of 104 feet, a width of 237 feet, and a depth of 83 feett. As a result, it can easily accommodate symphonic programs as well as ballets and operas. The building also houses the Sala Ravelo, a small recital hall used for chamber music and recitals. This hall has an audience capacity of 170. The main hall has a system of modulated acoustics which utilizes the most advanced electronic equipment and carries sound to the furthest corner. Some of the greatest orchestras in the world have performed here, including the New York Philharmonic.

This theater is now the permanent home of the OSN. Their concert programs and schedules are available at box office or at Bellas Artes, the headquarters for the National Symphony Orchestra's administrative offices, at the corner of Maximo Gomez and Independencia Avenues. The OSN is made up of both Dominican and foreign musicians, and frequently has guest appearances by leading international soloists. The governing principle is that music has no nationality, and so Maestro Carlos Piantini has been able to bring together talent from all parts of the music world.

Piantini is himself an international figure in music. After a career as violinist with the New York Philharmonic, he made his conducting debut in 1969 with the New York Philharmonic at Lincoln Center, and has since conducted that symphony orchestra on several occasions. His career brought him home to the Dominican Republic, where he was Artistic Director of the National Theater in 1973. That inaugural season and the years which followed were certainly the most memorable. Companies like the New York City Ballet, the Harkness, and the Royal Danish danced on the Teatro stage; the London Chamber Orchestra and the New York Philharmonic played; and Metropolitan Opera stars like Gilda Cruz-Romo and Justino Diaz sang. In 1979, Piantini was appointed Associate Director of the Caracas Philharmonic Orchestra. Subsequent to this, he returned to Santo Domingo in 1984, to direct and develop the national orchestra into one of the best. He frequently travels as guest conductor to the United States and the music centers of Europe, but home is the Dominican Republic and his work with the OSN is an important part of Santo Domingo's cultural life.

Series tickets are available for the OSN concerts. Individual performance tickets may be purchased at the Teatro Nacional box office every morning. Ticket prices are a bargain as they rarely exceed 10 *pesos*. Season tickets go for as little as 98 *pesos* for 14 concerts. There are an average of four concert programs each month. The ticket office at the theater is open from 9:30 a.m. to 12 noon (tel. (809) 682–7255).

CULTURAL INSTITUTIONS

PALACIO DE BELLAS ARTES
Independencia Avenue, corner of Maximo Gomez Avenue
Santo Domingo
Tel. (809) 682–6384
Grand old building, now used as second recital hall for local and international performances. Also houses rehearsal facilities.

CASA DE FRANCIA
Calle Las Damas (Colonial sector)
Santo Domingo
Tel. (809) 685–0840

This cultural center is sponsored by the French Embassy in the Dominican Republic. They offer French films, art exhibits, and a variety of cultural programs in the French language throughout the year.

INSTITUTO CULTURAL DOMINICANO AMERICANO
21 Abraham Lincoln Avenue
Santo Domingo
Tel. (809) 533–4191

The Dominican-American Cultural Institute was founded in 1947 for the purpose of fostering cultural exchange and educational ties between the U.S. and the Dominican Republic. In addition to language classes, art exhibits, conferences, and films, the institute, during the administration of Mrs. Helen Hughes, inaugurated a beautiful cultural center and theater which schedules performances during the year. Call their cultural office for info.

CASA DE TEATRO
110 Avenue Arzobispo Merino (Colonial sector)
Tel. (809) 689-3430

This non-profit cultural center was founded in 1975 to promote Dominican art. Exhibits of paintings, sculpture, photography and other activities are held regularly, under the direction of Freddy Ginebra.

A grand home in Santo Domingo

Chapter 10

EDUCATIONAL OPPORTUNITIES

NURSERY SCHOOL AND PRE-SCHOOL

LUCY'S LAMB PRE-KINDERGARTEN
88 Gustavo Mejia Ricart Street
Santo Domingo
Tel. (809) 567-2553
Classes in English and activities for children 2 to 5 years old.

INSTITUTO CULTURAL DOMINICO AMERICANO
21 Abraham Lincoln Avenue
Santo Domingo
Tel. (809) 533-4191
English pre-school program complete with outdoor play, videotapes of Sesame Street, arts and crafts. Classes are in English.

MONTESSORI SCHOOL
Sosúa
Ages 2 to 5. Small multi-lingual classes. Monthly enrollment, outdoor activities.

PRIMARY AND SECONDARY SCHOOLS

Santo Domingo has excellent English language schools for children. They do not, however, have boarding facilities. Some do offer exchange programs; it is advisable to inquire directly. Three of the best known:

CAROL MORGAN SCHOOL
Sarasota Avenue
Santo Domingo
Tel. (809) 533-1765
Pre-kindergarten through grade 12. Fully accredited by the Southern Association of Schools in the United States. Standard U.S. textbooks in use.

COLEGIO LOS ANGELITOS/SAINT GEORGE SCHOOL
552 Abraham Lincoln Avenue
Santo Domingo
Tel. (809) 565-5433/567-4907
Pre-kindergarten through grade 12. Combined program of English and Spanish instruction. Excellent facilities.

ESCUELA CARIBE
Jeffrey Valerio, Director
Jarabacoa
Tel. (809) 574-2760
U.S. (800) 458-9127
An experience in education in beautiful natural surroundings.
Totally tutored academics mixed with field trips, getting back to
nature. Agricultural projects and work with mountain children as part
of learning experience. Special programs for underachievers. Co-ed
program (ages 12 to 17).

LANGUAGE SCHOOLS

Most of these operate monthly classes. Enrollment and classes paid
for in *pesos* are inexpensive.

ALIANZA FRANCESA
Centro de los Heroes
Santo Domingo
Tel. (809) 532-2935
French classes for children and adults. Bookstore and library.

APEC
55 Maximo Gomez Avenue
Santo Domingo
Tel. (809) 687-1000
Spanish, English, and French classes offered for children and adults.

INSTITUTO CULTURAL DOMINICO AMERICANO
21 Abraham Lincoln Avenue
Santo Domingo
Tel. (809) 533-4191
Spanish and English classes offered for children and adults. They
also can refer you to private tutors.

INSTITUTO SUPERIOR DE IDIOMAS
415 27 of February Avenue
Tel. (809) 688-5336
Several locations throughout the city. French, German, Italian, Por-
tuguese, and Spanish classes offered.

BALLET AND MODERN DANCE

ACADEMIA DE BALLET SANTO DOMINGO
402 Bolivár Avenue
Santo Domingo
Tel. (809) 685-6645
Ballet and modern dance at all levels for adults and children.

ACADEMIA DE BALLET JEANETTE LANTIGUA
298 27 of February Avenue
Santo Domingo
Tel. (809) 566-0553
Ballet and modern dance and dance exercise classes for adults and children.

MEDICAL SCHOOLS

A number of the medical schools of the Dominican Republic have a substantial enrollment of students from the United States. The obvious reason for this is that the cost is a fraction of the cost of medical training in the United States, with tuitions averaging US$5,000 to US$6,000 a year in the Dominican Republic. Among those in operation are the following:

UNIVERSIDAD MUNDIAL DOMINICANA (a branch of World University)
(Dominican World University)
1516 Romulo Betancourt Avenue
San Carlos Building
Tel. (809) 533-9039
The medical school is conducted entirely in English. The School is registered as an eligible institution at the Educational Commission for Foreign Medical Graduates and with the World Health Organization.

UNIVERSIDAD IBEROAMERICANA (UNIBE)
129 Avenida Francia
Santo Domingo
Tel. (809) 689-4111
Training in health sciences. Medical school offers classes in Spanish language. Popular with European students.

UNIVERSIDAD CENTRAL DEL ESTE
San Pedro de Macoris

Tel. (809) 529–3562
Major medical school with excellent modern facilities. Substantial enrollment of American students.

HOTEL MANAGEMENT SCHOOL

UNIVERSIDAD CATOLICA MADRE Y MAESTRA
(Catholic University Mother and Teacher)
Abraham Lincoln and Bolivár Avenues
Tel. (809) 567–5000
In addition to liberal arts and medical science program at its beautiful campus in Santiago, it operates a Department of Hotel Administration in conjunction with Cornell University's Hotel Administration School. The University of South Carolina at Columbia has an exchange program with Catholic University at its Santiago campus.

ART CLASSES

CENTRO DE ARTE CANDIDO BIDO
5 Dr. Baez Street
Santo Domingo
Tel. (809) 685–5310
Classes in drawing, watercolor, and oil painting for adults and children.

GALERIA DE ARTE MODERNO
Plaza de La Cultura
Santo Domingo
Tel. (809) 682–8280
Classes in painting, drawing, and art appreciation.

APEC
72 Maximo Gomez Avenue
Santo Domingo
Tel. (809) 687–8386
In addition to language classes, APEC offers instruction in painting, ceramics, and graphic illustration.

ALTOS DE CHAVON SCHOOL OF DESIGN
La Romana
An affiliate of Parson's School of Design, see also the section on Altos de Chavon/Casa de Campo. Classes are offered in English in all aspects of design and fashion illustration.

Chapter 11

INVESTMENT, THE ECONOMY, AND BUSINESS IN THE DOMINICAN REPUBLIC

ECONOMY AND INVESTMENT OPPORTUNITIES

As the largest representative democracy in the Caribbean, the Dominican Republic has a government structure that resembles that of the United States.

President Joaquin Balaguer leads a progressive administration which encourages a system of free enterprise and stimulates foreign investment, particularly in the areas of tourism, off- shore manufacturing, and agro-industry.

The Dominican Republic was one of the first Caribbean nations to qualify for benefits under the Caribbean Basin Initiative (CBI), a program started in 1982. The country's domestically produced exports qualify, under CBI, for preferential tariff treatment in North American markets. The CBI trade incentive aims at the elimination of U.S. duties on products imported from the Caribbean Basin for twelve years beginning January 1, 1984 (see below, "Caribbean Basin Initiative").

As a result of a number of incentive laws covering investment in tourism, agro-industry, and industry, foreign investors have found a favorable atmosphere in which to invest in these sectors of the Dominican economy.

There are currently over 300 companies engaged in foreign investment in the Dominican Republic, including multinationals, (industrial free zone) off-shore manufacturing companies, and joint ventures in the areas of tourism, agribusiness, and mining.

BUSINESS OPERATING CONDITIONS

The first step necessary for the serious consideration of new investment opportunities is to determine actual operating conditions and costs. The following sections present information regarding the major factors associated with doing business in the Dominican Republic. The IPC (Investment Promotion Council) has sought to provide information that is as accurate and up to date as possible. However, certain conditions—especially costs—will vary over time and in different locations and situations.

277

LABOR IN THE DOMINICAN REPUBLIC

GENERAL INFORMATION

The Dominican labor force is one of the country's greatest assets. The people are congenial, willing to work, and wish to work in harmony with employers. Workers are highly capable, and take their work seriously. Employee turnover is generally very low. The abundant and competitively-priced work force has been an important driving force behind the recent growing investor interest in the country. Salary levels and social benefits presently in effect are very competitive with other countries of the world, and this is why the country is enjoying a surge in foreign business investment.

In recent years the country has experienced a dramatic deterioration of profits from its sugar industry. This can be traced to a world-wide surplus of sugar. For most of the early years of this century, sugar produced the lion's share of foreign exchange. Now, many countries of the world have improved equipment and farming methods that have caused this unfortunate turn of events. The reduction in this source of foreign exchange has effected internal investments in other areas of industry adversely and that in turn has increased the numbers of unemployed. Although this results in difficulties for the economy as a whole, it bodes well for foreigners contemplating the possibility of doing business in the country. There is a great available labor pool of intelligent, interested, hard-working and readily trained workers. There are unskilled, semi-skilled, technical, and managerial personnel available. The trade union movement is in its infancy, having developed chiefly in the years following the death of Trujillo. A relatively high unemployment rate minimizes the union's impact.

The demand for skilled workers is growing faster than the demand for unskilled workers. As a result, the government and private enterprise recently formed the "Institute for Technical Training" to help alleviate shortages of skilled labor. A major problem is that a large number of the unemployed live in urban areas where the potential for improvement of their situation is limited. That is one reason that the government is dispersing the new Free Zones for manufacturing throughout the country.

LABOR STATISTICS

Population:	6,600,000
Labor force:	1,460,000
Organized labor:	175,000
Unemployment:	Approx. 28%
Literacy rate:	72%

The Dominican Republic has a large supply of unskilled, semi-skilled, and skilled labor. The major areas of employment are:

Industry:	19%
Agriculture:	8%
Services:	28%
Other:	45%

LABOR AND WAGE LEGISLATION

Dominican labor laws, codified during and just after the dictatorship of General Trujillo, have established a framework of basic rights and obligations of workers and employers. Labor unions and employers may create associations to negotiate on labor relations. A union can be created by 70 or more workers and three or more corporations may form an association of employers. A "Corporation Union" is formed by workers of a particular corporation. The worker no longer belongs to the union once he leaves the employ of the corporation. A "Trade Union" is formed by workers of a particular trade. An eight-hour workday is considered normal by law, and 44 hours constitutes a workweek. When those limits are exceeded, the employer must pay overtime. For up to 68 hours per week, employees must receive 130% of their regular pay. Employees who work on a piecework basis may not receive less than the minimum wage.

Overtime. An overtime rate of 30 percent of salary is paid Monday through Friday from 44 to 68 hours per week. The overtime rate for Saturday and holidays is 50 percent. On Sundays and for work over 68 hours per week, overtime amounts to 100 percent of base salary.

Holidays. There are eleven holidays per year.

Vacations. Employees with more than one year of continuous service are entitled to two weeks of paid vacation. Employees with more than six months of continuous service who are terminated through no fault of their own are entitled to a pro rata share of the base year rate.

Christmas bonus. Employees earning less than 200 *pesos* per month are entitled to a Christmas bonus each year equivalent to one month's salary, or 8.33% of their yearly earnings, whichever is greater.

Severance pay. Termination of work contracts is allowed for many reasons. In cases of termination for reasons other than cause, workers are entitled to severance payments computed according to the duration of employment. An employer who terminates the employment contract of employees with three or more months service must pay severance payments according to the following schedule.

LENGTH OF EMPLOYMENT   SEVERANCE PAY

3 to 6 months	5 days salary
6 to 11 months	10 days salary
12 to 23 months	39 days salary

24+ months: 15 days salary for each year of service up to a maximum of one year's salary.

The schedule does not apply to employers who have a legal justification for terminating an employee.

Average wages. The average hourly wage in industry is 3.25 *pesos*.

Probationary Period. During the first three months of employment, workers may be terminated without being paid termination benefits. During this period, workers may be paid 40% of the minimum wage.

Social Security. All employees earning less than 528 *pesos* per month (US$92) are eligible for Social Security. The Social Security tax is paid 7 percent by employers and 2.5 percent by employees.

LABOR ORGANIZATIONS

Organized labor in the Dominican Republic represents 12% of the labor force, or an estimated 204,000 workers (mostly in the agricultural sector). Labor has experienced great difficulty in expanding unionism due to the high rate of unemployment and underemployment in recent years. As a result, unions are financially weak and have a hard time sustaining extended strikes or bargaining ploys. In recent years, striking transport, health, and sugar workers were unable realize gains of any serious magnitude and attempts to gain broad general support met with limited success.

The two most powerful labor organizations are the General Union of Dominican Workers (UGTD) and the General Confederacion of Workers (CGT). Others are the Christian Democrat-oriented Autonomous Confederation of the Union Class (CASC) and the AIFLD-linked National Confederation of Dominican Workers (CNTD).

FOREIGN WORKERS

Foreign citizens may not represent more than 30% of the labor force in any enterprise. However, there are exceptions to the rule in cases in which the employees are part of management or where the local labor force does not have the required skills available.

SUMMARY

The future looks bright as far as foreign investment entities utilizing local Dominican labor are concerned. The fact that the country can be categorized as "developing" indicates that it will be some years before labor costs reach heights that lead to reduced competitiveness. Companies doing business in the Free Zones of the country are happy to report excellent productivity, good labor relations, and profitable operations.

NATURAL RESOURCES

The country abounds in gold and silver, ferronickel, bauxite, coal, tin, marble, salt, gypsum, and limestone. It is the second-largest gold producer in the Western hemisphere.

TRANSPORTATION AND COMMUNICATIONS

The Dominican Republic's transportation infrastructure provides an excellent operating relationship with the U.S. and Canadian marketplaces. Daily direct air service from Santo Domingo to New York, Miami, and San Juan is offered by American Airlines, Eastern, Pan American, and Dominicana. Service to and from the Dominican Republic is also provided by a number of European and Canadian airlines. All airlines provide both passenger and cargo services. U.S. citizens may enter the country without a passport or visa.

Santo Domingo and other major cities are served by modern port facilities. The Port of Haina, located just outside Santo Domingo, is one of the most modern container ports in the Caribbean, with a 2,600-foot long, 35-foot draft wharf, a new 40-ton container crane and a 60-acre container yard. Transportation to over 12 U.S. ports as well as to Canada, South America, Europe, and the Far East is available on a weekly basis. Major lines include Sea Land, Evergreen, CTMT, Navieras de Puerto Rico, and Hapag Lloyd. Other major commercial ports are located in La Romana and San Pedro de Macoris on the southern coast and Puerto Plata on the northern coast. The country's Industrial Free Zones are all located near a principal port.

Turning to telecommunications, direct international dialing is available in most parts of the country using the 809 area code and dialing as in the United States or Canada. WATS service is also available. Satellite transmissions offer reliable facsimile and data transmittal services. Most banks operate electronic banking locally and with U.S. and Canadian banking counterparts. Domestic telephone service is provided by Compania Dominicana de Telefonos (CODETEL), a wholly-owned subsidiary of GTE.

Courier services are provided by BIC PAC (Island Couriers, Alcazar Plaza, tel. 567–9547/49), representatives of Federal Express. They offer door-to-door delivery of documents anywhere in the world, with 24-hour service to and from the United States.

The Dominican Republic's 12,000-kilometer road network is considered among the best in the region. Most major cities and ports are linked by modern paved highways.

BUSINESS START-UP PROCEDURES

The steps required for establishing a new business are not complex, and basically involve registration with the Internal Revenue Department, the Ministry of Industry and Commerce, and the Dominican Chamber of Commerce. Manufacturing facilities require a certificate from the Industrial Registration office of the Ministry of Industry and Commerce. Investors are advised to obtain local legal counsel to carry out these steps as well as to form a corporation.

Firms or individuals interested in exporting must obtain an export license from the Dominican Export Promotion Center (CEDOPEX). To acquire a license, one must file an application identifying the business address, products to be exported, capital, bank references, and port to be used. The applicant must be accompanied by (1) the operating permit issued by the Internal Revenue Department; (2) a resident permit, in the case of a foreigner; (3) a history of previous export permits (if applicable); (4) a financial statement; (5) a list of stockholders, addresses, quantity and value of shares owned by each person; (6) a power of attorney issued to the person representing the firm or the person filing the application; and (7) a financial reference letter from a commercial bank.

Firms that have been granted industrial classification "A" under the Industrial Incentive Law (Law No. 299, described in further detail below) need not submit a copy of the operating permit since they are exempt from this requirement. Instead, they must present a copy of their authority to operate as an "A" category firm. This classification applies to firms operating in one of the Industrial Free Zones and producing goods solely for export. Firms generally can obtain export licenses quickly.

TAXATION

Corporations are taxed on a graduated scale ranging from 10 percent on low incomes to 49.4 percent on incomes of over US$250,000. In addition to corporate income taxes, the government levies a flat tax at a rate of 20.6 percent on remittances abroad. Depreciation allowances are 2 percent annually for buildings, 10 to 12.5 percent for most machinery and equipment, and 5 percent for heavier machinery. Losses may be deducted from profits obtained in the succeeding three years. However, losses may not be carried back. Individuals are subject to a personal income tax. The base tax is 2 percent, supplemented by a tax on a progressive scale, ranging from 3 percent for income of less than US$2,000 to a maximum marginal rate of 70 percent for income above US$900,000 per year.

INVESTMENT INCENTIVES

The Dominican government has enacted a series of laws to encourage new investments and exports through the provision of fiscal incentives. The basic legislation governing all foreign investment is Law No. 861, which grants foreign investors the right to remit capital and profits and exchange local currency. While the Dominican Republic welcomes foreign investment in most sectors of the economy, Law 861 limits or excludes foreign participation in certain sectors including water, electric power, post office, telecommunications, advertising, radio and television broadcasting, and internal transport not directly linked with imports and exports.

MAJOR INCENTIVE LAWS

The Industrial Incentive Law (Law No. 299) seeks to promote new and existing domestic and foreign investment. This law classifies three types of business for the purpose of granting benefits and concessions.

A. Industries engaged in the manufacture of products exclusively for export. It is generally required that the facility be located in one of the Industrial Free Zones.

B. All new high-priority industries for national development, particularly in import substitution activities.

C. All new production or expansion of existing industries engaged in the processing of local raw materials or in the manufacture of products for domestic consumption where demand exceeds supply available from current plant capacity.

Classification A enterprises are entitled to a 100 percent exemption from income tax, import duties on machinery, plant, and equipment, and import duties on raw materials, semi-finished products, or materials used in the composition or processing of the container or packing materials. Classification A firms also receive 100 percent exemption from all corporate capitalization, formation, and document taxes.

Classification B enterprises are entitled to up to 50 percent exemption from income taxes on investments, and 95 percent exemption from certain import duties and taxes.

Classification C enterprises are entitled to up to 50 percent exemption form income tax on investments and up to 90 percent exemption from certain import duties and taxes.

The length of time that these classifications and incentives apply varies according to the geographical location of the enterprise. For firms located in Santo Domingo, the duration is eight years, for Santiago 12 years, for the Haitian border 20 years, and 15 years for firms located elsewhere in the country.

The Export Promotion Law (Law No. 69) applies to the export of nontraditional products having a high local content value. Traditional exports (sugar, coffee, cacao, tobacco, metals, and minerals) are excluded. Products exported from Industrial Free Zones are excluded since they are generally provided similar incentives under Law 299. Under this law, imports of raw and semiprocessed materials, packaging materials, and molds and dies destined for use in export production enter duty-free for not more than twelve months.

The Agro-Industry Law (Law No. 409) offers agribusiness income tax exoneration up to 100 percent of net taxable income, and up to 100 percent duty-free entry of machinery and raw materials. The actual level of tax exoneration is based on the geographical location of the project, the percentage share of raw materials of national origin, and the level of vertical integration of the project. Foreign participation in agribusiness operations is limited to a maximum of 49 percent.

The Tourist Incentive Law (Law No. 153) was enacted to encourage tourism development. The law applies to both new and established investment in facilities in designated tourism development zones. For a period of 10 years, the law provides 100 percent tax exemption, exoneration from construction taxes and taxes on incorporation or capital increases, and municipal taxes on licenses, and 100 percent relief from import duties.

A traditional Dominican ranchhouse

INDUSTRIAL DUTY-FREE ZONE INVESTMENT

SETTING UP SHOP IN THE DOMINICAN REPUBLIC

When investors in offshore free zone operations name their key reasons for investing in the Dominican Republic, in addition to climate, favorable geographic location and excellent communications systems, the most frequently mentioned plus factor is the workforce.

"The quality of the workforce in terms of a positive working attitude is what sets the Dominican Republic apart," says Arelis Rodriguez, Executive Director of the Foreign Investment Promotion Council. This is why there is a waiting list of investors who want to set up their companies in the country's Industrial Free Zones.

Of a population of almost 6.5 million, the Dominican Republic has a labor force of approximately 2 million. There is a substantial clerical and unskilled workforce. Today, many Dominicans are trained and employed in the sensitive production of medical supplies, electronic equipment, diamond cutting, crystal, clothing, and furs. There is also a surplus of skilled technical and often bilingual personnel. Codetel, for example, has employed Dominicans to work in their new computer graphics division in which detailed blueprints of sophisticated utility installations and telephone systems are transferred into computer data banks for Florida, Texas, Illinois, Indiana, Michigan, and California. These computer graphics are rendered here at a fraction of what it would cost in the United States. At the San Isidro Industrial Free Zone and Office Park, AMR Caribbean Data Services, a subsidiary of American Airlines, is operating a data entry facility for satellite transmission to the United States of ticket sales and records.

A number of new IFZ's are in the works and it is estimated that by the end of this decade there will be about a quarter of a million people employed in these parks. Investors are attracted to the Dominican IFZ's for reasons other than qualified workers. The facilities are first-rate with state-of-the-art infrastructure at the new installations. The IFZ investor enjoys complete fiscal tax freedom for up to 20 years, with unrestricted repatriation of profits. There are currently 160 companies in the Dominican IFZ's; these employ a total of 52,000 workers. The seven IFZ's in operation are located in La Romana, San Pedro de Macoris, Itabo Haina, Santiago, San Isidro

Top 10 Trade Partners with Dominican Republic, 1985 (Imports F.O.B. in Millions of U.S.$)

IMPORTS

Country	Imports
Belgium-Luxembourg	$7.1
Netherlands	$10.2
France	$13.5
United Kingdom	$19.5
Canada	$24.0
Argentina	$24.5
Brazil	$27.6
Spain	$43.0
Germany	$46.4
Japan	$85.3
United States	$690.5

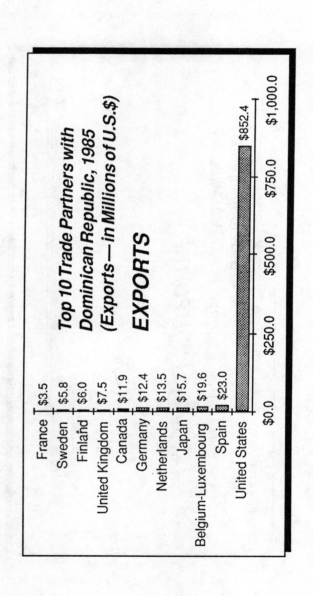

Top 10 Trade Partners with Dominican Republic, 1985 (Exports — in Millions of U.S.$)

EXPORTS

Country	Exports
France	$3.5
Sweden	$5.8
Finland	$6.0
United Kingdom	$7.5
Canada	$11.9
Germany	$12.4
Netherlands	$13.5
Japan	$15.7
Belgium-Luxembourg	$19.6
Spain	$23.0
United States	$852.4

Industrial and Office Park, Puerto Plata, and Bani. There are five more under construction and plans for over a dozen more in various stages of study. These IFZ's are all located in or near urban centers with easy access to banking facilities, transportation, seaports, and airports. The proximity to cities allows for greater availability of personnel, who are engaged in the manufacture of goods ranging from electronic components, medical equipment, crystal, and furs, to cigars and clothing. Operational costs are very reasonable and the facilities offer on-site power plants, customs, and security.

Free Zone exports are expected to generate US$309 million. This, in spite of government regulations allowing firms to sell 20% of their production locally as long as the product is not manufactured here in the country.

An impressive list of major corporations have recently joined the roster of those already working in the Dominican Republic's IFZ's for years. These companies include Baxter Travenol, Hanes, Bristol Meyers, GTE, and Westinghouse.

The Park at San Isidro is one of a kind as it provides a service industry facility based on computerized data systems that are costly operations in the United States. This systems service will employ Dominicans in high-technology jobs such as computer graphics, systems development, data entry, and program maintenance, which are essential to credit card companies, airlines, banks, insurance companies, and telephone and communications companies. ITT is planning a $3-million satellite at the San Isidro Park to expedite transmissions to the United States. José Ceron, the director of the San Isidro Park, believes that by the year 1992, as many as 20,000 workers will be employed at the park for high-tech work. The Dominican Republic will then be the first to offer ''Office Park'' services in addition to offshore manufacturing at its IFZ's.

Confidence in the investment potential here comes from all parts of the world, not solely the United States. Richard Hsu of Chem Tec Enterprises recently broke ground for a new privately-funded IFZ in San Pedro de Macoris. For the last two decades, Chinese investors have had their eye on the Dominican Republic and have made serious investments in real estate, tourism and, more recently, in agribusiness and offshore industry. Chem Tec Enterprises was established for the specific purpose of developing IFZs here. The new installation has an area of 400,000 square meters and will house 10 industries in its first stage, with an investment of US$20 million. Mr. Hsu and his associates were drawn here by the favorable climate, political stability, and geographic situation, but he was amazed at the quality of the available labor force. In the late 1970's he first contemplated the

Key Economic Indicators (in Millions of U.S.$ unless noted)

	1985	1986	1987
DOMESTIC ECONOMY			
Population (millions)	6.2	6.3	6.5
Population growth (%)	2.3	2.4	2.4
GDP, current dollars	4,663.0	5,590.0	5,572.0
Per capita GDP current dollars	752.0	873.0	888.0
% change consumer price index	38.0	9.8	19.8
PRODUCTION & EMPLOYMENT			
Labor force (1,000s)	1,900.0	2,000.0	2,000.0
Unemployment (avg. % for year)	26.0	28.0	27.0
Government deficit as % of GDP	4.0	2.2	2.8
BALANCE OF PAYMENTS			
Exports (F.O.B.)	740.0	720.0	750.0
Imports (C.I.F.)	1,286.0	1,250.0	1,350.0
Current account balance	-237.0	-180.0	-145.0
Foreign debt (year end)	3,500.0	3,700.0	3,700.0
Debt service paid	268.0	720.0	740.0
Debt service ratio as % of goods and services	20.0	51.3	48.0
Average exchange rate for year RD$ vs. US$1	3.1	2.9	3.9
FOREIGN INVESTMENT			
Foreign direct investment (new)	50.0	50.0	80.0
Total (cumulative) foreign investment	320.0	370.0	450.0
U.S. investment (cumulative)	200.0	235.0	285.0
U.S. share of investment (%)	63.0	63.0	63.0
U.S. – D.R. TRADE			
U.S. exports to D.R. (F.A.S.)	472.0	500.0	540.0
U.S. imports from D.R. (C.I.F.)	551.0	574.0	560.0
Free Zone Exports (D.R. to U.S.)*	205.0	238.0	309.0
U.S. share of D.R. exports (%)	74.0	78.0	75.0
U.S. share of D.R. imports (%)	36.0	40.0	40.0
U.S. bilateral aid (economic)	172.0	105.0	118.0
U.S. bilateral aid (military)	5.0	4.0	4.0

*Free zone data includes value of goods assembled from U.S. components; it is not included in Dominican export-import data.

Principal U.S. exports (1986); Foodstuffs, textiles, machinery, chemicals. Principal U.S. imports (1985); sugar, coffee, gold, furniture, garments.

Sources: Dominican Republic Government, International Monetary Fund, U.S. Embassy.

U.S. Imports from the Dominican Republic (in Millions of U.S.$)

Description	1984	1985	1986
Coffee	79.8	78.9	115.9
Gold or silver bullion/ore	153.7	119.7	111.9
Sugars, syrups and molasses	209.3	150.1	104.4
Cocoa beans	79.3	64.4	62.9
Chains of precious metals	11.8	28.1	43.8
Men's cotton suits and slacks	0.0	7.8	41.2
Women's knit apparel	0.0	8.6	27.8
Beef and veal, fresh/chilled	2.3	18.4	27.1
Ferronickel	37.5	41.2	21.9
Lace/net body support garments	21.0	21.0	21.3
Cigars	20.6	17.5	18.5
Electrical switches	13.8	14.2	14.4
Women's cotton blouses	0.0	3.6	13.7
Articles of coated paper	7.9	10.8	12.2
Beet or cane molasses	14.2	7.5	11.5
Jewelry and parts of	0.0	6.3	11.2
Men's cotton knit suits/shirts	0.0	2.6	10.8
Coton shoe uppers	0.0	3.1	10.5
Dasheens, fresh/chilled/frozen	7.4	9.9	8.8
Men's cotton pajamas	0.0	3.8	8.5
Women's man-made fiber coats	0.0	1.6	7.9
Leather articles	2.3	5.5	7.4
Deformed concrete reinforcing	0.0	0.0	7.4
Women's man-made fiber overcoats	0.0	0.0	7.3
Wearing apparel, fur	3.7	4.2	7.3
Lace underwear	5.1	6.2	6.8
Total Exports to the U.S.	1042.9	1013.7	1110.8

possibility of developing an industrial project similar to those he established in Taiwan. The new IFZ project will hold 80 industries in four phases. The initial ten will include manufacturers of electronic equipment, textiles, agricultural processing, and canning. The facility will provide complete infrastructure and communications systems, medical services in-house, and facilities for employees such as a restaurant and recreational areas.

The first phase should be ready by June 1988. Already, there are many potential investors from Hong Kong, Taiwan, and the United States looking into this latest venture. The second phase, set for a later date, will be located in an 800,000-square-meter facility in Santa Fe, on the road from San Pedro to Hato Rey.

All this is a good omen for San Pedro, already enjoying a renaissance with its famous medical school and university, and its well-established first Industrial Free Zone, which currently employs more than 20,000 people.

According to a recent *Wall Street Journal* supplement on the Dominican Republic, Frost and Sullivan, a New York-based political risk assessment firm, gave the Dominican Republic their top rating as a secure investment site; in their opinion, the surest and safest in all of Latin America. Total foreign investment in the country reached US$450 million in 1987. Of that number, total U.S. investment was US$285 million, representing the investment of over 120 North American companies during the past four years, more than in any other country in the Caribbean and Central America. The Dominican Republic continues to attract investors practically by word of mouth and the positive experiences of those who have been operating in the free zones of the country for decades.

Meanwhile, a new breed of investors eagerly await their opportunity to open up shop in the Dominican Republic.

AGRIBUSINESS

AGRICULTURAL DIVERSIFICATION IN THE DOMINICAN REPUBLIC

Because of depressed world prices and drastic reductions in the quotas of the U.S. market, the traditional exports of sugar, tobacco, and coffee have given way to nontraditional crops now emerging. These include cut flowers, decorative plants, fruits, and vegetables of seemingly endless variety. Over 65,000 acres of land formerly devoted to sugar production have been converted to the cultivation of

Agricultural Exports to the U.S. by Major Commodity Groups
(in Thousands of U.S.$)

	1983	1984	1985	1986
Total agro exports	366,394	458,914	378,062	384,893
Meats and products	9,400	2,206	17,469	25,661
Dairy products	6,460	6,584	5,184	4,786
Grains and feeds	1,611	1,796	2,562	2,758
Fruits, nuts and vegetables	30,468	35,813	39,129	42,624
Sugar and related products	178,562	217,430	153,137	114,410
Tobacco, unmanufactured	7,738	17,453	9,816	9,787
Bananas and plantains	2,013	1,583	1,127	783
Coffee, including products	67,485	78,097	75,476	113,021
Cocoa and products	55,843	80,877	68,008	66,298
Essential oils	—	—	306	216
Drugs, crude/natural	—	—	212	207

Source: U.S. Department of Agriculture.

nontraditional products, while in La Romana, research is being conducted into new uses for sugar as a source of fuel and energy.

In 1986, total exports of Dominican agricultural products to the U.S. reached US$385 million. The reasons so many entrepreneurs, both local and foreign, choose the Dominican Republic for agribusiness ventures are numerous. Production factors such as an ideal climate, excellent rainfall, fertile soil, an abundance of available land, different elevations, and the possibility of having multiple harvests in a one-year period are attractive. Social factors include abundant hardworking labor, political stability, and close ties to the United States. Economic factors include the competitive wages, Caribbean Basin Initiative incentives, and the most export-oriented fiscal policies in the region. Add to this the excellent transportation and communication links to the U.S. and the picture for investment is inviting.

More and more, diversification programs are taking a priority rating and these nontraditional ventures vie for importance with the cash crops of old.

In March 1988, California-based Dole Food Company signed an agreement with the State Sugar Council of the Dominican Republic (CEA) which will result in a major pineapple growing and processing venture. Dole Food Company is the largest of three divisions of Castle and Cooke, Inc., a Los Angeles company that employs 36,000 people worldwide. During the fiscal year ended January 3, 1987, Castle & Cooke revenues were $1.74 billion and their net income totaled $44 million, which gives an insight into the category of investors currently moving into the country. The project will be developed by Dole Dominicana, S.A., a Dominican corporation in which CEA will be a shareholder. CEA will provide approximately 13,000 acres of land formerly used for the cultivation of sugar cane, and lease the land under a longterm lease agreement. Dole will invest over US$13 million in equipment, installations and working capital. Commercial planting will begin later this year, and exports of fresh pineapple and juice concentrate will commence by 1989. Within five years, the company plans to employ some 3,000 workers as well as contracting for many services with local vendors. Exports will be focused primarily on the east coast of the United States, taking advantage of the duty-free provisions of the Caribbean Basin Initiative. The Dominican Republic was chosen as an investment site because of the country's rich agricultural potential, proximity to the United States, competitive labor costs, and political stability.

Plantings will be located in the areas of Buena Vista, San Pedro, Payabo Arenoso, and Bermejo, approximately 40 kilometers north of Santo Domingo. In addition to this new venture in the Dominican

A large pineapple plantation

Republic, Dole has pineapple operations in Hawaii, Honduras, Thailand, and the Philippines. With this Dominican venture, Dole estimates that within five years it will export up to 100,000 tons a year of fresh fruit and juice concentrate. Dole's general manager in the Dominican Republic is Stanley Black, who has previously served in management in Central America and corporate headquarters for the company.

In addition to this multi-million dollar investment made by Dole, there are numerous projects of smaller but substantial scope in agribusiness.

Halifax Trading S.A., for example, is involved in the production of green pigeon peas, frozen tropical fruit pulp and chunks, papaya chunks, tropical fruit pulps, grated coconut, coconut cream, and fruit pie filling. The company currently has two production centers located in extremely fertile regions with three or four yearly harvests, depending on the variety of crop involved. One of their plants is located to the south in San Cristobal, while the other is in Moncion, to the north. These two production areas provide a two-cycle capacity which takes advantage of the seasonality of tropical fruits and minimizes the risk of crop failures. It also allows for meeting the "insatiable" demands of the growing North American markets. With a production capacity of 456,000 tons a year, Halifax has exceptional facilities for processing and packaging their products under private label contracts. All production meets high USDA standards for quality control. Among their clients are Goya, Del Monte, and American Foods.

Domex S.A. was founded in 1981 by Ofer Rozenfeld, who had successfully grown fruits and vegetables in his native Israel. He currently produces melons, tomatoes, and pineapples on 2,000 acres of land in the Azua area, and averages about one million boxes of fruit for export to the United States every year. He believes Dominican produce is held in high regard on world markets because of the exceptional flavor of the fruit and because of strict quality controls observed in production.

Chinolas Dominicana S.A. exports large quantities of passion fruit to the U.S. market. Passion fruit grows wild here, but the company pioneered commercial planting three years ago. The demand for passion fruit and its nectar far exceeds the current supply and the company intends to double their production capacity by next year.

Local business entrepreneurs are also moving speedily towards diversification. The Vicini family, in the vanguard of the national sugar industry for generations, now sponsors vegetable production on part of the land that was formerly used exclusively for the sugar crop. The Bonetti family, an established name in Dominican business, is responsible for projects as diversified as cut flowers and African palm oil for export.

Byron Smalley and Oscar Cohen of Cariplant S.A. have enjoyed more success with their ornamental plants venture than even they thought possible. They supply both the U.S. and European markets with tropical plant varieties ordered by the thousands for their beauty and resilience. Their production includes three varieties of palm, yucca plants, three species of *dracaena marginata* (the colorful Dragon plant), *massangeana* (cane), crotus, *dieffenbachia* tropic snow, and even a Dominican variation of a bonsai lookalike. Carefully packaged cuttings are shipped to U.S. nurseries, as restrictions prohibit the importation of potted plants to the United States. Europe has no such import restrictions and Cariplant is able to ship potted plants in different stages of maturity to the European market. The demand for tropical plants is great and they already have plans for expansion. Five kilometers beyond San Isidro, the Cariplant farm and nursery is situated on over 300 acres of plantation that had once been used by a previous owner for sugar production. Byron Smalley has turned a lifelong interest into a lucrative export product and Oscar Cohen says he encourages potential investors to look into nontraditional areas of agricultural potential that, as in the case of Cariplant, can lead to some surprising results and excellent yields on the investment dollar.

Then there is the story of Southland Dominicana, which is already producing, canning, and exporting okra and has in a very short time become one of the largest okra suppliers to the U.S. market.

It seems opportunities for investment are endless and, Wilson Rood, Executive Director of the American Chamber of Commerce and publisher of *Dominican Business*, recently suggested that investors should look into areas of new opportunity and that more studies should be directed at these unexplored areas and less at repetition of what we already know. "For example," said Mr. Rood, "We have read articles on the feasibility of growing and producing the castoroil plant in desert areas. We have heard of factories in other countries making Tiffany-style lamps. The hand wiring of electric motors might be another good possibility. These are but a few examples. I believe that some productive research could be done into areas of business or agriculture that could be carried out by Dominicans at a considerably lower cost than in the United States. The textile business has already done this. There surely are many others out there. The field is wide open!"

There are approximately 3,000 agricultural and industrial export products currently eligible for incentive treatment and the Dominican Republic enjoys "most favored nation" status in the United States market for export of everything from soup to nuts. Considering this and the as yet untouched potential of new areas of business, maybe it is time to get in on the ground floor.

REPATRIATION OF PROFITS AND CAPITAL

All foreign investment must be registered with the Central Bank. Up to 25 percent of annual net profits from a registered foreign investment in the Dominican Republic operation outside a free zone may be repatriated. Companies operating in free zones have no restrictions on the repatriation of capital or profits.

For foreign firms operating outside of a free zone, repatriation of capital is permitted when an investor sells his shares, participation, or rights to national or foreign investors or when the enterprise is liquidated. In the event of liquidation, repatriation of capital gains from the sale of assets is limited to 2 percent annually from the date on which the foreign investment was registered up to a maximum of 20 percent of the total.

OTHER INCENTIVES

The U.S. government has adopted a range of trade and tax measures which can provide considerable benefits to investors in the Dominican Republic.

CARIBBEAN BASIN INITIATIVE

The Caribbean Basin Economic Recovery Act (CBI) of 1983 seeks to promote economic revitalization and expanded private sector opportunities in the Caribbean Basin region. The main provision eliminates U.S. duties on goods entering the United States from any beneficiary country until January 1, 1996. Duty-free treatment applies to products which meet the following criteria:

1. The article is exported directly from the beneficiary country.
2. The appraised value of the article must consist of at least 35 percent value added in one or more beneficiary countries (U.S.-made components may comprise 15 percent of that 35 percent, leaving 20 percent which must be added in beneficiary countries.).

3. Any product must be substantially transformed into a "new and different article of commerce" in one or more beneficiary countries.

Goods not eligible for duty-free treatment include textiles and apparel; certain leather items such as footwear, handbags, luggage, and work gloves; canned tuna; petroleum or products derived from petroleum; and certain watches and watch parts. The CBI also allows U.S. tax deductions for reasonable expenses of business conventions held in eligible countries.

For more information on the "Caribbean Basin Initiative," contact:

CARIBBEAN BASIN INFORMATION CENTER
U.S. Department of Commerce
14th and Constitution Avenue, NW
Washington, D.C. 20230
Dominican desk
Tel. (202) 377–2527

CARIBBEAN BASIN PROMOTION CENTER
c/o Mr. Richard Paullen
Chicago Association of Commerce and Industry
200 North LaSalle Street
Chicago, Illinois 60601
Tel. (312) 580–6944

This agency brings together potential investors and importers from the United States with firms in the Dominican Republic.

GENERALIZED SYSTEM OF PREFERENCES (GSP)

The U.S. Generalized System of Preferences provides duty-free access to U.S. markets for manufactured and semi-manufactured goods from eligible countries. About 3,000 products are currently eligible for GSP treatment, and the Dominican Republic is an eligible coun
If you are considering investment in the Dominican Republic, there are a number of private and government agencies that can be of help (see below).

BANKING AND BUSINESS SERVICES

The banking system is headed by the Central Bank of the Dominican Republic, which is controlled by the Monetary Board and supervised by the Superintendent of Banks. The Monetary Board, presided over by the Governor of the Central Bank, determines monetary policies and also directs the Central Bank's operations. The Central Bank acts as the bank of issue and also regulates the country's credit and money supply and foreign exchange rate.

Private banking is conducted by a large number of private institutions in four categories: Commercial banks, mortgage banks, savings and loan associations, and development banks. Commercial banks dominate this system and control about two thirds of the banking system's total assets. Among the 15 commercial banks operating in the Dominican Republic are a number of major international banks, including Chase Manhattan, Citibank, the Royal Bank of Canada, and the Bank of Nova Scotia. Commercial banks provide a full range of personal and corporate financial services.

Savings and loan associations hold about one fifth of banking assets, take in savings deposits, and offer mortgage and collateralized loans. With about one tenth of banking assets, mortgage banks provide short-term financing to builders and long-term financing to homeowners. Mortgage banks also extend medium-term (ten-year) funding for commercial construction. Development banks, which control about 6 percent of banking assets, offer medium and long-term loans to productive ventures in industry, agribusiness, transportation, and tourism.

BANKING FACILITIES

Commercial banks generally operate between the hours of 8 a.m. and 4 or 5 p.m., and most of them have branches in addition to their main office. Located in Santo Domingo, a few of the larger banks are listed here.

Citibank (closing time is 2 p.m.)
1 John F. Kennedy Avenue
Tel. (809) 566–5611

The Chase Manhattan Bank
John F. Kennedy Avenue (corner of Tiradentes Avenue)
Tel. (809) 565–4441
565–8871

Bank of America (National Trust and Savings Association)
103 Calle El Conde
Tel. (809) 689–6121

Banco de Santander Dominicano
John F. Kennedy Avenue (corner Lope de Vega Avenue)
Tel. (809) 566–5811
566–9111

Bank of Nova Scotia (Scotiabank)
Lope de Vega Avenue (corner of JFK)
Tel. (809) 566–5671

Banco Popular Dominicano
a subsidiary company of Grupo Financiero Popular
252 Isabel La Catolica (colonial landmark house)
Tel. (809) 682–9131
689–9141

BUSINESS TRAVEL IN THE DOMINICAN REPUBLIC

Most major companies have main offices in Santo Domingo proper. This allows for most business transactions to be done there. If, however, the businessman is doing business in the Industrial Free Zones, then it may be necessary to rent a car to visit them, since they are distributed throughout the country. The country is small enough to reach most destinations in good time by rental car or bus. If your time is limited, private charter planes are readily available at Herrera Airport in Santo Domingo, or you can have one arranged to pick you up at Las Americas Airport upon your arrival for delivery to your destination. The number of private airports in the country, however, is limited. Your best bet is a taxi from Las Americas Airport to Santo Domingo, and a rental car from one of the many agencies there. Make your car rental agreements in advance if possible, through a travel agent.

TRAVEL EXPENSES

Costs for individual travel and stay in Dominican Republic are reasonable when compared with many other countries. Santo Domingo is the most expensive city, but costs can be reduced by staying at less expensive but still adequate hotels (For more on hotels, see chapter 6). The only costs that are relatively high are those of private airplane charters. Taxis are very reasonable. The following chart shows what a businessperson might expect to spend during one day in the country.

A BUSINESS DAY IN THE DOMINICAN REPUBLIC

EXPENSE SUMMARY

COST	ITEM
Hotel room	US$60.
Lunch, better restaurants	15.
Taxis	15.
Dinner, better restaurants	20.
Telex/telephone to U.S.	20.
Interpreter (if required)	30.
TOTAL	165.

A budget of about $165 per day for basic living expenses is typical for business travelers. Car rental costs will increase this considerably (see section on car rentals). For a 10-day business trip originating from the eastern coast of the United States, the prospective traveler should plan a total outlay in the range of US$2,500 including airfare, but excluding expenses for entertainment, liquor, incidentals, gifts, or other non-business-related items.

QUALITY OF LIFE

The Dominican Republic offers excellent living and working conditions for resident and visiting business executives and their families. Comfortable housing, along with the latest in appliances and furnishings, is readily available for lease or purchase in Santo Domingo and other major cities. Santo Domingo offers a number of business-class hotels, with tourist class hotels available throughout the country (see chapter 6).

The Dominican society's appreciation of and demand for modernization is reflected in the range of products and services available to businesses and consumers. Santo Domingo's shopping district offers the latest in American and European fashions, while supermarkets and shops throughout the country stock most major U.S. brand name products. Businesses make use of the latest in office automation and communications equipment, including computers, facsimile machines, and desktop publishing systems.

Santo Domingo's cable television service provides viewers with access to more than a dozen U.S. channels including the major networks. Newspapers and magazines such as the *Miami Herald*, *The Wall Street Journal*, *Time*, and *Newsweek*, are readily available on a same-day basis. English and bilingual educational facilities from kindergarten to high school level are available in most major cities, while the country boasts an excellent system of university education consisting of over two dozen public and private institutions (see chapter 10).

THE AMERICAN CHAMBER OF COMMERCE

THE AMERICAN CHAMBER OF COMMERCE OF THE
DOMINICAN REPUBLIC
Wilson Rood, Director
Hotel Santo Domingo
Santo Domingo
or
P.O. Box 95-2
Santo Domingo
Tel. (809) 533-7292/532-7414

The American Chamber of Commerce provides excellent counseling services in areas of investment. Memberships costs U.S.$200 and entitles the member to business counseling and a number of important business publications that include English translations of all the important investment and incentive laws.

You could well be eligible for a tax write-off on your entire trip if you are seriously interested in doing business in the Dominican Republic. The American Chamber of Commerce has current information on this and members enjoy substantial discounts at hotels.

The United States corporate presence in the Dominican Republic, stagnant for many years, is now increasing rapidly. The traditional multinationals such as the oil companies and big banks were always here. The big change came when Gulf & Western bought out South Puerto Rico Sugar, which was later acquired by the Fanjul family of Palm Beach.

In recent years, notably during the past three, there has been an even more significant change. With the Caribbean Basin Initiative came a revolution of free zone companies; now some 160 of them employ over 50,000 people. Such big names as Westinghouse, Hanes, and Travenol are now here and others are on the way. The agribusiness developments with such non-traditional products as citrus, melons, and shrimp farming are developing rapidly with over 100 under way (see the section on Agribusiness below).

The U.S. business presence has been represented for years by the American Chamber of Commerce of the Dominican Republic. Founded in 1923, it is one of the oldest chambers of commerce in Latin America. It was fairly dormant during the Trujillo years, and until after the revolution of 1965. Starting in 1966, the Chamber became active in promoting business, and became well known as the top forum in the country for speakers at the monthly luncheons. These have included the President, the governor of the central bank, secretaries of state, and economists. Until 1977, the chamber maintained a small membership, as only U.S. companies or citizens could serve on its board. The new statutes drawn up that year changed the picture, and now there are Dominican board members. All Dominican companies that are members must do business with the U.S.

The chamber now has 2,000 members and six regional offices throughout the republic. It has broadened the scope of its activities which now include:

*Consultations on laws, decrees, and other provisions and their consequences for the Dominican and American private sectors.

*Defense of members' common interest, particularly regarding prices, taxes, labor legislation, trade, and markets.

*Immediate action in the face of measures taken in the U.S. which might be harmful to the interests of the Dominican private sector.

*Access to the Caribbean Basin Information Network (CBIN) through the chamber's computer. Market and business opportunities can be traced.

*Up-to-date information on regulations that affect trade between the United States and the Dominican Republic.

*Monthly luncheons featuring distinguished speakers from the public and private sectors of both nations.

*Seminars by experts on such topics as taxes, export regulations, marketing, business opportunities, and customs.

*Filing applications with the U.S. consulate for renewal of tourist and business visas for members.

*Mediating between Dominican and foreign firms who want to settle their differences out of court.

*Issuing of letters of introduction to members traveling to the United States.

*Supplying lists of local agents, representatives, or distributors of U.S. companies. Also, Dominicans and Americans interested in forming partnerships.

Membership with the American Chamber of Commerce includes subscription to most of its publications, such as: *Investor's Handbook and Business Guide*, a practical reference guide with information on Dominican laws and regulations of interest to businessmen; a directory of members; *Dominican Business,* a bi-monthly magazine containing articles of interest to the business community; *Monthly Bulletin*, a leaflet with a list of business opportunity leads and pertinent announcements; and *Forming a Dominican Company*, a useful booklet by lawyers Luis Heredia Bonetti and Jonathan Russin, which outlines the requirements involved in establishing a company in the Dominican Republic.

Overseas membership applications are available upon request, and the Chamber's publications listed below are available to nonmembers through mail order.

Investors' Handbook and Business Guide to the Dominican Republic
(current edition in English)
Airmail/overseas: US$20

Directory of Members
(in English)
Airmail/overseas: US$10

Dominican Business
"Business and Economic Newsletter"
This is an excellent bi-monthly Chamber publication with all the current business news.
Airmail/overseas: Check with them on subscription rates as this is a brand new publication.

HELPFUL AGENCIES AND ORGANIZATIONS

FOREIGN INVESTMENT PROMOTION COUNCIL
Consejo Promotor de Inversiones Extranjeras
Antonio Caceres, President
Arelis Rodriguez, Executive Director
American Life Insurance Company (Alico) Building
Abraham Lincoln Avenue

Second Floor
Santo Domingo
Tel. (809) 532-3281 through 86
Telefax: (809) 533-7029
U.S. address:
P.O. Box 25438
Washington, D.C. 20007

This nonprofit organization was founded in 1983 to help foreign investors get through the "red tape" of investment procedures. It also promotes projects for investment opportunities in the Dominican Republic, particularly in nontraditional sectors such as new areas of agro-industry in the country.

Department of Tourism Infrastructure of the Central Bank
INFRATUR
Director: Juan Antonio Elmudesi
Banco Central de La Republica Dominicana
Pedro Henriquez Urena Street
Santo Domingo
Tel. (809) 685-6151, 689-7121

This division of the Central Bank channels loans made by international financial institutions such as the World Bank and the Interamerican Development Bank to the Dominican Republic for the purpose of developing its tourism potential. Infratur is particularly responsible for the infrastructure and financing of tourism projects in the Puerto Plata region of the country. Their *Information for Investors* manual and Law 153, which covers incentives for investment in tourism projects, are available free of charge in English as well as in Spanish editions through their offices. They also have a number of attractive brochures on the country's tourism development areas.

Dominican Center for Export Promotion
CEDOPEX
in the Dominican Republic:
Plaza de la Independencia
P.O. Box 199-2
Santo Domingo
Tel. (809) 566-9131

CEDOPEX office in New York
One World Trade Center
Suite 86065
New York, N.Y. 10048
Tel. (212) 432-9498

CEDOPEX office in Miami
100 Biscayne Boulevard
Suite 611
Miami, Florida 33132
Tel. (405) 358-8174

This center was established to promote nontraditional export products from both the agricultural and industrial sectors. The center provides potential investors with current information regarding regulations related to agriculture, agribusiness, and manufacturing.

Dominican Republic Tourist Information Center
485 Madison Avenue
New York, N.Y. 10022
Tel. (212) 826-0750

They carry all the current brochures and information printed on the country and its major attractions. They can also give you a complete updated listing of tour operators working with the Dominican Republic.

Consejo Nacional de Zonas Francas
(National Council of Industrial Free Zones)
43 Jose Brea Pena
Santo Domingo
Tel. (809) 567-3371

Ask them for a recent publication: *The Gateway to the U.S. Market* on Industrial Free Zones in the Dominican Republic. This publication is sometimes also available through the Banco Central.

Secretaria de Estado de Industria y Comercio
(Ministry of Industry and Commerce)
Mexico Avenue
Santo Domingo
Tel. (809) 685-5171

Corporación de Fonento Industrial (Corporation for Industrial Development), Santo Domingo

Ministry of Tourism
George Washington Avenue
Santo Domingo
Tel. (809) 682–8181

Corporación de Fomento Industrial
(Corporation of Industrial Development)
27th of February Avenue
Santo Domingo
Tel. (809) 533–8151

FOREIGN INVESTORS OPERATING IN THE DOMINICAN ECONOMY

Some of the many U.S. firms doing business in the Dominican Republic:

Abbott Laboratories International Co.
Alcoa Exploration Company
American Airlines Inc.
Arco Caribbean, Inc.
Avon Products, Inc.
Bank of America NT & SA
Bristol Myers Dominicana, S.A.
Citibank, N.A.
Colgate Palmolive (Dom. Rep.) Inc.
Consolidated Cigar
Coopers & Lybrand
Eastern Airlines
Ernst & Whinney
Esso Standard Oil, S.A. Ltd.
Exxon Corp.
Falconbridge Dominicana, C. POR A.
Ford Motor Credit Co. International
Gillette Dominicana, S.A.
Gulf & Western Americas Corporation
Gulf Oil Corporation
Honeywell Dominicana, C. POR A.
IBM World Trade Corporation
ITT All American Cables and Radio
Leo Burnett Advertising
McCann Erickson
Otis Elevator Company

Peat, Marwick, Mitchell Company
Price Waterhouse & Company
Ray-O-Vac Dominicana, S.A.
RCA Global Communications, Inc.
SeaLand Service Inc.
Singer Sewing Machine Company
Texaco Caribbean, Inc.
The Chase Manhattan Bank, N.A.
Twentieth Century Fox, Inc.
Wackenhut Dominicana, S.A.
Westinghouse
Xerox Dominicana, C. POR A.
Young & Rubicam Damaris, C. POR A.

Street vendor offering freshly hardboiled eggs

Chapter 12

APPENDIX

SPANISH LANGUAGE GUIDE

BASIC GRAMMAR

You will find it necessary on occasion to understand at least a few of the most basic words and phrases to function adequately. The information we have assembled here will get you by even if you find yourself with individuals or groups whose only language is Spanish. Don't be overly self-conscious about your difficulties with pronunciation. Think how impressed you are when a visitor to your country attempts to use your language in its basic form. Remember how enjoyable it is to be helpful to such a person, and you will then know how Dominicans feel about helping you. Most will be pleased to be of service.

ARTICLES

Nouns are either masculine or feminine. Articles agree in gender and number with the noun.

DEFINITE ARTICLE (the):

	SINGULAR	PLURAL
masculine	*el coche*	*los coches*
feminine	*la casa*	*las casas*

INDEFINITE ARTICLE (a/an):

feminine	*una pluma*	*unas plumas*
masculine	*un libro*	*unos libros*

NOUNS

Most nouns ending in ''o'' are masculine. Those ending in ''a'' are usually feminine.

Nouns ending with a vowel add an ''s'' to form the plural; nouns ending with a consonant add ''es.'' To show possession, use the preposition ''*de*'' (of).

el fin de la junta	the end of the meeting
el principio del dia festivo	the beginning of the holiday

el portafolio del caballero	the businessman's briefcase
los zapatos del hombre	the man's shoes
el apartamento de Juan	John's apartment

*(*del* is the contraction of *de + el*).

ADJECTIVES

Adjectives agree with the noun in gender and number. Those ending in "o" and "a" form the plural by adding "s."

blanco(a)	*blanco(as)* (white)

Most other adjectives form the plural in the same way as nouns do—by adding "s" to a word ending in a vowel and "es" to a word ending in a consonant. As a rule, the adjective comes after the noun.

un barco inglés	'an English ship
unos barcos inglés	some English ships

Possessive adjectives agree with the object possessed, not with the possessor.

	singular	plural
your	*tu*	*tus*
my	*mi*	*mis*
his/her/its	*su*	*sus*
our	*nuestro(a)*	*nuestros(as)*
your	*vuestro(a)*	*vuestros(as)*
their	*su*	*sus*

his/her father	*su padre*
his/her/their apartment	*su apartamento, sus apartamentos*
his/her/their books	*su libro, sus libros*

Comparative and superlative: These are formed by adding *más* (more) or *menos* (less) and *lo más* or *lo menos*, respectively, before the adjective.

high	*alto*	higher	*más alto*	highest	*lo más alto*

ADVERBS

Adverbs are formed by adding *-mente* to the adjective or to feminine form of the adjective, if it differs from the masculine.

| sure | *cierto(a)* | surely | *ciertamente* |
| easy | *facil* | easily | *facilmente* |

Sometimes adjectives are used as adverbs. For example, *alto* can also mean "loud."

PERSONAL PRONOUNS

	SUBJECT	DIRECT OBJECT	INDIRECT OBJECT
I	*yo*	*me*	*me*
You (fam.)	*tu*	*te*	*te*
You	*usted*	*lo*	*se*
She	*ella*	*la*	*le*
He	*el*	*lo*	*le*
We	*nosotros(as)*	*nos*	*nos*
it	*el/ella*	*lo/la*	*le*
You (pl. fam.)	*vosotros(as)*	*os*	*os*
You (pl.)	*ustedes*	*los*	*se*
They	*ellos(as)*	*los*	*les*

In most instances, subject pronouns are omitted, except in the polite form (*usted*, *ustedes*) which means "you." *Tu* (singular) and *vostros* (plural) are used when talking to close friends, children, relatives, and between young people. *Usted* and the plural *ustedes* (often abbreviated to *ud./uds.*) are used in all other situations.

POSSESSIVE PRONOUNS

	SINGULAR	PLURAL
mine	*mio(a)*	*mios(as)*
yours (sing. fam.)	*tuyo(a)*	*tuyos(as)*
your (polite)	*suyo(a)*	*suyos(as)*
his/hers/its	*suyo(a)*	*suyo(as)*
our	*nuestro(a)*	*nuestros(as)*
your (pl. fam.)	*vuestro(a)*	*vuestros(as)*
their	*suyo(a)*	*suyos(as)*

DEMONSTRATIVE PRONOUNS

	MASCULINE	FEMININE	NEUTER
this	*este*	*esta*	*esto*
these	*estes*	*estas*	*estos*
those	*esos*	*esas*	*esos*
	aquelles	*aquellas*	*aquellos*
that	*ese*	*esa*	*eso*
	aquel	*aquella*	*aquello*

These are also used as demonstrative adjectives, but accents in the masculine and feminine are dropped.

VERBS

Here you must be concerned with the infinitive and the present tense.

ser (to be)*   *haber* (to have)

yo soy (I am)	*yo he* (I have)
tu eres (you are)	*tu has* (you have)
usted es (you are)	*usted ha* (you have)
el/ella es (he/she/is)	*el/ella/ha* (he/she has)
nosotros somos (we are)	*nosotros hemos* (we have)
ustedes son (you are)	*ustedes han* (you have)
ellos/ellas son (they are)	*ellos/ellas han* (they have)

*There are two verbs in Spanish for "to be." *Ser* is used to describe a permanent condition. *Estar* is used to describe location or a temporary condition.

THREE OF THE MAIN CATEGORIES OF VERBS

	infinitive ends in *-ar* *hablar* (to speak)	infinitive ends in *-er* *comer* (to eat)	infinitive ends in *-ir* *reir* (to laugh)
yo	*hablo*	*como*	*rio*
tu	*hablas*	*comes*	*ries*

usted	habla	come	rie
el/ella	habla	come	rie
nosotros	hablamos	comemos	reimos
vosotros	hablais	comeis	reis
ustedes	hablan	comen	rien
ellos/ellas	hablan	comen	rien

IRREGULAR VERBS

	poder	ir	ver	conocer
	(to be able)	(to go)	(to see)	(to know someone)
yo	puedo	voy	veo	conozco
tu	puedes	vas	ves	conoces
usted	puede	va	ve	conoce
el/ella	puede	va	ve	conoce
nosotros	podemos	vamos	vemos	conocemos
vosotros	podeis	vais	veis	conoceis
ustedes	pueden	van	ven	conocen
ellos/ellas	pueden	van	ven	conocen

NEGATIVES

Negatives are formed by placing *no* before the verb.

Es nuevo (it is new)   *No es nuevo* (it is not new)

QUESTIONS

Questions are often formed by changing the intonation of your voice. The personal pronoun is left out, both in affirmative sentences and in questions.

I speak Spanish   *Hablo español*.
Do you speak Spanish?   *¿Hablas español?/¿Habla usted español?*

Note the double question mark used. The same is true of exclamation marks.

How late it is getting!   *¡Que tarde se hace!*

BASIC PHRASES

Yes, please	*Sí, por favor*
No, thanks	*No, gracias*
You're welcome	*De nada*
Good morning	*Buenos días*
Good afternoon	*Buenas tardes*
Good evening/night	*Buenas noches*
What do you call this?	*¿Cómo se llama esto?*
What is your name?	*¿Cómo se llama usted?*
	or
	¿Cuál es su nombre?
Do you speak English?	*¿Habla usted inglés?*
I understand.	*Comprendo.*
I don't understand.	*No comprendo.*
Where is the Sheraton Hotel?	*¿Dónde está el Hotel Sheraton?*
Where is . . .	*¿Dónde está*
How much is this?	*¿Cuánto es esto?*
I am hungry.	*Tengo hambre.*
I am thirsty.	*Tengo sed.*
I am tired.	*Estoy cansado* (man)
	Estoy cansada (woman)
Where is the closest restaurant?	*¿Dónde está el restaurante más cercano?*
I am lost.	*Estoy perdido(a).*
Can you show me the way?	*¿Puede usted indicarme la dirección?*
What is the telephone number for that restaurant?	*¿Cuál es el número de teléfono de ese restaurante?*
What is the address for this store?	*¿Cuál es la dirección de esta tienda?*
Fast	*Rápido*
Slow	*Despacio*
The bill, please.	*La cuenta por favor.*
Credit card	*Tarjeta de crédito*
Cash	*Efectivo*
For you	*Para usted*
I'd like some orange juice.	*Quiero un jugo de naranja.*
I'd like a soft drink.	*Quiero un refresco.*
I'd like a cup of coffee.	*Quiero una taza de café.*
Black coffee	*Café negro*
Coffee with milk	*Café con leche*

I'd like a beer.	*Quiero una cerveza.*
Where is the telephone?	*¿Dónde está el teléfono?*
I want to make a long distance call.	*Quiero llamar larga distancia.*
What time is my flight?	*¿A qué hora es mi vuelo?*
The Pan Am flight.	*El vuelo de Pan Am.*
The flight is late.	*El vuelo está tarde.*
The flight is early.	*El vuelo está temprano.*
Where is the exit?	*¿Dónde está la salida?*
I need a taxi.	*Necesito un taxi.*
Suitcase	*Maleta*
Beach	*Playa*
Golf course	*Campo de golf*
Tennis court	*Cancha de Tenis*
Swimming pool	*piscina*
I need a receipt.	*Necesito un recibo.*
To the right/left	*A la derecha/izquierda*
A little	*Un poco*
A lot/very	*mucho/muy*
cheap	*barato*
expensive	*caro*
very expensive	*muy caro*
hot	*caliente*
cold	*frio*

MARRIAGE, DIVORCE, AND OTHER SERVICES

MARRIAGE IN THE DOMINICAN REPUBLIC

The legal requirements for marriage in the Dominican Republic are as follows.

1. The marriage must take place before an official of the civil registry.
2. Both parties must be at least 18 years of age, or otherwise provide parental authorization.
3. Birth certificate or documents identifying and indicating the age of each party must be presented.
4. Must present a notarized statement declaring that both parties are single, stating full names of both parties, professions, and address.
5. In the event of a previous marriage, divorce papers must be presented.
6. Two witnesses must be present at the marriage ceremony. They must be of legal age and should not be related to either of the contracting parties.
7. The cost of the legal work involved in a marriage will be approximately US$300 to US$400.

All the legal arrangements may be handled through a local law firm. The American Chamber of Commerce and the U.S. Consulate can recommend a number of prestigious attorneys. Following is a list of some of the highly-respected bilingual law firms operating in the Dominican Republic that can handle your legal requirements:

Headrick & Rizik
51 Elvira de Mendoza
Tel. (809) 685–4137
        685–2936

Kaplan Russin Vecchi & Heredia
Tiradentes Avenue
Tel. (809) 566–5101

Milton Messina & Asociados
55 Fantino Falco Street
Tel. (809) 562–6461

Pina Acevedo
56 Independencia Avenue
Tel. (809) 689–6209
         689–6750

Troncoso & Caceres
253 S. Sanchez Street
Tel. (809) 689–2158
         689–5817

HOUSES OF WORSHIP

In the Dominican Republic, church and state are separate and therefore, if you so desire, you may arrange for a religious ceremony in addition to the legally required civil matrimony. Catholic churches abound all over the city. In the colonial sector, the "Convento" and the Church of the Mercedes have special charm. There are ministries of other denominations located in the city of Santo Domingo.

ADVENTIST

The Adventist Church
18 Calle San Juan Sanchez Ramirez
Gascue
Tel. (809) 689–9035

BAPTIST

First Baptist Church
Sarasota Avenue at the corner of Calle Higuemota
Bella Vista
Tel. (809) 532–4963

EPISCOPAL AND UNION CHURCH

Union Church
253 Independencia Avenue
Tel. (809) 689–2070

JEWISH

Hebrew Synagogue Center
5 Sarasota Avenue
Tel. (809) 533–1675

These ministries offer services in English. Contributions are made at your discretion to the congregation and the officiating clergy.

INVITATIONS

There are a number of "Fotomecanica" print shops located throughout the city of Santo Domingo. Most of them can handle fast orders for printed invitations.

A very reliable and inexpensive one is:

Fotomecanica Cipriano
53 Luperón Avenue
Tel. (809) 685-9756

PHOTOGRAPHERS

If you wish to arrange for photographic services at your wedding or have a studio portrait done, there are a number of excellent professional photographers located in the capital:

RAUL CUBILLAS (bilingual)
International Photography
Tel. (809) 562-7267
beeper: 567-9551, ext. 1534
In Miami: (305) 447-4677
New York (718) 624-5566

ONORIO MONTAS
Mograf, S.A.
Tel. (809) 682-7073, 685-1389

HECTOR BAEZ STUDIO
19 Sarasota Avenue
Tel. (809) 532-3202

ROBERT ALVAREZ (bilingual)
Tel. (809) 567-1859, 566-5021

RECEPTIONS

All the major hotels in the city have reception facilities for anything from the very intimate wedding reception to a full-scale one. They will handle all arrangements, including music if you wish to have musicians perform at the reception, wedding cake, flowers, decorations. They usually have two cost arrangements: one if you provide the liquor and another if they provide it. Discuss these possibilities with the sales and banquet managers.

It has recently become very popular to have wine and cheese parties at receptions, rather than having a buffet or formal dinner. Hotel sales personnel can give you a clear idea of the various options and costs.

If you want classical music (violin and piano, trio, or quartet) call the National Symphony Orchestra office and they will give you the names of some of their members who are available to perform for special occasions (tel. (809) 682-8542). **The Solano Orchestra** is also available for weddings and receptions (tel. (809) 689-5271/688-7419).

DECORATIONS

DIGNA'S
Plaza Naco Shopping Center

They offer a large selection of party supplies.

CASA CONSUELO (Rental service for weddings)
A Garcia G 164 Sd.
Tel. (809) 685-1030

DIVORCE PROCEDURES

Laws 142 and 1306 are the divorce laws which apply to foreigners who wish to divorce by mutual consent in the civil court of the Dominican Republic.

Legal requirements of divorce are as follows.

1. "Quick" divorces can only be handled in cases where there is mutual consent.
2. One of the parties must be present at the hearing.
3. The absent party must grant a power of attorney to a local lawyer to represent him/her.
4. Both parties must sign a notarized statement (the absent party will provide the present party with a power of attorney to sign for him/her) in which an inventory of their joint property is stated, which of the two will hold custody of the children (if any) is stated, and the current address of both parties during the divorce procedure is stated.

5. The following documents must be presented to the court: Marriage certificate and birth certificates of the children, duly validated by a Dominican Consul.
6. The party who travels to the country should plan at least a two-day stay for the court proceedings which take place on weekdays.
7. Approximate cost of the entire legal process, including the lawyer's fees should be between US$1,000 and US$1,500 at the time of this writing.

The American Chamber of Commerce and the U.S. Consulate in Santo Domingo can provide a list of reputable law firms. Those already listed above in the section on marriage are bilingual firms with a solid reputation.

Special thanks to attorney Mary Fernandez de Senior of Headrick and Rizik for her legal consultation on the requirements for marriage and divorce proceedings for foreigners in the Dominican Republic.

HAIRDRESSERS

All the major hotel properties have one on premises. If you want to venture out to one of the local "salones," Santo Domingo has several excellent establishments. Treat yourself to the works: wash and blow-dry, with manicure and pedicure, usually costs between 20 and 35 *pesos*.

Hermanos Duenas
First floor of Plaza Naco; for women

Hermanos Duenas
Second floor of Plaza Naco; for gentlemen and children (Charlie speaks English, gives an excellent cut, and said this was not just for men and children—he has a large following among women, too).

Salon Rosita
Independencia Avenue, corner of Pasteur Street
Tried and true. One of the established hairdressers, a short walk from the Sheraton and the Jaragua hotels.

Salon Manolita
Independencia Avenue (next door to San Geronimo hotel)
An established traditional hairdresser. Reliable.

Nolasko's
271 prolongation Bolívar
A unisex establishment soon to open a branch at Plaza Central.

Los Gemelos
Tiradentes Avenue (near Plaza Naco)
Santo Domingo

Los Gemelos II (for men)
84 Lope de Vega Avenue

In Puerto Plata

Le Salon Erika
Puerto Plata Beach Resort

In La Romana

Le Salon Erika
Casa de Campo

(both branches are equally fine and are located at the resort properties for your convenience).

MEDICAL NEEDS

As in any travels, you may run the risk of digestive disorders. Fortunately, most of the major hotels have medical services on premises. Stomach ailments can be greatly curtailed by drinking bottled water with lime. Two good brands are Agua Cristal and Agua Sana, but each restaurant and hotel will have purified water upon request.

Do not overdo the sun. Be particularly careful of windy days on the beach, even if it is overcast, since serious burns can still occur. If you have problems, get an Aloe-based product (Savila) at one of the local pharmacies. They also carry a full line of sunscreen products, but these are imported and expensive so it is far better to bring your own.

Should you require a specialist for any health problem, one suggestion is that you check with your consulate. They can recommend the most reputable clinics and doctors. In many cases, some of the oldest clinics in town, although they may not seem like much on the surface, have the most established physicians. Clínica Abreu, for example, is certainly in this category. Most of their specialists speak English and many were trained in the United States, Canada, or Europe. One advantage you will discover just by looking in the phone directory, is that physicians in the Dominican Republic list their home telephone numbers for emergencies. Most of them also make house calls.

CLINICS

Partial listing of hospitals, here called *clinicas,* in Santo Domingo. The telephone directory carries a complete listing of specialists:

Clínica Abreu
Independencia Avenue
Tel. (809) 688–4411

Centro Medico UCE
Maximo Gomez Avenue
Tel. (809) 682–0171

Centro Otorrinolaringología y Especialidades
27th of February Avenue
Tel. (809) 682–0151

Clínica Dr. Abel Gonzalez
Independencia Avenue
Tel. (809) 682–6001/08

PHARMACIES WITH 24-HOUR SERVICE AND DELIVERY SERVICE

FARMACIA DR. CAMILO
31 Calle Paseo de los Locutores, near Winston Churchill Avenue
Santo Domingo
Tel. (809) 566–5575

FARMACIA TIRADENTES
15 Tiradentes Avenue, near Hotel Naco
Santo Domingo
Tel. (809) 565–1647

FARMACIA SAN JUDAS TADEO
57 Independencia Avenue
Santo Domingo
Tel. (809) 689–6664

EMERGENCY TELEPHONE NUMBERS

In case of accidents, and medical or legal emergencies, it is prudent to keep these phone numbers with you:

POLICE	682–3000
	682–3151
FIRE DEPARTMENT	682–2000
	682–2001
AMBULANCE SERVICE	566–1131
RED CROSS	689–4288
AIR AMBULANCE	566–2141

EMBASSIES

CANADA
Consular Offices   689–0002

UNITED STATES
Embassy   682–2171
Consular Offices   687–6060
                                    685–6629
Late emergencies   682–2171

A complete listing of Foreign Consulates are found in the yellow pages of the telephone directory under *consulados*; embassies are listed under *embajadas*.

Your hotel has 24-hour security service on the premises, and the front desk should be able to assist you in problems that may arise while you are in the hotel. Ask them to call the house doctor in a medical emergency or check the section on clinics for a listing of hospital and physician services.

REAL ESTATE RENTALS AND SALES INFORMATION

If you are interested in rentals of vacation villas or the purchase of property in Sosúa, there are a number of real estate companies that handle rentals for the season or can show you what is available for your investment interests. Among these are:

Bommarito Realty
Sosúa
Tel. (809) 571–2101

Island Investments
Pedro Glisante Street
Sosúa
Tel. (809) 571–2597

U.S. NON-PROFIT ORGANIZATIONS IN THE DOMINICAN REPUBLIC

ACCION International, AITEC division
Adventist World Development and Relief Agency
All American Cables and Radio
American Bible Society
American Dentists for Foreign Service
American Field Service International Programs
American Institute for Free Labor Development

American Public Health Association
American Red Cross
Amigos de las Americas
Association of American Chambers of Commerce in Latin America
Boy Scouts of America
Brother's Brother Foundation
Care, Inc.
Catholic Medical Mission Board
Catholic Relief Services-United States Catholic Conference
Christian Medical Society
Church World Service
Community Systems Foundation
Compassion Inc.
Coordination in Development Inc. (CODEL)
Damien Dutton Society for Leprosy Aid Inc.
Darien Book Aid Plan
Direct Relief Foundation
Eisenhower Exchange Fellowships
Evangelical Mennonite Church Inc.
Experiment in International Living Inc.
FCH Services
Family Planning International Assistance
Ford Foundation
Free Methodist Church of North America
Girl Scouts of the U.S.A.
Goodwill Industries
Greater Newark Chamber of Commerce
Heifer Project International Inc.
Inter-American Foundation
Intermedia
International Agricultural Development Service
International Educational Development Inc.
Island Resources Foundation
Jaycees Jubilee Inc.
Lions Club
MAP International
Mennonite Central Committee
Missionary Church Inc.
Missions Health Foundation Inc.
Moravian Church
National Council of Catholic Women
Overseas Education Fund of the League of Women Voters
Pan American Development Foundation

Partners of the Americas
Pathfinder Fund
Planned Parenthood
Population Council
Private Agencies Collaborating Together Inc. (PACT)
Project Concern International
Public Welfare Foundation
Redemptorist Fathers (C.S.S.R.) Province of Baltimore
Rockefeller Foundation
Rotary International
Daughters of Mary Help of Christians (F.M.A.)
    (Salesian Sisters of St. John Bosco)
Salvation Army
Margaret Sanger Center
Save the Children Federation Inc.
Southern Baptist Convention
TAICH
20–30 Club International
Unevangelized Fields Missions inc.
United Church Board for World Ministries
United Methodist Committee on Relief
U.S Chamber of Commerce
Vaccines for Children International Inc.
Volunteers in Technical Assistance
West Palm Beach Chamber of Commerce
Winrock International
Women in Development Inc.
World's Crafts Council U.S.A. Inc.
Worldteam
World Opportunities International
Young Men's Christian Association

TOURIST CARD (FACSIMILE)

NO. **232169**

VALOR US$10.00
VALUE

TARJETA DE TURISTA / TOURIST CARD

BIENVENIDO A LA REPUBLICA DOMINICANA/WELCOME TO THE DOMINICAN REPUBLIC

LLENESE FIRMEMENTE EN LETRAS DE MOLDE/PLEASE PRINT FIRMLY

NOMBRE COMPLETO _____ _____
FULL NAME   APELLIDOS/SURNAMES   NOMBRES/NAMES

FECHA DE NACIMIENTO _____ _____ _____   SEXO ☐ M
DATE OF BIRTH   DIA/DAY   MES/MONTH   ANO/YEAR   SEX ☐ F

LUGAR DE NACIMIENTO _____   NACIONALIDAD _____
PLACE OF BIRTH   NATIONALITY

OCUPACION _____   ESTADO CIVIL ☐ SOLTERO/SINGLE ☐ CASADO/MARRIED
OCCUPATION   MARITAL STATUS

DIRECCION PERMANENTE _____
PERMANENT ADDRESS   CALLE Y NO./STREET AND NO.

_____   _____   _____
CIUDAD/CITY   ESTADO/STATE   PAIS/COUNTRY

DIRECCION EN LA REP. DOM. _____
ADDRESS IN THE DOM. REP.

PUERTO DE EMBARQUE _____   VUELO NO. _____
PORT OF EMBARKATION   FLIGHT NO.

MOTIVO DEL VIAJE/PURPOSE OF TRIP

RECREO ☐   NEGOCIOS ☐   CONVENCION–CONFERENCIA ☐
PLEASURE   BUSINESS   CONVENTION–CONFERENCE

OTRO ☐ _____
OTHER   (ESPECIFIQUE/SPECIFY)

No. PASAPORTE/PASSPORT No. _____

_____   _____
FIRMA/SIGNATURE   INSPECTOR DE MIGRACION

INFORMACION DE SALIDA/COMPLETE ON DEPARTURE

PUERTO DE DESEMBARQUE _____   VUELO NO. _____
PORT OF DISEMBARKATION   FLIGHT NO.

(SOLO PARA USO OFICIAL/ONLY FOR OFFICIAL USE)

OBSERVACIONES:

Weights and Measures

1 mile	=	1.60934 kilometres
1 acre	=	0.405 hectare, 4,046.8564 sq. metres
1 square mile	=	2.5899881 square kilometres
1 pound	=	0.45359237 kilogram
1 gallon	=	3.785306 litres
1 metre	=	3.28084 feet
1 kilometre	=	0.621371 miles
1 kilogram	=	2.20462 pounds
1 litre	=	1.05669 quarts
20 litres	=	5.2 U.S. gallons
40 litres	=	10.4 U.S. gallons

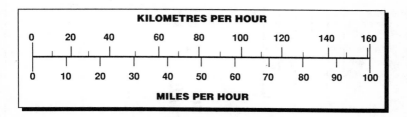

Metric Conversion
Distances/Liquids

Kilometres into Miles
1 kilometre (km.) = 0.62 miles

km.	10	20	30	40	50	60	70	80	90	100	110	120	130
miles	6	12	19	25	31	37	44	50	56	62	68	75	81

Miles into Kilometres
1 mile = 1.609 kilometres (km.)

miles	10	20	30	40	50	60	70	80	90	100
km.	16	32	48	64	80	97	113	129	145	161

Fluid Measures

litres	imp. gal.	U.S. gal.	litres	imp. gal.	U.S. gal.
5	1.1	1.3	30	6.6	7.8
10	2.2	2.6	35	7.7	9.1
15	3.3	3.9	40	8.8	10.4
25	5.5	6.5	50	11.0	13.0

INDEX

LIST OF MAPS

LIST OF TABLES AND CHARTS

THE MANY FACES OF THE DOMINICAN REPUBLIC

From the splendor of its modern, palm tree-lined boulevards to the intimacy of its historic neighborhoods, the Dominican Republic is a land of many faces. The signs of growth and modernization are everywhere; yet the modern vies with the traditional — old-fashioned roadside vendors linger, even on highways. Always on the go, Dominicans use all means of transportation, whether on four legs or on two wheels. Outside the bustling city, they engage in their favorite pastimes: enjoying the coastline, wandering in the countryside with its tropical allures, and relaxing with a friend, always offering a smile to visitors of their paradise nation of the Caribbean.

The Malecon in Santo Domingo

Signs of construction in Santo Domingo

Roadside sales of fruits and vegetables on the Autopista Duarte

Motorcycles and bicycles compete with automobiles in the city

The Dominican Republic was the first country in the west to see horses from Spain

Swimmers near las Americas Airport

A giant Banyan tree on the northern coast

ACKNOWLEDGEMENTS

To José Pagan

Mr. Pagan was a key player in the production of this guide. It was he who introduced Marc and Gretchen Paulsen to this beautiful country. As a student in Portland, Oregon, he met the Paulsen family, and a friendship developed that led the Paulsens to visit his home in the Dominican Republic. The Paulsens were reacquainted with the important part in history that the country played in the development of the Western Hemisphere, and were surprised to find so little information currently published describing the Dominican Republic and its fascinating past and present.

When the decision was made to remedy this situation by writing and publishing a guidebook, it was Mr. Pagan who helped bring the many people together that formed the foundation from which the many necessary elements were assembled. Mr. Pagan's family is well known in the Dominican Republic. His father was an important builder, and was responsible for the construction of most of the major bridges in the country and for the Isabel de Torres Cable Car facility on the northern coast. The elder Pagan served as an aide to President Balaguer in the 1970s during a period when many of the present trade programs were put into place. José's brother, Ruben Pagan, is currently involved in major construction projects within the country.

José Pagan speaks five languages. He has worked in the offices of the Ministry of Tourism and American Airlines, has traveled broadly, and is currently in the process of completing studies in international law.

To Fredric M. Kaplan

Mr. Kaplan, founder and president of Eurasia Press, provided the editorial and publishing guidance that brought this project to fruition.

THE AMERICAN CHAMBER
OF COMMERCE
OF THE DOMINICAN REPUBLIC

Now in our 65th Anniversary

invites you
to visit our offices
and do business
in our country.
The best investment
you can make.

**For further details read the economic
section on the Chamber**

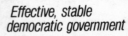